The Sara Bellum Review

Carl Fanning

authorHOUSE®

AuthorHouse™
1663 Liberty Drive
Bloomington, IN 47403
www.authorhouse.com
Phone: 1-800-839-8640

First published by AuthorHouse   07/27/2011

ISBN: 978-1-4567-3347-6 (sc)
ISBN: 978-1-4567-3348-3 (hc)
ISBN: 978-1-4567-3346-9 (ebk)

Library of Congress Control Number: 2011901815

Printed in the United States of America

U. S. Library of Congress Control Number: TXU1—169—216 ...02-05-04

The Sara Bellum Review is dedicated
to
Elmer and Nell Fanning

Contents

Introduction

Webster's Dictionary defines *topic* as "The subject of discussion, essay or thesis." The object of this book is to put a new spin (top) on an old word and in the process stimulate the reader's thinking.

Meet the topics or prompts; all 4076 of them.

First, we'll tell you *what they are not*:

The material includes no guilt trips over the living room carpet; no psychological battles to mop up; nothing bellicose. You'll find no exploding cars, berserk chainsaws or hairy creatures dragging you off into the Gothic gloom.

Nor will you be reading a novel with its attendant characters, plot and setting or any of the ingredients that normally go into prose fiction. *The SBR* is in a category apart from the skills of a George Eliot, Steinbeck or the insight of the Persian poet Rumi. Such writers championed the narratives of the heart. This material "marches to the beat of a different drummer."

Does the text contain anything controversial?

For the most part we have stepped neatly around most of today's heavier issues. We are however aware of the fact that some readers are skilled at reading between the lines and others cannot get on with their day without finding an ant in their morning coffee. With this in mind we did endeavor to maintain a certain level of discretion. *The SBR* was not written to engender arguments or to resolve age old issues.

And, incidentally, we fared quite well without the *devices* that much of the media relies on when their content is lacking in substance.

Of course, naysayers responded to this textual scrubbing with a unanimous "it'll never fly."

We disagreed.

We invite you to take a walk with us on what we call the high road and if that rings a bell you'll be in good company. The road is not crowded. The air is fresh.

Meet Sara Bellum. She is the author's voice, overseer, part time Renaissance women and the commentator behind the asterisk. (I also water the flowers.*)

And now we'll turn this over to her.

"Hey ho . . . I am pleased to announce that I just received a call from John Donne the English poet. He was sitting inside the Tower of London and during the conversation, he, among other things, recalled his famous line: 'Ask not for whom the bell tolls. It tolls for thee.'

"After hanging up, I thought, how apropos and a perfect segue into this text. 'The bell tolls for thee' or better yet, the ringing is a wake-up call for us to embrace the ever dynamic life of the mind . . . so let's get started, onward and upward.

"Now, we'll tell you what the topics are about?

"In general *The SBR* was compiled to amuse, entertain and race the bubbles to the top of the water cooler. And there's more, much more so let's draft a metaphor.

"You are about to experience a word carnival. Look out, *Ring*ling Brothers: Barnum, Bailey and Bellum are in town. Be sure to read their brochure. Their itinerary includes verbal acrobats and clowns juggling figurative language. You'll find a dog that jumps through the hoopla and a bearded lady who assures the crowd that the topics will grow on them. Looking up you'll notice the trapeze artists swinging through a series of lofty ideas.

"The carnival is always educational. It opened the door for the writing team to discover its forte; to play ping pong on a tennis court. We found a Petri dish on the table and were able to explore our culture. We gazed at vultures, listened to lectures and lived our future in the present now.

"From imagery to history, the team wrote yarns as big as a barn and tails that follow a comet. We were stargazers, trailblazers and lasers. We noticed that sunshine can be easily bent out of shape. We talked of prisms, isms and guitars; cars, trains and a 1952 pickup loaded with names; names that are elastic, even borderline bombastic. Be looking for houses and spouses or computer mouses. [sic]

"We used a vocabulary taken from the back shelves of a word supply house and smiled as the book took on a life of its own and apart from a plethora of puns, we haven't committed any major literary sins. Some of the entries may have double meanings: none contain any hidden messages.

"From A to Z, upward to high school, out and beyond, you'll find that *The SBR* offers a mix, a variety worth pondering.

"For high school classrooms, specifically, A Day in the Life, Look Around, Musings and Point of View to name a few may be the most student friendly. These four categories feature various shapes, tones and colors and they offer easy arenas with which to work. At this level, the entries are simple and accessible. They are tailor made for journal writing, class discussion or musing over. If a topic presents too much of a challenge, if at first you don't understand, move on to the next one.

"And, one more thing, the bell's about to ring, which means that we are about Donne.

"To recap, the topics are well crafted, taken from our daily playground and do offer a variety of viewpoints. You'll find something for everyone here that works, something that may even be funny and as we all know humor is the best medicine. Example: After spending some time in the Pun category, the Hatfields and the McCoys decided put down their guns and are co-authoring a book called *Why Feud-alism Doesn't Work.* Enjoy."

(Quotation marks enclose plays, poetry, songs and direct quotes or language that is obviously spoken. *Italics* are used to indicate words to be emphasized and book titles. *We* refers to the writing team.)

Abstract

1. (Re: The aforementioned John Donne: time travel is the latest cell phone application if you're with the right company.*)

2. "I will not go back to that monster," she screamed and pulled his hand off the steering wheel which caused the car to spin out of control and slam into an oncoming train. The impact sent the car into a series of rolls. It came to a rest in an upright position and instantly burst into flames. Pandemonium ensued. What little traffic was on the streets at that time of the night came to a sudden halt as people rushed to the scene to offer help. Within seconds emergency vehicles could be heard in the distance . . . ." (This paragraph doesn't belong here. It's in the wrong book. Obviously, a publisher's mistake.*)

3. Why would a dog laugh at tree bark?

4. A marble sinking in honey has caused the breakup of several icebergs off the coast of Africa. (Are we only getting one-tenth of the real story? *)

5. Step in, close the door, hang up your coat and find a chair. Now, what do you expect to happen? (According to the sylla*bus* that brought us here, we'll watch a movie on how to work with abstract topics.*)

6. Roman numerals were ordered to March through a calendar all the way to December.

7.   Vertical bridge / Horizontal ladder. (One step at a time.*)

8.   How much does an elephant's glance weigh?

9.   Should you bury green pixels in a picture of the desert to grow an oasis?

10.   How long is the shelf life of elf food? (Myself, I do not know.*)

11.   Should you run out, you can always fill up on luck at the Leprechaun Station.

12.   "Between a rock and a hard place" is an awkward position from which to work.

13.   What exactly does the wheel of fate repairman do?

14.   Anytime you see an empty glass on a table, rest assured that somebody will see it as half filled with apple juice processed by the Abstract Fruit Co.

15.   During this specific eclipse of the moon, a volleyball tournament attracted more fans than did the baseball playoffs.

16.   When Apex Climington reached the top of the mountain he looked around then down and noted to his guide, "You know, there is a lot of gravity down there." "Yes," agreed Dewey Pullman, "but if you'll *fall*-low me and we can avoid most it."

17.   You have been told umpteen times there is no way to save a stump short of painting a tree on it.

18.   We X-rayed a Crackerjack box and found all the whistles to be in top condition and ready for the popcorn playoffs.

19.   Kendal found a cool and dark cellar corner where crickets silently kicked into the shadows and back.

20.   Beaumont Mathis was sitting on the edge of a tunnel looking down a long line of zeros.

21.   Percy Oglethorpe thought it would be perfect to plant an abstract tree near a stand of under-berry bushes.

22.   What would the truth look like hanging in effigy? (Let's take Polly Graph out of retirement long enough to get her opinion.*)

23.   Is there any way to separate Tuesday and Wednesday? (I'll tell you at midnight.*)

24.   Enjoying the moment, he took a picture of the clock.

25.   The search continues for the valve used to keep the atmosphere inflated.

26.   Is anybody listening to all the invisible sounds?

27.   If your high school was located next the railroad tracts, how many students hopped the train at the beginning and didn't return until the end of class?

28.   What are the demographics of those people flying in and out of Norm Airport?

29.   The dealer failed tell Carson Seymour that the steering in the early model Abstract was not designed to handle conventional traffic problems.

30.   Katrina wants to know why anyone would carry with them a bag of dogfight snarls. (Growls are not exactly howlingly funny.*)

31. Do some information backgrounds need to be landscaped?

32. The art of good health places a frame around the vitamin/mineral chart.

33. Can a quick glance detect movement when there shouldn't be any?

34. High levels of *vicarious* are being detected in many living rooms. (Vivian Carlyle, are you living your life through an electronic median? *)

35. That night during the Hare Krishna session, three rabbits managed to escape from behind the Magic Curtains.

36. Is there a measuring tape for a minute? (Yes, and it takes about sixty seconds to get to the end of it.*)

37. Is the Great Wall of China longer than most history books?

38. Nothing happened to the person heard saying "excuse me" to a tree.

39. We have various flavors of dilemma depending on your appetite for solving problems.

40. From the vast pool of people, a few are constantly evaporating.

41. The words were lost in the quiet of the woods.

42. We now have a jet stream that can assemble a line of air currents.

43. A human squall line of sneezes was required to dry the paint on an allergy relief billboard. (Horse shoe! *)

44. Can you hang your clothes out to dry on the line that separates the ocean from the sky?

45. World records are set when Olympic high jumpers are quicker than the pull of gravity.

46. After climbing a wall of facts what would an "away-without-leave" scientist find?

47. Bermuda Triangle buffs are to hold a reunion on May the thirty-second near the unanswered coast of the Question Mark Peninsula.

48. Can a teeter totter operate in reverse? (When you're on the up side of things, it's much easier to see what's been going down.*)

49. What are you likely to see floating across the lake at midnight? (A bottle with a boat in it.*)

50. What exactly will be at your fingertips once you're connected to the cable for Utopian Utilities?

51. Cassie T. Saturday was hired to shadow the man's silhouette on his day off.

52. The poker game being played on the prison floor dealt a full house to the warden.

53. If you want to know the last thing I said before I closed the freezer door, you'll have to open the door. (I-ce.*)

54. Can you tune your mirror to bring in *Alice in Wonderland?* It all depends on how you look at it.

55. One symbol asked of another, "What do you represent?" "I'm part of a drum set," it clanged.

56.   The first Warm Air Compact Disc ever recorded was air dropped to ice-bound mountain climbers.

57.   Try extracting the thought patterns that fell to the floor with the whittle shavings.

58.   In the summertime, *I. G. Lew*is has the coolest home on the block.

59.   If swords are your reward, write a story about the wooden cat that fenced a scarecrow out of the cornfield.

60.   We know of a group of people who believe that manikins can stare back.

61.   The crew wanted to know how far the captain could see with unaided binoculars.

62.   Some activities fall neatly under the rubric of a social centrifuge or separating the boys from the men.

63.   Dace looked up from the kitchen table and her apple cider and wondered why someone had left a cedar log on top of the refrigerator.

64.   If you don't mind, we need to know what you keep in that storage unit in your back yard. If it's empty just ignore the question.

65.   Headlines; Egyptian Glue Fight in Local Mummery (Let's stick to topics that the reader can identify with.*)

66.   Willard can hear much better now that his ears have been pierced.

67.   In a cold room, can you feel the presence of a pyromaniac?

68. A leather belt left behind by Kroger Porthos is hanging in the closet of an economics class.

69. Little Martin wants to know why a daffodil can cast a shadow that looks like a monster.

70. To win the organics battle, cantaloupe rinds can be catapulted into a medieval compost.

71. Similar to a propeller blade, if you spin your savings fast enough they'll disappear.

72. We are waiting for our coffee to get cold so it will look as if we have been here a while.

73. Two iotas were on the numerical swim into nothing: "I, ot-ter, as good as proclaim it *ocean 'ork' day* and when we're finished we'll all swim away." (Do I read an otter called Iota or a miniscule amount? We're guessing that such whimsy is only as confusing as you make.*) (Ocean-ork-graphy?*)

74. Can you bring me a cup of tea and a buttered scone while I think about the food service industry?

75. Two circles that are mathematically clamped to your driveway should repel any neighborhood squares.

76. The world's largest telescope lens has to be periodically cleaned for star dust.

77. Want ad: Reward Offered for last laugh. Man is serious about finding it.

78. Prenelope Plummage flew in from Portnoy, Utah, with plenty of time to ruffle some feathers at the Peacock Dance Hall. (This sounds like the alliterative dance of the consonants.*)

79. An elaborately designed pulley system was used to move the Canadian border three inches to the north.

80. Lewis Spanner always places a copy of "Popular Mechanics" in his tool box to harden the wrenches while in storage.

81. Would one million zeros lined up in single file create a tunnel? (This is a waste of zeros. We need them to publish books on mathematics.*)

82. We applaud those mechanical hands that get the dishes so clean inside the kitchen machine.

83. Do parakeets read the bird section of the newspapers on the bottom of their cages?

84. The head *friar* at the Trappist Monastery jumped and singed his frock when it was suddenly announced over the intercom that he was about to see a vision. (Did he knock over the barbeque grill? *)

85. Did you study? Have you been tested? (You'll find more levels here than you will in a carpenter's tool box.*)

86. A cardiovascular hammer can pound a round episode of concern into a lengthy copper wire called worry.

87. You can now get a quiver full of anti-gravity arrows for shooting stars.

88. Are you the connection between the past and the future? (We all bring a sense of presence to the table.*)

89. Would you like credit for your ability to relate to people *vis-à*-vis?

90. How often do you check the frequency that is bar coded into your humanity card?

91.   A big league meal might consist of a batter up that singles into pancakes then slides onto home plate.

92.   President Perco took a sip from his coffee and wondered why the various members of the procrastination club were so consistently late.

93.   The name brand Circus has been around for a long time therefore when they tell you they have a new line of suites and ties, be assured that you have the ticket to success.

94.   Do intelligent people conduct themselves any different than a maestro would a symphony?

95.   To most people *light is information* translates into electricity to read the morning newspaper.

96.   Alison and Robert decided to travel light on our their honeymoon by taking the Physics Express. (Will you be back last week? *)

97.   Gremlin jockeys will soon be available to ride in the Mischief Preakness. (All they have to do is show up and if they don't win, they'll place third.*)

98.   "Mary, Mary, quite contrary . . ." if you plan to grow silver bells, it'll cost you ten cents a gong to buy the seeds.

99.   Sometimes you have to punt the topics over their heads and get on with the game.

100.   Time is running out for Bell Laboratories in their search for an *hour* that will hold more than current models.

101.   "You know, I'm as hungry as my name is Lumber Jack and up ahead you'll see one in a chain of restaurants owned by Paul Bunyan. He calls it the Lumber Meals and the hot plate special today is a smorgas*bord*. By the way after

you've eaten, you'll notice on the way out a twenty foot high log dispenser for those patrons who need a tooth pick. So pull over."

102. Walter Ripley's pond leaks and he can't believe he has found a plumber who makes field calls.

103. If you're going to sell a bag of paramecium food, you'll have to shrink the pet shop into a deer print at the edge of the pond. (I once gazed for three days at the Amoeba Borealis.*)

104. Julius was trying to kill some time when he tore the month from the calendar, folded it into a paper airplane, pushed it into flight and gazed on as three days bailed out.

105. As reported by the Bucket Brigade: Any time a fire is restricted to a campsite or imprisoned behind rocks, it tends to get a little put out by it all and will eventually attempt a break out.

106. Only when our gazes begin to leave visible energy tracks will we know what people are staring at.

107. A side view of physics: As of twelve o'clock, unlock tomorrow and all things above gravity line thirty-two feet will float away. (We do like to keep both feet on the planet.*)

108. If you want to understand the joke you'll have to drive faster than ten miles per hour. The "Oh, I get it" Lodge is about to meet at Humor City Hall and you're still fifteen miles away.

109. What would the tintinnabulation of a bell sound like in a car-tune? (Let's not lose the longest most colorful word in the book listening to music while driving down the textual highway.*)

110. *Jeri* and *Bill* wanted us to write a topic about their favorite pet. So we put it in a cage and stood back as it ran in circles.

111. What is the record for the longest sustained Alpine echo? (All records aside and furthermore I cannot write an onomatopoetic echo.*)

112. Can the wind blow your line of vision? (If my eyes are following my flying hat.*)

113. If a person's glance is composed of a specific wave length of energy, the individual who is pulled into or meets your eye contact might be on a similar wave length as yourself. (The views expressed in this text are not necessarily . . . . *)

114. Isn't the past carefully wound around an ever expanding roll of Memory Wrap?

115. Why fret? We have a gentle breeze and a full moon and a musician who will take the boat across the canal to a land of relaxing tunes.

116. You need mathematics in your tool belt if you ever plan to construct a passable bridge between space-time and the next higher dimension. (This bridge does have a weight limit.*)

117. What controls the outcome when you flip a coin? (If it lands on tails, his name is Chance and we are at odds with him.*)

118. A most colorful waitress can certainly feed the imagination.

119. You don't have to be lost at sea before you can use a lighthouse as a point of reference.

120. The best way to find the lighthouse is to turn onto Freeman Switch Road. (Is that where *whats* his name works as a custodian?*)

121. The man in the front row seat with a beanie on his head stood up and asked, "Hey, Indy, what kind of pit stop is necessary to rotate a thinking process?"

122. The calisthenics of consciousness can help you zoom back and forth between micro and macro. (Such a saucy entry; Yes, I understand that we need to put these Italian noodles back in the little oven and heat them.*)

123. Some people were quite pained by the pun when we wrote this entry on the *chakra* board. (Would seven acres of okra sound any more strange?*)

124. The idea foundry is fueled by *information*. (The original topic called for *alchemy* to end the sentence. Thinking it was buried too deep in the chemistry department, it was omitted. Let's let the reader decide.*)

125. Do you know what takes place in the space that inaudibly unfolds between two musical octaves? (They did move a grand piano in about three hours ago.*)

126. Are you located in the successful slot on the ambition wheel?

127. The scenario twelve pill will help to understand the magnetism that draws an individual to a snow capped mountain range.

128. The mystical man turned to me and said, "alloy" and went on to ask if I was familiar with the many faces of gold.

129. On at least one, three, five and seven occasions we have talked about how odd things have been going.

130. In the still of the night, a dreamer catches the first train out of the Brain Station and is free. (Free to launch his craft onto the Sea of Tranquility.*)

131. He said he was sitting at the time table when suddenly he heard something that happened two days ago.

132. Did Gigi byte off more than she could chew when she boasted that she had an ever-expanding memory?

133. Wouldn't you agree that your dreams are your personality?

134. Have you ever climbed the stairs of a crowd of curious onlookers? (When you get to the top you can see what the people were staring at.*)

135. Your essence card will never expire.

136. Anyone who can breathe senses that the air is more than transparent. (Is there something in the air? *)

137. With a little ironing, the obvious can be worn inside out.

138. Is ABBA the rhyme scheme to the first four lines of a poem or a Swedish band?

139. An armadillo shaped bat was used to spank car shaped balls into the outfield that borders the Diamond Junction turnoff. (Did you find this thing in somebody's attic? *)

140. Has science left the holographic apple half eaten? (Science has a shrinking appetite for fruit.*)

141. When you reach the summit of Abstract Mountain you'll understand why so few people attempt to climb it.

142. The new pharmaceutical labeling is required to tell you when the placebo effect will wear off.

143. Would a thermos bottle filled with comedy soup have you laughing during a cold snowy evening?

144. Have you located the pixel in the cartoon frame that doubles as a rabbit hole?

145. What will you hear if you turn up the sound on a volume of air?

146. Did we mention that The Depth Perception Family includes their neighbors Height and Width in the family Dimension?

147. The O'Clock patrol ticketed a '09 Time Buggy that was moving too fast into the future.

148. Is there a form of intelligence or life in a sedimentary rock? The answer would be as abstract as the rock is dense.

149. Even the blue sky is up to you and what you choose to see. Anything that appears abstract was never meant to be.

150. Somebody broke a bottle of Sunday morning and suddenly it's noon.

151. Songs written in the subways made the boll weevil extinct. (By the Extermination Recording Co? *)

152. Why would it take more than a nickel's worth of sense to understand that some things are more than mere coin-cidence?

153. "Do you have many physicians who have hiked the Cumberland Gap?"
"We have one out there now and it's been three days

since we've heard from him. He's somewhere out in the Boone-docs."

154. What does it mean when the king of clubs flies out of the bedroom, down the hall, through the living room and out the door?

155. The illusion knob on a depth preceptor device allows you to determine the extent to which you believe that which you see is real. (Let's pour this one back into the think tank.*)

156. We will pay money for information leading to a broader understanding of why we think we are so limited. (This must have been a sign stapled at eye level to a utility post.*)

157. Did you know there is a valley between your structured thoughts and a forest where magic wands are grown?

158. How do you highlight the waves of grain that need to be cut? Bolt the steering wheel of a tractor on top of a lighthouse and rotate the beam. (This topic might go to seed.*)

159. Were you aware of how hard it is to grasp the idea of thinking?

160. Does x = minus b plus or minus the square root of b squared minus 4 a c over 2 a qualify as a second degree planet inhabited by equations? (Located in the Algebraic Constellation.*)

161. While counting sheep to get some sleep, several early twentieth century physicists noticed that one of the animals understood the nature of a quantum leap. (Ergo, the Golden Fleece was used to spin a wool coat.*)

162. Nodules of oblivion were found in the secretions of sleep. (We've tried it all including Cliff's Notes and no matter what we do, we still manage miss the message with this topic. The only option left is to throw it into the kitchen sink and turn on the water.*)

163. Caution! Are your ears open to the daily swarm of noise that drops it's decibels onto the highways, the streets and into the homes? It saturates your television, radio, even spills from the clock when the alarm goes off telling you it's time to turn it off!

164. Citizens are urged to walk briskly through the din of the rush hour monotone. The dull roar bounces from the bricks and sidewalks, rolls from the pavement, recoils at corners and glances from the lion's share of headlines at the local newsstand. It's a beta stimulator that includes drowsiness, apathy and indifference to din warnings. (I hate to turn these to down, so listen up . . . Re: 78 and 79: Somebody has had a little too much coffee this morning.*)

Art

1. Is there magic in art?

2. Beauty is the artist's studio.

3. With art as his vehicle, Van Gogh was frequently parked next to a corn field. (Can metaphors be painted? *)

4. Mona Lisa painted a dark moustache on a portrait of Leonardo de Vinci.

5. Shouldn't the artist want you to identify with his or her paintings? (I think I understand this topic.*)

6. Campbell Soup anyone? After an art form was detected on a painter's drop cloth it became *modern*.

7. To give your painting a certain *mys*tique, place the canvas behind a waterfall for about ten minutes.

8. Artemis High is the mayor of Frame City, a rapidly growing town located in the Talent Mountains about fifteen thousand feet above sea level.

9. Time spent in an art gallery will elevate your sights much quicker than a shooting gallery.

10. "The Barber of Seville" has raised his prices.
    "That's nothing to sing about."
    "No, but the music certainly grows on you."

"Who are you talking to?"
"Anybody who needs a haircut."

11. Dehydrated pigment was added to the palette to create a desert scene.

12. The idea is to put a well balanced diet of art onto your contem-plate.

13. Would the ultimate art experience be to paint a picture of an art gallery? (When it sold, it could open some doors for you.*)

14. The drafty old shack had one broken window through which you could see the Matterhorn.

15. Does the mountain scenery offer a power surge that illuminates the artist's canvas?

16. He wasn't fired: he was told to re-design after painting the chimney a foot lower than the highest part of the house.

17. While studying art at the Louvre in Paris, take a magnifying glass and quite possibly you'll see a herd of rams climbing the north face of the Matterhorn.

18. After forty days of rehearsal, *plank*-ton were nailed into place and before an audience of two, "Noah" was performed on a lake stage.

19. Michelangelo learned he could only work in the winter time when he decided to paint a snowflake on the ceiling of the Sistine Chapel.

20. When the gallery burned, they suspected arson until Dugan O'Miley remembered the painting of a log cabin with smoke rising from the chimney.

21. "Hi! I'm Rochelle and when I'm not being personified, I paint landscapes. Today, you'll learn tie-dyeing on a snow covered canvas. Start by working the underbrush out into the open field. Next, pull some yellow tones from a heated palette and smudge in the flames. Tomorrow, we'll watercolor a rill from the melted snow."

22. When people of the north slice lake ice for their igloo windows, aren't they in effect framing a still life view of the world? (And in the spring when the windows trickle back to where the water birds are waiting to feed we'll call it Art Ducko.*)

23. Do you sup-poise that in the past centuries artists were the cameras for their times?

24. When they punched in the hole for hanging the calendar, they punched a star out of a night picture.

25. Did Lao Tze ever paint a moustache on a bust of Buddha? (An excellent way to open a can of conversation? *)

26. We saw a portrait of a mime in the "Art Imitates Life" corridor at the Metropolitan Museum of Art. (Shouldn't there be a mirror hanging in the same hallway?*)

27. To prevent aesthetic depletion take two capsules of beautiful scenery.

28. An industrial strength jack would be required to elevate some of what passes for modern culture.

29. We were so busy cutting out pieces of paper that we forget to submit our example of a decoupage.

30. One momento, did you not see that the portrait of a pentimento smile masking a frown? (The big word means that one painting has been painted over by another.*)

31. Take a good look at the painting. Do you see any water dripping from the webbed feet of the mallards as they lift up from the surface of the pond?

32. A note from the Gallery: The artist who painted the giant Redwood scattered leaves across the floor under the frame to enhance the sales.

33. Let's consider it a carnival when people must learn the art of juggling three different occupations.

34. If each note of music has a corresponding color tone, then paint your mountains with the loftiest crescendos.

35. An art building with a fence around is for those students who wish to draw their swords.

36. Did you read the lengthy paragraph that described Mt. McKinley? If you look close you can see how an avalanche has collapsed parts of the text structure to the timberline. By placing the picture next to a heating vent, the snow will melt and you can recover the words.

37. Will chem-trails be seen crisscrossing the skies of impressionistic twenty-first century art work?

38. To understand the language of light, you must first learn the alphabet of visual thinking. ("Only the shadow knows . . . ."*)

39. Take a close look at your favorite picture as it hangs from a tree limb at the top of a mountain.

40. The bigger picture doesn't fit in the gallery of conventional thinking. (We hope this entry is palat-able.*)

41. Blue/green minutes of paint dripped from a canvas of melting clocks onto Salvador Dali's smock. (This refers to one of Dali's classic paintings.*)

42. If a picture is worth a thousand words, where are the words? They live in pigment houses whose rooftops blend together to make up the color tones.

43. A line of ancient Romans bungee-jumping from an aqueduct was painted across the girth of a jeroboam. (We do try to be flexible.*)

44. Would the universal paint be black with tiny white specks in it? (Will the paint begin to fade when the sun comes up?)

45. Any work of art that has a veneer of quality will endure the test of time.

46. Call your resident artist and ask this person why we never see a cat's cradle of telephone lines rocking the landscape pictures.

47. Thinking *broom* is the best way to sweep the floor with your vision.

48. Should you study painting in France long enough, your Paris-scopic vision should give you an understanding as to what's behind the artist's work.

49. Hasn't silence been painted into every picture you've ever seen?

50. Paint in the yellow eyes of the wolf, blinking dim then bright as he pads down the survival course and through the passing trees.

51.   The noise of the chainsaw sliced through the artist's concentration as he was greening a picture of a tree.

52.   To be less messy, the artist painted his studio the color of the drop cloth. (*Camou*, there will be a disconnect here if you cannot find *flauge* in the dictionary.*)

53.   A sketch artist drew a crowd after which he asked the group to sign their names next to the bottom of the frame.

54.   Headlines: Artist Needed to Complete Work on Draw-bridge

55.   Have you noticed the pictures on the walls as you make your way to the end of a long haul?

56.   How much art is surrealistic? (When Sir Real is available, we'll ask him.*)

57.   Throw your name in the hat and in three days we'll have a *drawing* and see who is the most talented.

58.   How can "Ear of Corn on Canvas" be complete unless the frame is made of shucks?

59.   Will someone from Oklahoma please open the door to more Ard? (No doubt, a suburb of Art.*)

60.   "For over thirty years," he lamented to his grandson, "there has been a nail in the attic wall with nothing hanging from it." "What color is that nail?" the young man asked.

       "It's indigo blue."
       "I have what you need. It's a picture of a man holding a hammer with music playing in the background."
       "What kind of music are you talking about?"
       "Handel's Messiah."

Color

1. A kaleidoscope of colors was seen making a spectrum of itself.

2. Out of the blue we found its definition.

3. Does it take a spectrum of collusion to commit a conspiracy of color?

4. All the regrets have been removed from the Rue Alley between the Red and Blue Intersection.

5. Songs about nature should be written on a green note. (In the literary circles, pages are also known as leaves.*)

6. The spines that bind literary classics are now being soaked in extract from redwood trees to insure that these giants will be red again and again.

7. We painted the well house a water color.

8. The wave length of blue should be measured and protein coated for easy observation.

9. The Roy G. Biv Band was hired to help celebrate the completion of petitions by black and white to become colors. (The name is an acronym for the colors of the spectrum.*)

10. How would a person translate a bird song into colors? (Will the whip*poor*will sing the blues tonight? *)

11. Did you know that the red muffler you're wearing around your neck is quite loud?

12. Magic? When the leaves changed colors this fall was it lost on the people queuing to see the latest Harry Potter movie?

13. "Somewhere over the Rainbow" has highly colorful overtones.

14. The cycles per second within the color spectrum were slowed to the point of producing a floral arrangement.

15. At the intersection of two specific wave lengths, the sound of blue is absorbed into the color of the sky. (If clouds don't get in your way.*)

Commercial Break

1. A one hundred year rust-free warranty should cover the teeth of modern gargoyles. (Speaking of gargoyles, I need some salt water.*)

2. Have you heard of the new run-in-place gerbil exercise plan?

3. How many commercial drinks have they improved by locking their formula in the basement of Fort Knox?

4. Sears Catalog Summer Sale features a lampshade that looks like an oak tree or the perfect way to adorn your forest floor with acorns.

5. While waxing airborne, Icarus demonstrated the new Sun Guard skin protection cream.

6. The retired Astroturf salesman cut to the chase.
    "Want to watch your grass does grow at night? Need to make it a personal experience? Try the new lawn viewmaster. It is specially equipped with headlights."

7. The lucky winner of the door prize will also receive a bag containing a key to the door.

8. Because you can't see the grass grow at night, we offer you a lawn mower equipped with head lights.

9. For quite some time now, apples from the Garden of Eden have been on sale.

10. At some point in the dialogue store we recorded the following exchange:
    "How much would you like to think?" asked the clerk.
    "Uh, $1.65 worth," replied customer.
    "One aphorism without the terse."
    "That'll work."
    "Here is your change. Are you ready for this? *Never buy a used car on a rainy day.*"
    "Thank you."

11. Hetch would like to introduce the new twist-to-open hen eggs with reusable shells.

12. Our time lapse camera reveals that you made it around the quarter mile track twenty-two times in fifteen seconds. (Your equipment must be in excellent shape.*)

13. The Gull Getaway Plan has nothing to do with holding up Fishhead's Marina located slightly east of Foyles Cove.

14. As advertised: Buy this gold plated hummingbird bed and we'll throw in an Audubon Society recording of their January meetings.

15. The only qualification you will need to receive the Lemming Credit Card is to fall in line with the others and take the plunge into a sea of debt.

16. Deliah's Scissor Emporium features the Samson Dip, a stylish new eye opener designed to bring down the temple.

17. We were sipping tea in a coffee house overlooking an amusement park when the waitress asked us if we needed a roller coaster.

18. With the earth body as a vehicle, does your foot ever get heavy on the exhilaration pedal. (Of course you'll be driving a late model Physicality III.*)

19. Wear a crash helmet if you plan to test drive the Mind Rover, the best selling item in the showroom.

20. The old Oracle camera with the zoom lens that once took beautiful shots of the future is now a picture of the past.

21. Try the new five-second commercial spot remover. It is guaranteed to work or you will be reading this ad again.

22. With Cryon optic insulation, you can foresee and insulate yourself from those icy social encounters.

23. As advertised: Sleeptoria Men's Wear now offers the snooze buttons.

24. Have you thought about the many advantages to having the new Water Floor Carpet covering in your kitchen? For starters you never have to worry about leaky pipes. Plus most heat waves are oven controlled.

25. The new look is called *the argument*. Beauticians get it by using tiny little blades for splitting hairs.

26. Nina Finegar's Creative Rub is a handy balm that generates a corpuscle uprising among the inmates of the brain.

27. As advertised: "To guarantee the effectiveness of our drainage system, we will construct it during a simulated rainstorm."

28. We recommend this as a pleasant reminder: "On a frequent basis, you should check the quality of your symbols filter used for interior thought processes."

29.   "We can replace the dull, tired rhetoric of yesterday's speech. It's called a dictionary. It acts like a filter. This linguistic device is used to form your ideas. Low level clichés and profanity clog it. Colorful words, articulately pronounced, keep the device clean, the mind clear, and the thinking a-whirl. You are what you think. You can build a vocabulary now or think in the slow lane for the rest of your life."

30.   Plug, a member of the writing team, wants to know if we have mentioned *The SBR* in this section?

31.   Did you know that The Three Bean Company has converted Jack's fairy tale stalk into a cell phone tower? (Is there a corporate giant somewhere in this picture?)

32.   The new Pillsbury Doughboy T-shirts for math buffs features a Pi R squared design and is discounted $3.14 if purchased at Needmans.

33.   Have you tried our new hearing aid? Did you know that it filters out advertisements?

34.   When you flip the switch, a white light will indicate subject-verb-agreement. A second light tells the writer that the next few sentences will contribute to the central idea of the paragraph; batteries not included. A one-year warranty covers use under normal conditions to include when the student doesn't feel like thinking.

35.   Is it real? Deci Bell has invented a noise pollution machine that absorbs the dull drone of an airplane's din onto a compact disc.

36.   Will a software program on personhood ever be compatible with your computer hardware?

37. An ancient Egyptian heavy equipment company boasts that "no job is too big."

38. Available now: Highly sensitive radar gun that allows you to map the air imprint of a magnetic path created by the information flow between book and brain. (What if you're thinking is under the radar? *)

39. Our inflatable anti-advertisement shield offers a lifetime of resistance to parasite ads that vex or otherwise cause swelling of the sanity nodes.

40. A lot of fluff? Not exactly. Casey Bedford has come up with a new idea called the solar pillow. What does it do? How would you like to *see* your *dreams* come true?

41. For people who are prone to taking cap naps, we now offer a wrinkle free shirt with snooze buttons.

42. What's in vogue? What's hot with people in the know? Red temper flashes from Tantrum Unlimited that pierce your left lobe.

43. "Will we be able to confirm the shipping address on this last case in the morning?"
    "Yes, the last case of canned heat will be shipped to Point Barrow, Alaska tomorrow."

44. You'll get to know it as a mop saver. No wonder we have been awash with orders for the water floor carpet covering.

45. This is a reminder that the warranty has nearly expired on your basic two hundred word function list. We suggest that you order more or fad rapidly into a dim world of limited expression.

46. Tennis anyone? The word is out on the court. That word is a size eleven and it's built for the athlete who demands higher quality footwear. Try on the new Tenacious for your next tennis shoe.

47. Anna Conda presents the one square of jungle floor, complete with compost heap, red ants, parakeet droppings and a grapevine that grows to satisfy noisy neighbors.

48. Also advertised: "It's new, made from tungsten and has an eighteen inch daylight simulator that's so effective grass begins to grow after the third flashing."

49. "Isn't it the same old story? Your pen won't start. We invite you to stop in at The Ink Joint for some free critiques and help yourself to our carefree pot of percolating ideas. We're located one ream east of Writer's Block on the Individual Expressway. We are open to the closed mind."

50. If your belt is holding you up, take it out and slide it through the loops of a new cut of winter jeans. These fashion statements have pockets of warm air sewn into the waist line.

51. "Plenty of tickets still available," announced the Morality Cruise Co. which went on to report that when the Polly Graph clan wanted some elevated leisure, they scheduled a trip on a steamer headed for the Any Integrity Atoll.

52. If it's raining in your heart, if the weather is beating down on the ole pump house roof, try the new upbeat mingle shingles.

53. Higher flight: The writer as stewardess works the aisle to see that all the characters have their plot belts fastened and are ready to fly on Expression Airlines.

54. The more current TV models now have a fifteen foot wide viewer pocket called the *no thought zone.*

55. At the bottom of Big Rock Candy Mountain is a chocolate barn that contains Tootsie Roll fence poles, pralines, a barrel of caramel, wall to walnut bars, bales of brownies and three confection stalls for Milking cow Duds.

Creativity

1. Albert Einstein has been quoted as saying that creativity is more important than intelligence. He also said that process was more important than result.

2. As you cruise down the Topic interstate, you'll notice that about every five miles we have inserted a curve in the road designed to keep you awake and alert.

3. Is this your concept of the ultimate sentence?

4. Is a binary canary related to a parakeet?

5. Don't most people speak body language?

6. "Is there any violence in the book?"
   "Yes, there's a blank page you can tear out if so provoked."

7. Creativity is the magnet that attracts the proper sequencing of words. (Plus or minus a few adjectives. *)

8. Trifles, having escaped from a box of small talk, were feeding the ducks quacked to the side of a freezer. (Isn't this some kind of cracker? *)

9. "Are you new to this shoe?" asked the aglet of the grommet.

10. How many metric chews are there in a line of granola poetry?

11. Perry Schulz was free falling through this book about air when he landed on a copyright number.

12. With a guitar-shaped pen you could write quite note-worthy puns.

13. Publication request: We can no longer print stories about the high seas until the shipment of indigo ink arrives.

14. Have you ever been lost at the intersection of two paragraphs?

15. A writer's lost and found department contained a plot, setting, characters, dialogue, denouement and a stained coffee cup.

16. We asked Dewey Google his plan for finding a needle in the haystack in front of his barn.

17. "*Boggles* the mind," said the mystery writer to his keyboard as he began his days work by describing a painful noise down by the swamp.

18. Would the contents of an empty story change if you put it in a safety deposit box?

19. You can write anything about mental blocks if you can only think of how to phrase it.

20. *Re*: Can *Sus*an and *Tat*e breathe new life into that novel you're writing?

21. The dialogue offered here is accompanied by your choice of a variety of smells.

22. "Draw a rope over the river!" pleaded a character to the lethargic cartoonist.

23. If he could speak, what would the manikin say? ("I can explain this blank look on my face." *)

24. Of rhymes and contour lines, put on your metric shoes if you plan to climb a poem with elevation.

25. The language of a high tech manual was reassembled in a junior high word shop.

26. A bewildered peacock was hiding in a paragraph describing the fauna of Mexico.

27. A desert scene was the perfect basis for the family Green to play the part of an oasis.

28. That saddle shaped chair he sat in while writing horse stories has left his mind addled.

29. The black ant tackled the red ant well below the driveway yard line causing it to fumble a wasp wing from its mandible.

30. A landslide described in a geology book completely covered an adjacent volume describing log homes.

31. He fastened an ink pen to a weather vane to determine which direction his writing should be going. (I hope the weather vane is supported by a keyboard.*)

32. Four feet of any given line of poetry is exactly enough to two people to hit the dance floor in celebration of the free verse jubilee.

33. We know that natatorial means water, so when you catch up with that strange creature the *gubernatorial*, be sure to

feed it peanuts and keep it well hydrated. (You're sitting on the edge of a large pool of politicians.*)

34. A southern fan whipped and rippled a stream of anti-freeze all the way down Grid Street and into Torradia. (Somebody's cool aunt lives there.*)

35. When a writer needs for an idea to strike, he will hold a metal pen in front of his eyes and brainstorm.

36. To avoid information leaks try spraying a proofreader's solution on conjunctions to make sure they are tightly connected to the rest of the sentence.

37. While talking about his castle, the king seemed chagrinned: "We never had a problem with pirates until we emptied the sand from the moat and filled it with sea water.

38. To this day people are still talking about the mess that was made the day the rumor plumbing line developed a leak.

39. Polly Money, a board game vendor on Park Avenue, was reading the instructions by the railroad when police arrested her with the option of either going directly to jail or paying two hundred dollars.

40. Somebody opened a neglected copy of an American History book and a wasp flew out of the livery stable where Paul Revere kept his horses.

41. Onomatopoeia is a snap when you write a paragraph on green beans that tells you how to break off both ends and once in the middle before throwing them into the pot. (Splash.*)

42. Carpe Diem tried to seize the day during intervals at a carnival where she forced a Tuesday grip on the time slide into Wednesday.

43.   Once the author had completed the chapter detailing our climb to the top of the mountain, we gazed out across the margin at the most beautiful peaks of expression ever described by a pen.

44.   Don't leave home without wrapping your new Eccentri-card in a used paper towel, then stuffing it into a plastic bag next to a picture of Houdini.

45.   How long are we expected to dance before we learn the definition of *terpsichore*? If someone would please open the door to the muse, we could be waltzing out and spinning about tossing curvets, doing pirouettes, gamboling and doing whatever we chose. (I'll bet. *)

46.   When plant season begins, grab your weapon, stalk the target Iris, deliver the hardware to the stem, clip the stamen and depollenize before the filament flares: From there you remove the anthers before anybody questions the point we are making here.

47.   The sailor from the south: "Would yawl care to join me for a three hour tour on what has been defined as my "jolly boat . . . which carries a mainsail and two or three jibs with a mizzenmast far aft?"

48.   Do you know about the machine that edits any paragraph at least a yard in length. First you must pour in a can of all-purpose punctuation to keep the motor running smoothly.

49.   "Was it a car or a cat I saw?" questioned the old man after witnessing a late model Jaguar speeding down Palindrome Street and nearly snuffing the ninth life of a cat. (The big word is defined as a sentence that reads the same forward as it does backward.*)

50.   Are you looking for shoes that will fit your footnotes? Be informed that that brand of humor is so old it is no longer being made.

51.   "Why would any single person have to buy three tickets to see tonight's performance at the Theatre of the Absurd? Furthermore, what is the name of tonight's opening play? Did I hear you right? It's called: 'What is the world record for the longest time a picture has hung on a wall?' One final question: How will we know when the performance has ended? Oh! I see. The picture will fall."

52.   Ima Lissenin slipped an argot into a slang shot and hurled it through the tidy talk to the center of the targot.

53.   When the man in charge is in concert with the problem, we see pipes put in place and water flowing musically to and fro: we give the plumber credit for being organ-ized.

54.   "A man, a plan, a canal: Panama" was stenciled on a ship that can sail forward as easily as it can backwards.

55.   "Now stop it!" warned Alice as she watched her cat chase a roll of worsted across the living room carpet. Not to be bested, a kitten picked up a needle and began weaving it into a mitten . . . or sew it was written.

56.   We approached the orchestra, borrowed the conductor's wand, took it into a green house and slipped it between an index finger and a green thumb.

57.   The mailman was working N Street when he delivered the alliteration: "Opun the envelope and you'll find a nice letter from your niece written from Nice."

58.   A torment of mockingbirds held an ad hoc squawk during the unraveling of an argyle sock.

59. "What was that noise? Did you hear a limb fall from a tree?"
    "No, that was a sound effect."

60. A late night shipment of fear pellets arrived at the stable that houses nightmares.

61. Rime schemes are as easy to scan as the a b c's.

62. When you have misted your plants, tell them so.
    You then excuse the pun and see how fast they grow.

63. Milly Mockingbird feathers her nest by teaching parodies to parakeets at the aviary clinic.

64. The Overalls Guild of avant-garde carpenters constructed as shaky old barn in the middle of Times Square.

65. A Harley Davidson Weather Cycle starts slow in the winter, then revs, clutches, is put in gear then accelerates into spring, gathers speed, shifts, and cruises into summer.

66. Myron, the compact disc thrower, hurled the orb the entire length of a digitized Roman Empire.

67. Fifth and Vine Street has a new Tarzan subway policy that requires a seven decibel elephant call from the passengers who think the city is a jungle.

68. My name is Chuck and I have been grounded from the Fast Food 500 because I had to lean on the pit crew for rotating the hot dogs during the race for supper.

69. Some words fell out of a tree and hit Sir Iambic Newton on the head, inspiring him to pen the "Gravity of Poetry."

70. A landscaper working in front of a historical building was overheard telling a genealogist that several branches of his family tree had been mulched.

71. The deeper meaning of a paragraph describing a pond was lost, so we dredged the depths with grapnels until we hooked the bottom line.

72. In England, the National Rifle Association would be charged about 2000 pounds for a thirty-minute radio discussion on the latest model Remington, provided they could find a target audience.

73. The song was such a stretch for the group that they had to attach a bungee chord to the bridge of a guitar to get any air time.

74. Several dead poems had their metric feet tagged, scanned, slabbed and reposed as footnotes in the muses' mortuary.

75. A publishing house now runs submitted smut through a slew of innuendo clarifiers, pebble blotters and pulverized erasure tips to insure safe public acceptance.

76. A murder of crows was arrested by the north wind. The jailbirds were given one *caw* to make and a perch on the de-fence while a lawyer promised that there would be no flight from prosecution.

77. Neurons and more neurons: billions of them, mind you are tuned into the slow-motion replays of penalties, information pile-ons and fumbles in a daily game of bias ball.

78. A tale in parallelism: Oscar Oblivious mud wrestled with allegories until one day he was singled out when the truth bit him on the rear. He promptly moved his reptilian brain to Bath, Maine, married the local luggage lady Vonda Virtuous and started a salamander collection.

79. A section of the population woke up to different speech patterns after a dialectic storm moved up the east coast last night.

80. Delmer Denton, former drill sergeant for the cavities squad was suddenly jettisoned out from under the bridge and down the throat by the force of a mouth wash.

81. "White Light" is latest movie to see. The flick is a visual extravaganza with a supporting cast of seven colorful characters. The film took the theatre by storm and when nothing was said and the audience was undone, it received a four star rainbow review. (The popcorn was good.*)

82. Have you thought about putting a shine on those penny paragraphs written to make small change in the continuity of a dime novel?

83. The author recommends that you run your bath water as a background sound to the story you are reading about Niagara Falls.

84. "King Kong" the pop song about Faye Ray is almost to the top of the Empire State Hit Charts despite competition from the rock band, the B 52's.

85. Since 2002 when he was attacked by a pack of puns, he has had to take single meaning word tabs to prevent the spread of this infectious humor.

86. A philosophical goose egg: Jack climbed the introspective beanstalk up through his cloudy thinking; upward and inward through those enchanted circuits that lead to golden castles.

87. He felt as if he had been hexed by the sand-"Witches of Eastwick" when a vague sense of mayonnaise began to spread over his bedroll. He rose up in his bunk and looked

around at a burnt toast of a day. As the malaise soaked in, he took a long look at his bread, hopped up and began to sop up the sounds of a distant gravy train.

88. The Grecian Urns, a Socrates-owned baseball team, put on their thinking caps and beat the IRS 1040s through a series of well-placed deductions.

89. Socrates' football team, the Grecian Terns, took off their thinking helmets long enough to pour a gallon of ice-cold hemlock over their coach's head after losing at this year's Logic Bowl. (Ouch!*)

90. His latest release from the Folsom Recording Studio is called "Grand Larceny" and includes such stolen hits as "Judgment Day," "You Murdered that Song" and "Time for Ar-rest."

91. A metaphor and a pun stepped out of their English roadster long enough to fish for lower gas prices in a car*pool*.

92. Our latest report from dirt marauders indicates they have been bathing with the new Kublai Khan saddle soap.

93. The day the Kick family rolled into Soccerville, USA, A.Giles rented a field house where they could set up their family practice.

94. The knight munched the turf on the chessboard into an L-shape all the way up to the edge of the castle until a bishop approached the horse from an angle, placed the king's reign over its muzzle and captured him.

95. A rim shot is a basketball joke that bounces off the front of the audience. The comedian gets the rebound and (drum) rolls it into the hoop.

96. A paragraph describing a newly constructed house experienced footnote popping sounds as the house settled toward the bottom of the page.

97. The family of finches that had nestled behind the awnings of a library was fed bookworms until it was big enough to check out a volume of insects.

98. A fictional character was seized by a sneeze attack brought on by the dust jacket covering the book.

99. General L. Acidophilus secured the culture by leading a battalion of the best bacteria in a victory over the caffeine regulars during the stomach uprising.

100. Ralph was floating in some white water R's when he was rafted into the marines. We are talking 'r' as in ridiculous, Ralph. You can't be rafted while poling a pirogue down the river.

101. English: We took a Cobblestone Survey to see how many people walked their turkeys to Ovenshire, Wales, for a parting of the wattles before dining with the Eaton Cranberries.

102. Thereafter, King Myopia ruled over his Boredom in a state of mind that had closed its borders to Huns, Puns and various Anglos of Humor.

103. To wipe the record clean, Larsen E. Swipe returned a stolen stile last used at a Walker Brothers Concert.

104. Was there ever a Count Pollen in a European country known for his flower gardens? (Would you settle for Sir Resin the nobleman who resonated within most history books? *)

105. When city planners ate from their plates at the intersection of Syrup and Pancake, they found their silverware waiting for them on a tray shaped like a parking lot.

106. Though it appeared to be rusting, the topic dealing with irony was only oxidizing its right to be read.

107. As a foot-note to all musicians: Lester Shue's tongue fell out when the orchestra leader found the right horn to fit the brass player's personality.

108. The city of Bloomington hired Flora Stamen to do specialized field work detailing the various methods by which flower metro-pollenate.

109. The teacher was late. The instructions which were on the billboard were largely ignored and so the raucous fun began. Three of the top ten geology students began pelting their lab with hits from the "Rolling Stone."

110. "Let me run this down for you," chided the skeptical brother. "Sis, the cash you won for your theory of Big Foot made a twenty-six-inch impression on believers who are still hot on the trail of this legend."

111. A recent graduate from Tadpole High in Croatia, the amphibious Roger Frog leaped beyond the pond memories to work on the riverfront for Stoad Tools, Inc.

112. General Pixel assured a color company of dots that when the public saw the big picture, he was certain his would stand out against the black-and-white resistance troops.

113. Mo was Tarzan's mentor at the Mentum Tribe during his exposure to the pendulum method of inter-jungle transport.

114. Right after breakfast, there was a siege at the sausage factory, so we asked the chef to write us a letter describing the pan-demonium.

115. The Rainbow Computer Company tells is that if you turned a dancing leprechaun loose on the keyboard, he might tap out the location to a pot of gold.

116. Erin McFadden adjusted the trajectory of the trebuchet and hurled an eight hundred pound war verb across the margin and through a castle wall on the opposite page. (The reference here is to a medieval weapon used to hurl rocks. It must be an action verb to carry so much weight.*)

117. When questioned, the equestrian-minded Ecuadorians of the Galapagos Islands agreed it would behoove them to train their horses to run.

118. "So, you think you're so special with that highly touted wizard brain; so special that you've decided not to go to the *convention* with us because you won't fit in. Well, let me tell you if my name was Magic Wanda I would bop you in the nose with a little stick and make you disappear."

119. If the movie is a comedy it will smell like a banana which means that:
   a. Some of the jokes will be slippery.
   b. You'll hear peals of laughter coming from the audience.
   c. Some jokes ripen with age.

A Day in the Life

Describe:

- the plot of your latest movie and give its title.

- your appearance.

- the last funny thing your brother or sister did.

- your favorite person.

- the heat during a week in equatorial Africa.

- the children you may someday have.

- your progress as a freshman to a senior.

- the end of the world as if it were tomorrow. (Some may argue that tomorrow arrives.*)

- a most unusual dream.

- a day in your favorite amusement park.

- an immediate family member. (And do it now, please.*)

- your first diving experience. (We're not looking for a deep story; only one that is self contained.*)

- the toughest job you've ever had. (Do not include English class.*)

- the contribution you will make to the world.

- the personality of the town where you live.

1. Why do students want to be popular?

2. What is the name of your next compact disc? Describe and tell why you wrote the songs.

3. You are an Olympic participant for a gold medal. The race is on when all of a sudden . . . .

4. Why do people talk so much? (Maybe you should ask somebody. *)

5. What is of the utmost importance to you?

6. What do you want to learn in this class?

7. Are you bored with the class or yourself?

8. Explain the relationship you have with your family.

9. Is your opposable thumb for or against picking up hitchhikers?

10. Switch rolls with somebody for a day and do a taste test.

11. Be a kitchen cabinet for a day.
How are you holding up?
Are you open to new ideas?

12. Thanksgiving is here and we have a cooked turkey on the table. Offer a eulogy.

13. This morning you shot an elephant in your pajamas. How did he get in your pajamas? (Compliments of Groucho Marx.*)

14. Packy Dormus cannot remember that last time he saw an elephant wearing pink pajamas. (Did the big animal have a package of peanuts in its pocket?*)

15. You are the director of the movie called "My Life." How are the other actors doing? (I'll bet some of them are real characters, aren't they?*)

16. You are Captain Luke Warm and your ship is trying to cross the Great Bathtub when something pulls the plug. Describe.

17. Nights provide the perfect dark room for examining your life film. (The topic was dated and yet film remains in good condition.*)

18. You have recently returned from Europe. Tell about your trip. (Did you make the trip this fall? *)

19. Olivia Molecule was often ridiculed for being so small until Atom Publishing accepted her novel, *The Invisible Women*.

20. You took the leap. You jumped from an airplane and now your parachute won't open. Or: You jumped from a plane that was still on the ground. (Free falling from an airborne aircraft is fairly inexpense.*)

21. Be a desert for a day and the caravan has left you? Describe. (So, finish your apple pie and ice cream and let's go check the camels.*)

22. If you found a bottle with a note in it, what would you want it to say? ("Let us out of here," signed Sofie and Kate.—co-signed*)

23.   My uncle Notch pulled a belt off the top of a door and the buckle hit him in the nose.

24.   What is the most difficult aspect of being a freshman? The easiest?

25.   You are William Tell's son. Your dad has been having eye problems. The apple is on your head. Write dialogue. (May I request a song by Arrowsmith? *)

26.   A load of humor lumber has been delivered to a comedian construction site. (I'll bet you ten pennies the reader nails this one.*)

27.   What is it like being in charge of traffic control in Central Africa? (When the light changes we might hear the joke about the charging elephant.*)

28.   Jimmy Driftwood was on the beach dreaming about New Orleans when a beach comber walked by whistling a war song.

29.   Who are your favorite writers? Why?

30.   Is writing one of your strengths? (We are Delilah, excuse me, delighted to hear you say that you wrote a research paper, Samson.*)

31.   Who are the funniest people in the world? (Anybody who can see the humor in things without wearing glasses.*)

32.   Are you into weight lifting? Can you curl ten pounds of conceptual thinking? (I will avoid the temptation here is to make a remark about *dum-bellum.* *)

33.   A casket maker looked up long enough to tell say that this was the most solitary *undertaking* he had ever done.

34. "Now, this won't hurt a bit," assured the dentist as he bore down with an eight inch drill.

35. On the spur of the moment he decided to build a horse barn.

36. "Thunderations," complained Thor's mother, "We gave him a hammer and hoped he would become a carpenter. But no! He had to go off to Hollywood and be in the movies and just look at the stormy life he's lived."

37. "Are we lost?"
"No."
"Well, what word would you use to describe the situation?"
"I'd say we were at a crosswords puzzle."

38. A butterfly landed on Marjorie's head as she was about to toast to the new Monarch.

39. A wildlife course is being offered for zebras who aspire to be basketball officials.

40. The dam broke when the Little Dutch Boy reached down to get his cell phone.

41. In the ancient Middle East, Leviticus Strausolamew made his living patching tents together from old worn out blue jeans.

42. "A man wearing a gorilla suit was sitting in a cage at the zoo."
"How do you know there is a man in it?"

43. For those of you who think you are *march*ing to the beat of a different drummer: Newsflash, this is April.

44. Apparently witches have carte blanche on Walpurgus night. (Raise your broom in the air if you know which night this is.*)

45. Exclusive yacht club members are excited about this year's ice cycle growing contest.

46. A person is in control of her domicile when she places bricks under the water drain to prevent erosion.

47. Walking through the random order of events, you are going to get some mud on your shoes.

48. Shouldn't you try to look the part that you are playing?

49. Headlines: Dr. Pino Keyo Performs Nose Surgery on Mendo City's Mayor (In all honesty, you may need some help with this one. Our dictionary man tells us that mendacity means *lying*.*)

50. Prerequisite bull session to becoming a sophomore in college: solve a global war or determine if the tree made any sound falling in the forest without any humans to hear it.

51. Do you plan to attend a college this fall that offers a course in golf? (Studying can be tedius.*)

52. Jack, immediately upon his return from the stalk in the sky, reported his *nestegg* earnings to the I R S. (Fee, fi, fo fum; they'll be doing my taxes in the auditor-ium.*)

53. Milton Strongback was always willing to give the hitchhiker a lift should he be carrying a heavy load.

54. When you hear three cheers you will know that the triumvirate was triumphant. (Yes, and we will provide them with a place to sit.*)

55. On this brighter cheerful day, the president was told to put a cap on spending by one of his sun visors.

56. Austin, the electric gardener, estimates that a bionic tree provides up to six million dollars worth of shade.

57. Hey, that guy sitting on the park bench is counting the membership birds in a large flock of pigeons.

58. Sliding along the bottom of an empty day, Frankie Portia stopped long enough to watch the Tarzan double demonstrate the use of a new mosquito repellent.

59. The chairperson of the furniture company told us that we were not allowed to pad our paychecks by sitting around all day.

60. Tomorrow we need to fasten more formations to the ceiling of the cave.

61. The Cement Awards are presented by the Foundation for People who *set up* late at night waiting for some concrete information via the news media. (Will a candid comment in a textbook make the evening news?*)

62. Richard'll tell us all about the steps we need to take to preserve our tradition.

63. You are a talk show host and your guest is Bigfoot. Is it a size twenty-two interview?

64. Vultures circled the paragraph that described the carnage.

65. Anytime Texan Paul Mercer wants a quick easy slide across Couch County he slips a vinyl saddle on his horse and takes off.

66. The person seen rappelling the Tower of Babel slipped at an interjection and landed on a syntax.

67. O. B. Servantes concluded one day that "if you stick around long enough this business of being human might get a little old."

68. Patterns Workshop: Tuesday will deal with subtle-ties. (Did I mention over our last cup of tea that this one was lost on me? *)

69. Both parties, Tweedle-dee and Tweedle-dum, agreed to wear name tags.

70. When a sheriff was found to be wearing an outlaw's shirt, the man with a star was told by the judge to "button it if you want to walk away with a size small sentence." (Or you can edit it.*)

71. A family of Taoists was seen filling its karma machine. (Let's hope they use a lot of positive energy.*)

72. How *fast* are you expected to run in the Diet 5K?

73. Spew, correction, few if anyone wants the job which doesn't change the fact that Volcano Inc. needs to be plugged. (Pardon the inter-eruption.*)

74. Did the macho man take a quantum leap into a sink full of dirty dishes? (" . . . and the dish ran away with the spoon."*)

75. According to the polls, a lot of people are neither positive nor negative about the issue.

76. *Nate*, do I understand you to say that you're getting married because you feel that it's your turn to go to the *altar?*

77. What does a cultural uniform look like? (Is that a blue collar question? *)

78. When a jet airliner was mistaken for a toy by the Jolly Green Giant, the passengers were forced to parachute to a *Thousand Islands.*

79. This statue wonders if there isn't a claws in some ordinance that prohibits pigeons from landing on it. (If not a clause it has to be a statute.*)

80. The successful rug doctor will prescribe thirty minutes per day with a vacuum cleaner for one of his walk-in patience.

81. A noticeable thin caveman emerged from his grotto to announce to the world that he been on a troglo-diet. (A troglodyte is a cave dweller and I'll bet you three soda straws and a milk shake that someone will trip over that last word on their way out of the cave.*)

82. You are telling me that there is a train conductor who rails about the noise that some cars make?

83. Blink if you agree that you need to practice making eye contact.

84. Headlines: Insect Trapped in Camera Inspires Japanese Sci-fi Flick

85. Anna Havanna found a cigar box filled with traditional values at a yard sale. (The 60's folk song "Puff the Magic Dragon" (Peter, Paul and Mary) will never be for sale no matter how many yards are being sold.*)

86. What interests you the most: people, things or ideas?

87. Are you waiting for something fantastic happen?

88. Piper wants to know if it will hide unsightly bathroom plumbing.

89. The plaster mold of a dog biscuit was used as model for a golf course.

90. After inciting a prolonged silence, the boring comedian decided to became a tent salesman.

91. "Sprinkler Today" informs us that the new outdoor water hydrant can really motivate a gardener to get with the flow.

92. Three people were dunked in the ensuing skirmish after Puggy did a cannonball off the diving board.

93. Will a mole hill have an emotional transition into a mountain?

94. Would it affect your electric bill if you had a duck quack for doorbell?

95. "I shot an arrow into the air and was arrested by the game warden."

96. Will there be fast food in Oz? Yes! And we know the perfect person to be the foreman. He is two and a half times more qualified than the nearest applicant. We should let the Ten Man in on the sizzling number-gers we'll be selling to all the Munchkins.

97. Some people claim they have found elf chairs under certain kinds of mushrooms. (We'll shii-take your word for it.*)

98. "Oh my gauche!" she muttered after spotting her boyfriend beating a set of drums in the middle of a traffic jam. "He's taken one of his galvanized oxygen pellets."

99. People who eat with chopsticks are also capable of producing a drum roll as they read their fate from a cookie.

100. Del Purvis without so much as a pause, volunteered to train nine people survival techniques for hiking through the Catskills.

101. The Marsupial Company has the kangaroo line of apparel in its pocket.

102. Write an operation manual for any machine. (You do understand how this topic works? *)

103. You are a kamikaze pilot. Describe your last flight.

104. You are a caveman. Describe life in the cave and your language. (Ugh! *)

105. Humpty Dumpty sat on a wall and was promptly reprimanded by a security guard for breach of a "no trespassing" sign. The very next day:

     Humpty Dumpty sat on a wall. Humpty Dumpty had a great fall. Consequently, the Dumpty family filed a law suit against the construction company for using mortar that failed to pass federal inspection codes.

106. Malia wrote a letter to herself outlining her ambitions to travel the world. She found a stamp for the envelope and within minutes had slipped it into the "out of town" slot at the post office.

107. Theavy metal band, the Scalded Banchees agreed to show up the morning after their recording session to help repaint the walls.

108. A recording of "The Three Stooges" sound effects could be heard in the background as slapsticks were falling from the comedy tree.

109. Christopher Columbus is your boss and you have a few things to say to him about a constant diet of pinto beans and corn bread. Explain. (Do you have a cook named Nina? *)

110. He decided to become a mechanical engineer after years of partnering with his father who repaired car motors by listening to them.

111. Enough of this talk about someone else, let's talk about me. (Most circles are self-centered.*)

112. Things that go bump in the night are in effect yesterday realigning itself to satisfy the requirements for what today should look like. (Don't you hear a bump when one day runs into another?*)

113. When he bought the farm the deed was delivered in a coffin shaped envelope.

114. The cop-per wired the metallurgist all the while telling him he was about to be hammered into conduction.

115. Ankh, if you're alive and well and a few minutes ago you left the library where you had been studying Egyptology.

116. The empty packages of corn, asparagus, radishes and lettuce were used as signs to indicate what crops had been planted where. (Did Carl take time off from his job at the Acronym Center to put in a garden?*)

117. Font vaulter Jordon Brinkley soon learned that the higher the number reached, the bigger the headlines in the local press.

118. The eccentric man called the pharmacy today and asked if we had a more potent placebo.

119. The eccentric man called back thirty minutes later to say that he felt much better after making the first call.

120. You'll meet the inspection team that will thoroughly examine your gift for gab kit before the censorship leaves the harbor.

121. Day after day in ancient Greece, Apollo harnesses his steeds and pulls the sun across the sky. (So it was in that culture. In our time he would be warned to use a sun screen.*)

122. She was basking in an early morning land of chimeras where dreams flow like ribbons rippling through a breeze when suddenly the alarm tattooed her senses like a staple gun into full awareness. (Wake up! *)

123. A sea change is big: He will be giving away all his gold today at three to join a monastery.

124. Once upon a time, the Troll Herald consistently reported gremlins at the Kremlin.

125. Mr. Sandman was seen sitting atop a glass furnace wondering why he had been fired and why his days in the desert were dune.

126. New demands made on the members of the Polar Bear Club. Not only do they have to wade into frigid waters, they also have to kiss the hand of the nearest fair young maiden as an act of shiver-ry.

127. The old man walked slowly along the seashore throwing bread to the gulls, side-stepping the flotsam and examining conches. Suddenly he stopped, sat down and

began to construct a sand castle. (Let's hope it has flood insurance.*)

128. On the one hand, how many people do you know work overtime to justify the stereotypes with which they are labeled; on the other is a glove.

129. Now we know that Merlin the Magician turned a novice into a seasoned writer by guiding him through the craft eight hours a day for five or six years. (Work shows.*)

130. Hospital intercom; "Superman to radiology."

131. Can you handle power?

132. Do you recall the day when Mrs. Carpenter decided to use her husband's level to balance a checking account?

133. Did Einstein ever get a flash of relativity while attending family reunions? (Rarely, because h*e* was too busy being the *m*aster of *c*eremonies.*)

134. The report cited deadly sins two and five as being responsible for hijacking the police chief's personality.

135. The cream of Zen Monk theorists usually snack on cosmic Koans. (Our treat: a koan is a puzzle used as an aid to meditation.*)

136. Seely saw Celes try to angle her protractor between two equal sides of the same field.

137. Omer Osmosis fell asleep on the couch and dreamt that his semi-permeable membrane was being audited for its properties of absorption. (I hate it when that happens.*)

138. If Monday will hold out a rope with one end in each hand, Giles will skip a day.

139. Speaking of Houdini, this linguistic whiz kid is quite the escape artist. After being tongue-tied and issued a gag order in the bottom of a mute tank, he still came out talking.

140. Not only is Ken Tinnue a leader in the *Keep Marching until April* movement, he and his wife Toby also moonlight as a pause in the middle of many long stories.

141. A Biberian belongs to that exclusive group of people who have never dropped oatmeal on their shirts.

142. You are a genius, Bubba, what is your next project? (Please don't tell me you need to go to the Mensa room.*)

143. If it's too wet on the outside, we may have to go inside to celebrate the July fourth light show.

144. "Hey Valise, What's in the luggage?"
"A few personal items."
"Can you be more specific?"
"Okay, I'm packing a looking glass that I consult anytime the situation calls for bringing out my personal best?"

145. "Don't walk into the store feeling listless. You'll buy a bag full of things that we don't need," Pat Tree Arch advised his teenage daughter, "and do not strap on the head phones and go grocery shopping while listening to 'Hungry.'"

146. We sent out a technology ship and using all the equipment we had at our fingertips plus a *ton of skill*, we did the impossible. We resurrected Davy Jones' Locker. Today that maritime storage unit rests in the basement of the Smithsonian.
"And what is in the locker?"
"You'll have to ask the treasury department."

147. Those old ice-cream makers were so cranky. If you wanted vanilla, you turned the handle clockwise. After that flavor

was made and you wanted strawberry, the handle would go counterclockwise and you'd be back where you started.

148. Ike was so eager to begin his evening program that he grabbed a mike and "KCOR is your off-the-dial time travel station to reach. Tune us in and get your ticket punched for songs that haven't been written yet. We'll discuss trends that are alien to our listeners and get with artists who haven't the slightest idea what we're talking about. And now we'll take a station break. Here's Compton Marcel."

"So you like your tunes; another reason to buy this baby. This car has *radials* that we guarantee will take you completely across the land of the music." (Groovy.*)

DNA

1.   Thanks to *He*loise and *Fe*lix we discovered after all these years that the safe was never locked.

2.   Drop a can of polish into your gene pool and be amazed at what surfaces with your progeny.

3.   For those who *chromofy*, the DNA double helix race should take you up the Ancestral Trail to, then twice around the Gene Pool. Advance from there to, then over the Nuclei Bypass where some Ribos will RNA your way to the X or Y finish lane. (And so it goes with the human race.*)

4.   Can you imagine what shape the stairway takes in the new Helix House?

5.   The DNA lamp can shed a lot of light on whatever you're doing.

6.   Have you ever heard of a DNA rod for conducting high frequency energy waves?

7.   A squirrel's genetic blueprint contains a helix tree whose branches support a steady supply of chromo-nuts.

8.   Instilling morality through intelligence is no more complicated than correcting the defects in the DNA helix.

9.   The all new hereditary jungle bars have been recalled due to defective chromosome grips.

10. Is there a chromosome repair shop in this town? (Yes, it's on N. Spiral Street or about a half mile from the airport.*)

11. We now have the all new chromosome hiking boots. Your jeans will slide comfortably over them. They have been trail tested twenty-three times and are equipped with durable water proof soles. ("Walk this Way" by Arrowsmith*)

12. A macho climber has called in for the twenty-third time warning us not to forget our jeans.

13. Chromosome electronics do provide plug-ins for mental juke boxes.

14. How many people know how to alter the inner seam of a DNA jean should they want to change their life style?

15. As you stroll through their water garden, you'll notice some people are quite good at creating that perfect balance of the elements to surround their gene pool.

16. We are all partici*pants* in the jeans game.

17. Saturday nights should include sitting and watching as a lighthouse helix beams DNA molecules to the good ship Levi.

18. We strongly recommend the release of Malcolm Chemical from his duties at the Center for Disease Control?

Food for Thought

1. Describe popcorn before and after popping. (Let's make a movie about popcorn.*)

2. Spaghetti spokes should bend with each fork in the road.

3. La Zahn, ya don't need a menu to tell you that we specialize in Italian cuisine.

4. Why does Pearl have such an appetite for oyster soup?

5. When you hit those new chocolate hockey pucks from the right angle, you can chip off a few M & M's.

6. You can tell when your tomatoes are ripe enough to be described in a chef salad if you'll use brackets (red, plump) that fade when the vegetable is ready.

7. Eaton Wigglesworth was terrible fond of his morning swim through a bowl of strawberry Jell-O.

8. Would a root beer float qualify to be in the ice cream parade?

9. If you were for-aging would you pay more attention to your eating habits?

10.   We read how a new diet calls for a bowl of homilies with a single kernel of truth.

11.   Would it take a forklift to move a mountain of pasta?

12.   We turned a clock on its face, poured the time out and it became a salad bowl. We then used a minute hand to toss in a three-second slice of tomato, a lettuce pause, some easy aging cots, minute pieces of bacon and one hors d'oeuvre.

13.   Do you need a tem-*plate* to see what a well balanced meal will look?

14.   According to the Texas Highway Department you can make an enchilata difference in the life of a bridge if you will line it with taco shells. (This one is saucy and we're getting hungry or should we cross that bridge when we get to it? *)

15.   What kind of pie requires 3.14 pints of fruit?

16.   Our favorite pasta time is Ra-*violi*-n music and spaghetti.

17.   We don't know of any forks in the road that will help you get through the Serengeti spaghetti. We do however offer dessert after the meal.

18.   If your thoughts are overweight, perhaps your thinking needs to go on a diet. Stop glazing at donut shops and soaking up junk food entertainment.

19.   Place an open menu on the roof of a restaurant and observe a higher order of leaves as they create the pattern for the daily special.

20.   You can slice through a lot of bologna with the edge of a question mark.

21. The poetry of breakfast is the smell of bacon and eggs and I reach for my oink pen as memories unroll in perfect hominy.

22. If you are looking for the building blocks to the Muscle District, get out your map of human nutrition and find Protein Town in the state of Bean.

23. "It has been roughage," says Asa Asparagus and wife Carrie Crouton, concerning their aspirations to be admitted to the American Salad Bar.

24. Will you find fossilized sugar cane in rock candy?

25. Similes can be as sweet as cookies.

26. "Listen, I am really hungry but those Frugal bars are way too expensive."

27. "Quick, give me a double scoop on a cone . . . uh, make that three, give me three; Whoops! It landed on your shoe, I see," faux pod an innocent snacker.

28. Musicologists are now using each of the thirty-two strings of a harp to slice an equal number of cheeses.

29. Are bass drums to the orchestra what potatoes are to the diet?

30. A telemarketer for the latest pre-tossed salad bar would be a *coll*-ard.

31. Dessert will be the aftermath of a meal served on a multiplication table. (Will it be peach pi? *)

32. On a scale of one to ten with cake being two and carrots being eaten; this is considered a balanced meal

33. Let-terians use an okra stamp to speed the delivery of good health into their diets.

34. Are you overly *dog*-matic about your vegetables? Take your point of view for a wok.

35. The smell of bacon wafting up through the midnight oil must certainly have inspired Nostril Domus to think about the Bay of Pigs.

36. "Here! Have a chocolate argue mint."
"No thanks."
"C'mon, try it. You'll agree with the taste."
"Okay, I'll try it." (This is a teaser. Since he willingly ate the candy, he obviously didn't agree with the taste.*)

37. Are you hungry for beauty? From atop the water tower in Plateria, we see a mountain of mashed potatoes with a river of gravy flowing through the valley below.

38. The use of calipers expedited the measuring and reduction of the size of the holes in Swiss cheese.

39. The house specialty for the Diamond Restaurant is their carrot salad.

40. "This is excellent sponge cake. Who made it?"
"Abbey Sorbine baked it. She's the lady standing over there next to the sink soaking up all the compliments."

41. A new item on the menu for cattle rustlers is purloin steak.

42. Fruits and vegetables are to vitamins and minerals what books are to information.

43. Common taters with dissenting opinions are listed as deep fried on the media menu.

44. A suggestion box contained a note that requested a quicker response to and improved efficiency in the handling of such notes.

45. A raw bean dropped in a pot of water might create a ripple of dietary sarcasm.

46. She was sitting on a drifting cumulus cloud eating a bowl of chicken soup when suddenly a seraphim appeared and asked what part of the bird goes into the broth? "Mostly wings," she replied.

47. Add sauce to a culinary doodle and the noodle becomes spaghetti.

48. Soak some the adjectives out of your more descriptive paragraphs and it will read a lot cleaner.

49. Can you pick a song called "Tomatoes" then slice the notes into a musical salad?

50. Back in his leaner days, before being admitted to the bar, Sly Slicero drove a late model Avocado when rolling into top seeded Patty Petite's place for a dinner date.

51. We need dining forks that will vibrate according to the quality of the food with which they are stuck.

52. You can level a mountain of cheese if you'll attach a grater to the nose of a dozer.

53. Wheat grew in such abundance that the trees overhanging the grain dropped piles of breadsticks between the furrows.

54. While kneading some bread to complete the communion, he did some genu-wine reflecting on genuflecting.

55. Since we all eat carrots to a different drummer and since nobody can nibble like the Ever-Ready rabbit, we should all plant carrots to his beat and give away a battery of them each spring.

56. Blue cheese sandwiches can be found at the celestial bar during any given month with two full menus.

57. How ironic that it's still in the grammar menu of "Food for Thought" because we have no words to describe adjective chili. (Are we talking about *cool beans*?*)

58. Want to figure out physics? Dip Sir Isaac Newton into a glass of milk.

59. Try the new Count Abacus tomato sauce. (I'd be happy to if you'll slide it cross the table.*)

60. Twice a month, Rose Berry opens the refrigerator door as dad takes the kids out for a pop cycle.

61. You must peel an intangible if you need some vitamin C abstract.

62. My grating cheese will usually land in the bottoms of a Mississippi salad bowl.

63. The waitress was serving time for having broken a law dish. (Somebody must have ordered a chocolate cake shaped like a clock.*)

64. Do skillets burn out?

65. We offered Tom Atoes complete control of the salad bar because he seemed to fit right in. (Really? You seem to have left out a few; *Carrie Ut*ley, Brock Alley and Tonya Crews? They all need jobs too.*)

66. Two flying monkeys from "The Wizard of Oz" have been grounded under suspicion of banana intoxication.

Future

1. Future dictionaries will list the emotional impact in terms of mergs beside each word: house will be 3.5 mergs; home, 7.5.

2. At some time in the future will it cost you $4.37 to expose a gallon of tea to three hours of sunlight?

3. In the future, we'll have quarter size crystal balls that can be worn around the wrist and will have the capacity to tell us when they will stop working.

4. "Step right up, show your ticket and get an hour's worth of fresh air inside this glassarium."

5. In the distant future will trained firemen be able to focus an anti-flame gaze at anything that's going up in smoke?

6. Futurists envision the day when fire will be controlled by the sound of a trumpet.

7. Plug this new and improved Rudolf nightlight in under any window and snow begins to fall. (Did someone say, "Look, it's raining, deer?" *)

8. In the future, interns will sell jars of grape jollv to people who have had a less than smiling day.

9. Words of the future are to be found in a prediction-ary that rests on a coffee table at the end of the December thirty-second lobby.

10. In the future you'll be issued a ticket if you don't slow down to the point where you can hear the audible speed breaks.

11. Forget the subway: Someday subatomic travel will be possible. (Can you draw graffiti on the wall of a physics book?*)

12. The year was 2098 and Rodney Upton was miffed: "You can't fly a kite in one of those inter-city wind tunnels. The tail will get caught in a wall vent."

13. The year is 2212 A.D. and archeologists have ample evidence to conclude that ancient *US-Asians* worshipped their gods from a complex known as Mt. Wal-Mart. Mythologists are however, mystified. It seems there were creatures known as Gummy Bears, small metal boxes that people held to their ears and voices sounding from the ceiling.

14. Bio active cards will be assigned to people in the near future. Punch one into the instant therapy unit, listen to your three magical notes and receive automatic psychological realignment. (We know of a turtle that seemed to enjoy its mud swings.*)

Generic

1. "You are about to venture into a land of prompts that roll and romp and bounce off the wall and that's not all. They pomp and pump from a well that never runs dry." (We never used this testimonial that was submitted by an anonymous donor.*)

2. Let's divide *bi-furcate* . . .

3. into two topics.

4. Are these entries original? (See p. 222, #70*)

5. A one man topic band has to toot its own horn.

6. Sometimes while walking along the shore line, we would stop, find a well-rounded three-line topic and skip it across a mental body of water.

7. 7. Try using one of these topics as a tool to describe life in high school.

8. The topic gearbox is calibrated at a two to one ratio of metaphors to puns.

9. We need a designated topic to drive home a Point-ibishi that meditation gets more mileage than alcohol.

10. This is a test topic. For the next sixty seconds, you'll receive information on what to do should you read something in the nature of an emergency.

11. We've started drilling from several topic derricks that have been erected off the coast of the Cortex Islands.

12. We drill for topics. If we can help you with a story you are writing, we will lease, not sell, the needed bits with added lubrication to set you on your way.

13. Do not touch this topic. There, at the end, is a white hot stick welding a heavy metal song to the top ten periodic chart of lists.

14. From this gate forward, check all thought processes for a valid passport as documented proof of recognized originality. (They must carry the embassy stamp of intelligence.*)

15. If the ideas will not come on, check to see if the topic switch is off in the breaker box.

16. Is it a faulty metaphor if you can't reach the fruit at the top of the topics tree?

17. In the throes of writer's block woes? For a solution mix one part topic with three-parts liquid plot.

18. What about the topic that's been camped at my front cortex for three days? Why? Because he's waiting for the pen light to come on?

19. A lot of water is necessary to plant, cultivate, and harvest a new crop of topics.

20. The topic squad will send a trained team to any area of the brain that reports a neuron fire.

21. The blueprint calls for eight synaptic discharges, four of which branch off into neighboring neural deltas to create a current topic.

22. A topic-tician slide rule takes properly aligned images to the nth degree of the metaphorical power.

23. The topics will be easier to identify if taken four to six at a time from a lineup. (Are some of the puns borderline criminal?*)

24. The judge held a hearing to determine if any of these topics had committed a crime.

25. Do the teachers at the Robin Hood School of Economics point with an arrow when using the blackboard?

26. We don't need any more gadget topics that you have to plug in to figure out.

27. Topics of all shapes, tones, hues and pitches use air tanks that are stored in Diverse City.

28. Sometimes, while walking along the shoreline, we would stop, find a well rounded three line topic and skip it across the waters of the mind.

29. How much nitro-creativity would it take to detonate one of these topics into a full blown story? (Would it blow somebody's mind?*)

30. A cogitator's repairman had to replace the *fuge* in the *centri* in order to separate the light from the heavy weight topics.

31. Many of these topics were produced by the Leprechaun Brain Trust.

32.   Each member of our staff carries a topic detector, which beeps when nearing potential material.

33.   Due to their dimmer voltage, foibles are difficult to work into the personality of a stronger topic.

34.   The Iron Man of the Tri-topic-thon trains at the Dali Lodge behind the Apex Mountain Range.

35.   When they arrive with a twenty-three degree text, the *Topics of Capricorn* have received the suns northernmost point of inspiration.

36.   Many of the entries have a built-in night light in the event a reader feels left out in the dark.

37.   Experts have visited this material and they all agree they were inspired to write a more creative appraisal of what they've seen.

38.   Most topics are equipped with a scanner that provides up to a ten sub-thought capacity.

39.   An introspective topic ponders what has been said, how it was received, the content of the grammar, should it change, how will the other topics react and what will it have to say in the future. (This entry won best generic top of the year award.*)

40.   We do not accept underwritten topics.

41.   You'll find a battery of these entries that can be recharged.

42.   FYI: Cynthia combines two different sizes to make a topic she can wear in front of the readers.

43. This topic developed an overwhelming feeling of grandeur when written into a bubble that floated high above a scenic landscape.

44. Our agent in Ancient Rome is Thoughticious Profundis who resides at their Topiceum.

45. Climb, clime, kalime to the top of the topic's tower and soak in a bird's-eye-view of the gallery.

46. We hesitated to write a topic about pork barrels because we couldn't decide if it would go into the Money category or Food for Thought. (The taboo light of politics is flashing. Do we leave it in or take it out? *) (My friends are all rooting for you to leave it in there . . . . Holly Bellum)

47. "What I don't understand," commented the police officer "is why she had such a difficult time describing how her verbal maps had fallen apart after she left them out in the rain." ("The rain in Spain falls . . ."*)

48. You can fuel up at any of our convenient Topic stations located on most inter-states of contemplation. These stations are also found after the fourteenth turnaround should you be pacing the floor.

49. Who will be the people's choice to win the Writer's Cup for Excellence in the category of topic creation?

50. Before we can add any new shadow topics to the text, we have to wait until the sun advances farther across the sky.

51. When the heartbeat of this book stops, will the words return to the dictionary?

52. A few people have asked us if some of these topics have hidden meanings. (You will probably find exactly what you're looking for.*)

53. A house of cards takes on an entirely new meaning if you'll use the ace of hearts for a front door.

54. A Sara Bellum unit is the amount of creative energy necessary to elevate one paragraph of text one letter grade in a writing class.

55. Does this book use the more simple topics as a Trojan horse to expose the younger readers to more complicated ideas? (More or less.*)

56. Set some roses on the table of contents while *The SBR* is completing the list of categories.

57. Tell *Caf*-tain Bor-*eine* that we may not be the crème of the crop or even on top but we still do not want to be lumped in with all those other coffee table books.

58. Your are reading the white tiger of creative books.

59. Any topic that seems out of place can be put in a trebuchet and hurled it back to the introduction.

60. According to Chinese art of decorating a living room, Feng Shui, this comment fits comfortable in the living room of the Main Office.

Grammar

1. Can you explain the power of a question mark? (Haven't they been known to completely transform a sentence? *)

2. Do you recommend rubbing some euphemism soap on those saddlebags that are filled with hard-to-break horse adjectives?

3. While you are pouring words into a thought mold, modifiers will *rebar* your efforts until the paragraph hardens.

4. Bill Fordyce was getting married so he back his truck into, then hitched it to three prepositional trailers, then pulled them out of the parking lot and down the street to the storage units.

5. Hey, Ezra, make sure your adjective tank holds at least two hundred Pounds of descriptive pressure.

6. The definition of a noun is converted into energy by a verb.

7. The president of all the modifiers lives in a white house.

8. The English teacher was known to open a dictionary plant he kept next to a window and then turn to the P's to help pollinate garden variety research papers.

9. Twenty spoken words are rolled into a subject-verb circle that moves around like a wheel spinning out a thought.

10. The sentence was balanced. The metaphors had lift. The motifs were tight. The puns had been doubly checked. All parts had passed the grammar test and the propeller compelled us to take it for a spin. Let's see if it will fly.

11. When kids are wading in a stream of words, they always want to roll a rock over to see what nouns verb away.

12. Read on. It's round; thump it. It's plump and juicy, wet, full of seeds and ready to be sliced open, munched and devoured. It's an adjective melon growing along the banks of the Grammar River.

13. "Have you bounced a triple negative off your logic trampoline lately?"
"No!" "And why not?"
"Don't need none nohow."

14. The nose of a grammar hound can detect a splice of comma from a meal eaten in an eighteenth century European novel.

15. By definition most adjectives do their best work with a noun.

16. Predicates in orbit around a subject produce a magnetic attraction for direct objects to complete the action.

17. Oden <rode> the bull for over eight seconds thanks to the use of verb clamps in complete sentences.

18. Did Noah's family make room for feminine and masculine parts of speech while aboard the ark of grammar?

19. Start with direct object hors d'oeuvres. Add a sprig of adjectives to garnish the prepositional patty melt. Heap on scalloped infinitives and buttered gerunds with added peas

for punctuation. Finish with chocolate commas dripped over a mound of ice cream modifiers.

20.   Orders came to start naming things so the Fifth Battalion of nouns equipped with their Latin derivatives went marking single file into the field.

21.   A comma splice near the colon had caused a hemorrhage in the flow of thought. The editors took a pole and decided to slide it between the main idea, tie them together and haul the paragraph off the page.

22.   If there was such a thing as a grammar car, we would question some people's ability to drive. (You will get a citation for an incomplete sentence.*)

23.   If the subject of your garden sentence is tomatoes, plant several prepositional phrases next to the predicate to support the vines.

24.   You would need the fastest modifier in the west to describe the lightning draw of a noun.

25.   An opening at the beginning of the paragraph allows you to slide down into a room that contains deposits from the various parts of speech. (Do you land on a bean bag? *)

26.   According to the Grammar Family, there is always an Uncle Cedent ready and willing to refer back to the subject should the Ante be busy with the local chapter on pro-noun-ce-ments.

27.   "I do declarative," exclaimed the subject to the verb, "You must see the imperative i.e. agree to marry me without any questions."

28.   People should grammar their cotton if they ever want it to make a fashion statement.

29. At the second consonant check point, *travelers* will be asked if they are carrying an extra L.

30. Now that you have written the rough draft of a sentence, tune it. Tighten the subject-verb strings until they sound agreeable. Switch notes that over modify. Then strum your phrases into a series of chords until they bring out the music in the sentence.

31. Would you prefer to live in a short story or a diagrammed sentence? Explain.

32. The Grammar Band uses backup modifiers to harmonize with the singing noun.

33. The grammar auction was interrupted by an impatient fellow who wanted to know when the bidding would begin on interjections.

(Editorial; Why is *that* being accepted as an antecedent for people? Ex. He is the man that failed the grammar test. People are not *that's:* the correct antecedent is *who.* *)

History

1. An empty jar of Peter Pan peanut butter was found near the tarmac at Kitty Hawk, circa 1912.

2. The hula-hoop has rolled into the cultural storage bin.

3. Give an account of George Custer's last battle as if you were there.

4. You are at Sutter's Mill, California, circa 1850. Describe the first nugget of gold that you see rolling around in the pan. (I can buy some new blue jeans and a note in the left pocket will tell us that the first jeans were sewn from the tent material used by the miners.*)

5. You are apprenticed to Johnny Appleseed. Describe an average day. (We had applesauce for breakfast.*)

6. Do you recall the winter of '36? Do you remember three feet of snow on the ground? Tell your story. (If you leave your hovel, you'll need to grab a shovel.*)

7. George Washington is about to throw a coin across the Potomac. Given, the money came out of your pocket: describe the proceedings. (How far will the dollar go? *)

8. Who is your most admired historical figure? (Leonardo de Vinci is convincing.*)

9. Describe your latest adventures with Davy Crockett.

10. Pony Express riders have agreed to start sharing their chocolate chip cookie samples with the Indians.

11. "Mrs. Hester, may I step out of the classroom for a minute to take some cough medicine. It's history extract and it won't take long . . . Doctor's orders."

12. Francine's favorite country, historically, is northeast of Spain.

13. Have you ever looked under the carpet that covers the margins in most history books?

14. A cowboy in fourteenth century England would sing a song to his madri-gal.

15. "Go west, young man, go west," advised the nineteenth century New York Tribune editor Horace Greeley, "and write the story about what happened to the buffalo."

16. The Wrong Brothers had been at Kitty Hawk, North Carolina in the early part of the century, aviation might never have gotten off the ground.

17. Welcome Johnny Conversation Seed, a man who carries a leather bag of ideas, several of which he will plant should he chance upon an area of fertile discourse.

18. A wax likeness of the Roman ruler Nero and his fiddle has a wick at the top of it.

19. The Union Pacific Yin and Yang depicts the droving of the golden spike that united the east with the west. Meanwhile, four hundred miles to the north, a calf was born that would one day kick over Mrs. O'Leary's lantern and burn half of Chicago.

20. If Edward the Eighth had had an Emotion Three camera, his lens guard would have captured the *shudder* speed of the crowd seconds before the lights went out for Ann Boleyn. (If you don't want any part of this, close the shutters.*)

21. After taking the audience step by step down through the real history of the human race, he looked up to see a fright of stares.

22. In 1896, Judge Roy Bean hung the Curtain clan for fabricating a story about a bolt .45 hand gun that had disappeared from his upholstery.

23. Before entering Socrates' house, the visitor had to tap *think* in Morse code on his wooden door.

24. What did we find when we opened the crates? Bias worms, fear molds, parasites and information fungi: all of which had been shipped through the Medieval Canal up and into the twenty-first century.

25. In 1867 a pioneer woman wiped the sweat from her brow and announced that "pushing a prairie schooner filled with lit-otes up the Rocky Mountains was not in the job description." (Would it be an *understatement* to say that we needed to define litotes? *)

26. "Guess what?" asked one Egyptian slave of another. "Once we finish the pyramid, we've been assigned to relocate the Rock of Gibraltar to block some mountain corridor east of Istanbul." (Don't forget to take your block and tackle and football helmet.*)

27. Highway snobbery in the North Atlantic Ocean robbed a lot of people of their lives when the Titanic sank.

28. After the Wright Brothers made the historical flight, a newspaper that ran the story was fashioned into a paper

airplane, launched from the top of a bicycle shop and flown 1/100th the original distance.

29. A ring of hemp rope binding a tea crate was salvaged from Boston harbor and used to secure the Liberty Bell to the town tower, circa 1770.

30. If the Greeks had been ahead of the game, they would have taken the thread of life that Atropos the Fate was about to sever and tied it around the clasp of Pandora's Box.

31. If the Romans had had wall sockets, they would have plugged their TV's in to watch the gladiator playoffs.

32. Ben Franklin might have used his own bifocal lens through which he focused a ray of sunlight to start a fire in the Franklin stove.

33. By at least one account, Teddy Roosevelt was flossing his teeth with a gold card during his charge up San Juan Hill.

34. Caulking guns should have been used to defend western European castles during the middle ages.

35. What happened to the wheelbarrow full of oak chips that were found under A. Lincoln's log cabin? They were time travelled back to G. Washington then packed around the sapling that replaced the cherry tree he chopped down.

36. Paul Bunyan often claimed that he had no axe to grind. Apparently the one he used had been smelted at Valley Forge and had never lost its edge.

37. Lizzie Borden took an axe and chopped several armloads of wood to heat the room where her defense attorney was preparing her case.

38.   Grady Bison has recently released a well researched book in which he, let's just say, takes aim at Buffalo Bill on more than one issue.

39.   When Hannibal led his elephants across the Alps, he put canned goods in all the available trunk space.

40.   If they had had electricity back in the dark ages, somebody might have switched on a lamp long enough to study a science book.

41.   The Whiskey Rebellion of 1794 was proof that ninety-five per cent of the Pennsylvania farmers who knew grain to be more marketable as liquor disagreed with Federal Taxes.

42.   When Alexander Graham Bell first introduced himself to his wife, she commented that the name had a familiar ring to it. (She should have put him on hold and then played some music to keep him occupied.*)

43.   In the event that she became bored, Mrs. Julius Caesar always took a copy of *The Rise and Fall of United States* with her to the coliseum.

44.   Several crates of teapots were loaded on board Robert Fulton's Claremont to generate backup power. (This report was filed by the eighteenth century "Mainsteam Press."*)

45.   A descendant of Bill Cody used his last five Buffalo stamps to mail *A History of the West* to a distant relative.

46.   In 1878, Annie Oakley won the Chester Award by shooting snipes, the ace of hearts,1 and finally buffalo shadows all within a one hour time frame. (We have missed her.*)

47.   Would you conclude that twentieth century mythology has an airplane (As opposed to Jupiter?*) pulling the sun across the sky each day?

48. Sir Walter Raleigh's leather belt was purchased at a Windsor Castle yard sale by the Barber of Seville and thereafter used to sharpen his shaving equipment.

49. In order to test their mettle, medieval knights carried Allen wrenches to tighten the clanks which prevented their horses from bolting.

50. During the middle ages, rock work began when fear of invasions became as big as the castles were tall.

51. Resurrected clay tablet number 26,556 that crumbled during the torching of the Alexandrian Library in Egypt might have informed us as to the connection between energy blockages and diseases.

52. "Fief Oner D. Horst, your first class will be in the castle where you will study the caste system. Should you plan to become a player, we'll see if your pro-moat-ivated, give you the oats of feality and then we'll look for the next bridge to cross." (Let's be *loyal* to the dictionary man and ask him what *feality* means.*)

53. An army of red wrigglers was assigned to a local com-post during the time of the great Lima Bean Throwout.

54. The Union Pacific probably started as a train set assembled in a New England basement by a pre teen using the Morganesque tools of the trade to get on the right tract.

55. We have found that there are several missing notes to the song of history.

56. How do the Beefeaters of England re-gard the Tower of London when it has only one person walking to and fro.

57. History has some attachments that are carefully screened from the reader.

58.   What do the hieroglyphs on the walls of the Egyptian tombs say? (Pharaoh checks will be given out when you place the capstone on that pyramid.*)

Imagery

1. This camel had to tie himself to a pyramid while listening to the Sandblasters an arid group whose music will blow you away.

2. What fun, let's go inshore to California and take in the after spawn fete of the four-minute grunion run.

3. Sidewalks do grow up to be streets and across the alley you'll find that ball bearings grow up to be bowling balls.

4. Captain Stamps and his flotilla of letter openers is slicing ever closer toward the Holiday Islands.

5. The sunset bounced from the chrome onto a purple can of rust remover.

6. If you look close you'll see that the Green Three-Legged Co owned by the Grimace Bro. bought a three by four inch advertisement in the lower left hand corner of Pandora's Box.

7. Countless ocean stories have rolled up on the white sandy beach and were lifted up into a moon beam.

8. Where can we find a melted popsicle home for tongue depressors? (Al is pining for us to use Liechtenstein.*)

9.   A car on blocks is parked in a field with a mason jar in the back seat and a bird nest is visible in the glove box. (This is no doubt a prepositional phrase it's going through.*)

10.   Euneda Stamp sent her boyfriend a hat shaped like a mailbox as a reminder to write her a letter. (Alliteration.*)

11.   Some people say it took a light from the white water; others say fire water. We don't know. What we do know is that the canoe was made of cigars. After three hours of floating down the Brimstone River, it might as well have been made of ashes.

12.   Did the Pumas Company promise the people of Eruptus that they could pour all their excess volcano sauce into one of their lava-tories?

13.   "My, that *def*-initely stretches my earlobe," announced Earl Head. (Is this a left—handed reference to bothersome noise?*)

14.   Would we be way off the coast if we alluded to the fact that you might find the solution to your problem in the Aleutian Islands?

15.   Swordfish have loosened their swashbuckles and now play mumble-ty-peg during the scabbard and blade fest. (You have to be pretty sharp to get this one. *)

16.   A barrage of complaints in a cardboard box was bouncing around like a Mexican jumping bean in Lonny Miffles' garage. (This contribution will not last two minutes at a yard sale.*)

17.   The girl on the bicycle was caught up in the fits and starts of city traffic and honking horns.

18. Why not? Shouldn't the cone from a witches' hat be reinforced with the excess straw that falls from her broom? (Hex-actly. *)

19. Aerial harnessed Mina-taur the bull to a pair of skis and went bouncing through some cumulus clouds. (Sounds like some major fun.*)

20. The apprentice pun smith always carries an anvil in the trunk of his vocabulary.

21. Monique salmon is credited with popularizing those unique seaweed t-shirts.

22. Leave a trail of breadcrumbs if you insist on searching for your gingerbread house.

23. Isn't it hard to pick up on the behavior of liquid mercury? (This should inspire a rock band.*)

24. Headlines: Boston's Garden's Pete Moss Squashes Record

25. The broken mirror reflected a black cat walking under a ladder on his way to crossing a few paths. (And so it goes with a super stitcher.*)

26. A lot of people have been fired after being caught hanging out in the rear of a kiln.

27. What kind of flowers would you send to a manikin's funeral?

28. Can you see the imagery of winter rain; wind-blown and forming ice trees?

29. A bacteria-shaped mob trampled a line of white corpuscles then swarmed into the main artery off the city.

30. Seven people gazed on as the wind turned the flaps on a marquee into an undulating chorus line of dancing elves. (I guess you had to be there.*)

31. What do you think about prism shingles that convert sunlight into shimmering colors?

32. The drilling rig, Mosquito, disappeared after finding itself between a navel radar scan and a hungry bat.

33. Call it a cover-up when you take the Blue Tarp Sea, fold it up, stuff it into a box and send it to Liver-pool for the winter.

34. Why would a chopper hover over a cabbage farm? (Sal-ly Ad-air might have the answer.*)

35. You can take off your copper wire shoes. We know of no such thing as a heavy metal orchestra that needs a conductor.

36. Water dripped down the eye of the blue rock, one of an aggregate of boulders forming a face on the precipice.

37. A rust spot on the crankcase of an old tractor resembled an aerial view of the farmer's land.

38. Do sprouts grow in the mien flow of a Chinese water garden?

39. The poet who employs pathetic fallacy will describe the rain falling from a face-shaped cloud in terms of human emotion.

40. Is it a good idea to model sheet music after the holes being poked in wet cement by a pogo stick? Wouldn't we be better off looking up and noting the patterns made by birds that are perched on the utilities lines?

41. Samson, the journalist, was feeling the strain from the Delilah Media Chain when he pulled two of his columns out from under the "Temple Top Daily."

42. Can you get hour's worth of flour out of the tin box that sits on the clock?

43. When communications break down, wispy little questions marks gain in size, grow fur, and begin to scratch at your back door during the night.

44. Dr. Whitney Rose and her five petals decided to climb the glass precipice on the west side of Mt. Greenhouse.

45. You mist "The Fog." This was a band of precipitation that rose before dawn, played their hit song "Density" and then moved on with their vapor tour.

46. When ole man winter touched down in the south he was piloted by a gaggle of geese.

47. Do not be afraid to rise above the fray.

48. Insomnia? Are you trying too hard to get to sleep?

49. However unscientific it may sound, water thinking might create a delta out-flowing of ideas.

50. A late-breaking tidal wave muddied the news when it inundated the press room at the Atlanta Herald.

51. Are they the same width? An iron horse was seen tailgating a Roman chariot down the rail tracks.

52. A telephone sitting on a table in the middle of a one hundred acre field began to ring and an owl answered the phone. (And it's always a hoot taking to you.*)

53. The webbed feet of a goose plunged into the blue surface of a lake.

54. After a rain is there a string of trout at the end of the fisherman's rainbow?

55. If water could stand on two molecular legs of hydrogen, it would have the best 5k time running down hill in a liquid state.

56. Five inflated cat balloons whose strings were attached to a mouse trap floated patiently over the Walt Disney Studios. (They are obviously quite caught up in their mission.*)

57. Have you ever tried sliding down a porcelain slope into a clear blue lake inside the Bath Mountain Range?

58. Most yards have a myriad of dragonfly take-off ramps.

59. Do the wheels on a skateboard keep you going in circles?

60. If you freeze the image of a raindrop splashing into a puddle it bears a likeness to the golden crowns of fairy tale lore.

61. The snap of a twig broke the silence in the upper reaches of a tree and rippled its message across the valley toward the river.

62. The Surreal Theatre is something many people only dream about. (Information provided by the Sir Real Pollsters.*)

63. The Three Branches of the Flashlight Theatre will soon be presenting "Night Sounds."

64. The sky is the limit when it comes to clouds offering the best definitions of imagery.

65. Certain images tend to migrate toward warmer thinking patterns.

66. *An eagle-shaped cloud glided across the sky* is a series of verbal notes poetically vibrated into a visual chord. (You could have fooled me.*)

67. Do frogs rest their legs on toad stools?

68. Poetry is the verbal distillation of imagery.

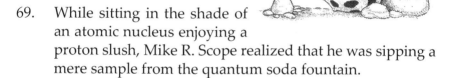

69. While sitting in the shade of an atomic nucleus enjoying a proton slush, Mike R. Scope realized that he was sipping a mere sample from the quantum soda fountain.

Irony

1. Ironic isn't it that the brainstorm knocked out the electrical system?

2. Whatever happened to the bamboo wood heater?

3. Don't wait for an invitation to join Hermit Club.

4. A Manhattan poodle refuses veal strips while the six o'clock news outlines a growing desert in Africa.

5. Ted Gates was in a quandary as he explained his problem to his mother after school. "We're studying centrifugal forces today and somehow I got separated from my note book just before class started."

6. The alarm clock factory started production twenty minutes late this morning.

7. Thurston Caine drove through a rain storm to buy some bottled water at a local grocery store.

8. Would it be a cubic centimeter of irony if the ice machine overheated?

9. He maps fjords to keep from becoming eccentric.

10. A shingle factory roof leaks.

11. To this day music is used to inspire people to go to war.

12. Dr. Luna tells us that a paper weight moon rock falls off his psychiatric desk once a month. (We feel much better after having told you this.*)

13. Live worms were found in a discarded tackle box.

14. "Mozzarella, man, jeez! Did you say that that mouse trap was made of cheese?" came the question from an unbelieving Nibbles Rodenta.

15. Not so long ago people would pause long enough to tell us what they were thinking about while milking a cow? Today, they hand us their "Bucket List."

16. Is it difficult to understand a simple term such as oxymoron?

17. Why do philosophical discussions always get bogged down in the quick sand of words? (We Kant tell you the answer to that.*)

18. That which appears to be the definition of irony is not always as it seems.

19. What high octane fuels do we store in think tanks?

20. Didn't Alfred Nobel the man for whom the Nobel Peace Prize was named also invent dynamite?" (Can we at least indirectly give him the credit when things get blown out of proportion? *)

21. Headlines: Ceiling Collapses at Lumber Warehouse

22. Should your plastic surgeon be stumbling over the cosmetics counter?

23. Three out of thirty remained to receive their free confidence kits. (Thirty is ten times bigger and a more confident number.*)

24. Relax, your shirt looks splendiferous. Besides we're travelling on a wrinkle free airline. (Good thing we're sitting next to the dictionary man.*)

25. Farley Falcon was put in charge of a rodent farm.

26. Somebody is always complaining about laughing gas.

27. A squid failed the Rorschach Test. (That's because he didn't have an inkling as to how he should answer the questions.*)

28. The word people keep talking about silence.

29. Should you study before taking the Greatness Aptitude test?

30. "Let's all get together and attend the National Hermit Club Summit."
    "Where will it be?
    "The Herman Tige Lodge."
    "Where is that?"
    "Nobody seems to know."

31. Do golfers ever get caught in sand traps?

32. Zachary wants the freedom to live in the cage of his choice.

33. Who could predict that the swimming pool would be filled with divining rods?

34. The cement truck had to drive around the rock slide.

35.   Gooden Stern doesn't believe in playing games when it comes to football.

36.   Do we need to develop a plan to get the world more organized?

37.   The court waived the lesser charge then sentenced the flag pole sitter to solitary confinement.

38.   Why is yesterday's fun today's boredom?

39.   Surplus crab pincers are being used to pin the nets from which they were caught out to dry.

40.   At a local high school, a mouse managed to byte through the Apple on a computer box.

41.   Indians captured the Lone Ranger and used his mask to tie Tonto's hands to a tree.

42.   Prometheus used a pocket lighter to study the master plan for stealing fire from the gods. (Did he study a book of matches? *)

43.   When they *read* about the higher rates being charged for anger management classes, three people walked out.

44.   Irony and here's the rub: (1) The one person who is capable of giving you advice is not here. (2) The one person who could do this to you and get away with it; does. (3) The one person, of all the others, you'd like to hear from, never calls. (This is a contribution from Sara Bellum's fifteen year old niece Holly who wanted to be a part of the text.*)

45.   A new study shows that studies are becoming less and less accurate.

46. A miniature statue of Rodin's "The Great Thinker" was put in a computer box and stored in a closet.

47. Should you raise funds to rehabilitate a local outbreak of greed?

48. Out topics lab indicates that most medical tests do not require any study.

49. Stay tuned for the latest media announcement informing you as to when you can turn your TV off.

50. The same people who drive with their headlights on during the day also tend to be chronic tailgaters.

51. Eisley became confused and was lost on his way to observation class.

52. A pearl necklace was found hanging from the foot of an oyster bed.

53. "Somebody out there should be knowledgeable enough to explain to us why we are so attracted to sugar," *sigh*ed the *ant*.

54. Most males would like nothing better than to pull their hair out when they are told they have chronic alopecia.

55. Yes, you can rake in the irony when someone opens the door to a watershed and an empty tub comes floating out.

56. The man from Mensa cannot decide if he wants to celebrate or cerebrate his membership in the club.

57. Twelve men labored for four hours to relocate a marble statue of Hercules. (So let's go shoot some marbles.*)

58.   Whale blubber fueled the lamps by which men told stories about their adventures at sea.

59.   Without any explanation, the captain charted a course for the Manipulation Islands.

60.   He had to sit down for a minute and think about the definition for intelligence.

61.   Iris Irony has a closet filled with wrinkled shirts.

62.   This book has a shopping cart full of excellent ideas waiting to be checked out.

63.   The expiration date on a piece of metal had rusted.

64.   The fact that some things are better off not being said should never be put in writing.

65.   Jonah wrote the story of his three days inside the mammal's stomach and sent it and the pictures to "National Geographic" after "Whale Digest" rejected it.

66.   When it came to safety issues concerning car tires and kids, a single vote was cast placing a rope around the tire and hanging it from a tree. (That would be the swing vote.*)

67.   After several decades of visually absorbing electronic bullets, computer buffs can't think of a single reason why they are having memory problems.

68.   Orson insisted that the speaker give him three good reasons why there is determinism.

69.   The otter dived under the protective umbrella of the water when a rain storm started.

70. A customer's thought bubble went out causing him to forget to buy light bulbs.

71. This study explains why water changes its tone as it fills a glass. (Are you thirsty for some good music? *)

72. How many times do we have to tell you; *spare* us the repetition? It's an old worn out tire, a retread. It's re-done-dant.

73. An "out of order" sign was seen on a cemetery gate.

74. A Norman Rockwell paint brush was auctioned off for the price of a "Saturday Evening Post."

75. Faulty wiring in a candelabra caused a fire that melted the likeness of Thomas Edison in Madame Tussaud's Wax Museum. (Whoops! *)

76. Michelangelo fell while painting the ceiling of the Cistern Chapel and landed on a huge roll of wallpaper.

77. The Daily Oracle lost much of its readership when it failed to accurately predict its last day of publication.

78. Marionette mayhem resulted when two puppets became entangled in an argument as to who was pulling the strings.

79. A hope chest washed up on Myrtle Beach with a life preserver on it.

80. Have you had any formal training in the art of relaxation?

81. The alligator, one of the oldest living creatures on the planet, swallowed a clock in the *Peter Pan* story.

82. He was reading a story about roller coasters when the G-force suddenly pulled the book out of his hands.

83. The maple syrup tester was asked how fast she needed a sap sample.

84. Some people get defiant when told they need to learn to *emote*. (This may be the only way to get a message inside the castle.*)

85. Most of the people questioned did not believe a horse should be tied to a Gallop pole.

86. Two archeologists refuse to settle a dispute as to who uncovered the pre-historic hatchet.

87. A cigar-shaped gun was used as evidence to solve the case of the tobacco murder mystery.

88. Hundreds of people gazed on as a broom floated down the flooded river and swept through the small town.

89. Headlines: Superman fails Physics Course (Did Jimmy Olsen write the story? *)

90. Most people do not have the slightest idea what their minds are capable of doing. (Most books have a core paragraph or a bottom line to it and this may be ours.*)

91. You will find relatively little profit while riding in the caboose of a train. (You have to look forward to making money.*)

Literature

1. You are Robinson Crusoe's man, Friday. Describe your master. (We need to tell him to get involved, look for some clubs to join. He should find a theatre group and play the part of a castaway.*)

2. Upton Sinclair once pulled a portable *Jungle* through the streets of Chicago.

3. On half mile outside the Edgar Allen Poe Museum is a sign that reads "Visitors Welcome. Swing left onto Pendulum Road."

4. If we are to navigate this ocean of literature, then put some wind in the sails.

5. The eighteenth reason for reading "Self Reliance" is to get you to buy the book on essays by Emerson without being told to. (Since there's no one else in the room to consult, let me put forth the question: Isn't that an essay? *)

6. A manual offering the step-by-step process for improving the human race was found in a magazine rack in the office of a used car lot.

7. Shakespearean sonnets should be stored at 98.6 degrees Fahrenheit. (Yes, they are all about humanity.*)

8. Information from the Alexandrian Library which burnt during Julius Caesar's time is finally starting to surface in

contemporary literature. (Not only is this knowledge long overdue, it's amazing.*)

9.   The twentieth century keeps "The Raven" by Edgar Allen Poe in an aviary and is available for speaking engagements.

10.   Allen Beecher used the pitchfork from "The American Gothic" to pry open the cellar door at the rear of the House of Usher. Once in, he found ample lumber with which to construct *Uncle Tom's Cabin*.

11.   How would a realtor describe the " . . . House of Usher?" (He might tell you that the market for it is depressed: wait until this *fall*.*)

12.   Only a cat-o-nine-tales should interview *The Three Musketeers*. (Is there a mouse in the house? *)

13.   We know of two people who sat for three days in front of a mail box waiting for their copy of *Godot* to arrive. (This is based on a novel by Thomas Becket about two tramps who are waiting for . . . . *)

14.   Headlines: Nile Valley Ranch to Use Pyramid-shaped Iron for Camel Branding

15.   Tell people you are writing a book and they immediately think coffee table or *How to Sew with Pine Needles*.

16.   A bookworm received its PhD in Irridation, as granted by the English Department. (By dent of their tendency to tunnel worms tend to aerate the soil.*)

17.   And so, Hamlet sat there munching some pastry and trying to decide if he wanted an aviary built behind his Danish castle. (This isn't about soliloquys, it's about bees.*)

18. Little Lord Font-leroy might be upper-class italics to a social typesetter.

19. A re-moat control device from Morgan le Fey Electronics can be used to move water from a channel into the big ditch that surrounds King Arthur's tele-castle.

20. Did a touring *Rip Van Winkle* ever ask for a wake-up call?

21. Should Peter Pan grow up, will he know how to fly?

22. Alice's caterpillar cleans his hookah pipe with rolled up blueprints of earth's first space station.

23. We were told that it took twelve feet of iambic lumber to construct a stanza upon which Keats's "Ode to a Nightingale" could rest before building a nest.

24. Little Bo Peep was arrested for voyeurism.

25. Roy's sister has a roasted rooster on the roster for the alliteration club meeting tonight.

26. He won the Pulitzer Prize for literature because he was able to step out of his writer's ego long enough to identify with the human experience.

27. The same ropes used to fasten Gulliver to the ground were later Swiftly sold at a London auction to one Lilli Vespution.

28. No doubt George Eliot was waxing on in terms of classical literature when she produced one in a string of novels called the *Mill on the Floss.*

29. At any given time in the prison library, someone might be guilty of reading a few chapters of *Crime and Punishment.* (You cannot check it out.*)

30. The literary club held a brush arbor discussion on Sinclair Lewis' *Elmer Gantry*. (The best way to understand *brush arbor* is to relax under a canopy of limbs and branches designed for outdoor gatherings.*)

31. If "beauty is truth, truth beauty . . ." it follows that the student of poetry can teach Keats. He rates with Yeats. His Words are worth gold and when he lyrics on time and with the rising fog, we know he is a sonneteer and a card-carrying Romantic.

32. "Do most people notice it when a *mouse* jumps out of the rim of a bac-*k tire*?" Alex posed the question to his girlfriend Andrea.

33. Back in *1984*, nobody, not even my big brother, could have predicted what we would find when we drilled an Or well next to the animal barn.

34. A likeness of a barracuda's dorsal fin should have been tattooed onto the ivory leg of Melville's mad Captain Ahab.

35. The whale oil that fueled Paul Revere's Bulls Eye lantern came from an ancestor of *Moby Dick*.

36. Excalibur now hangs over the fireplace at Morgan Le Fey's retirement cabin by the lake.

37. Calipers will not work. In *Measure for Measure,* the caliber of a person capable of extracting Excalibur from the stone is the unknown factor of the Arthurian Legend.

38. The Orphean Lyre tamed Tennessee Williams' *Cat on a Hot Tin Roof.*

39. Headlines: Goethe's *Faust* Files Chapter Twelve Bankruptcy (The Faustian character sold his soul to the devil.*)

40. All the allegories on the banks of the Nile may have been a statement whereby Mrs. Malaprop was watering down a reptilian instinct. (And we are all Ever so glade that she did.*)

41. The ravens all hid under the floor to escape a wall of screams from the Poe Sound Technician.

42. From the Audubon Archives we found an albatross with a pendant of Samuel Taylor Coleridge hanging around its neck.

43. We asked the Pinocchio twins, Mary and Annette, what is the measure of a person who isn't telling the truth?

44. He was so excited after attending the first meeting of the *Rip Van Winkle* insomnia support group that he couldn't get to sleep.

45. A wealthy British art dealer disappeared after somebody opened a box of Sherlock Holmes's London fog during a recent antique road show.

46. A needle through a hat can be thimbolic for sewing yarns.

47. Somewhere in a Ray Bradbury village, a paramedic unit was summoned to assist a man who looked as if he hadn't read anything in several days.

48. Ice cycles formed on his desk while Tolstoy's ink pen was exiled in Siberia.

49. All proletarian novels should be read while wearing a denim jacket. (And what will members of the class upstairs wear? *)

50. The Cowardly Lion went on to organize the Emerald City Crime Stoppers.

51. The yellow brick road turned into gold for L. Frank Baum, the author of *The Wizard of Oz*.

52. With approaching middle age, the *Sweet Bird of Youth* will migrate south.

53. If you want to take any books with you on the float trip you'll need this roll of *Huck Finn* wrap.

54. The *Robinson Crusoe* calendar is without a Friday the first two months of the year.

55. *Robin Hood* used an arrow to realign the wealth of poverty slices in a Middle English pie chart.

56. Swarms of mispronounced asterisks fell from the passages of Poe's prose forming the footnotes of despair.

57. Ali Ba Ba had one of his Arabian Knights UPS a box of sand to Western Europe where it would be melted into Cinderella's glass slipper.

58. "Hey, Odysseus," yelled the Cyclops, "I'll keep an eye out for you."

59. After the success of the book, the seagull *Jonathan Livingston Seagull* rose above the need to be fru-gull.

60. Once you find Melville, Rhode Island, take the Harpoon exit in a direct line to Ahab's Ocean Auction where they are having a white sale.

61. *The Three Musketeers* of physics would be Porthos (liquid), D'artagnan (solid) and Athos (gas). ("All for one and one for all" and on Wednesday, a free-for-all.*)

62. *The Hunchback of Notre Dame* Chiropractic Center has a new doorbell in opera-tion.

63. The Legend of the Holstein family can be found *Under Milkwood* in the dairy archives.

64. Next on my right is the model home of actors Ken and Barbie Android and their daughters Ann Ode and Di Ode. The family's latest release on the Ibsen label "A Doll House" promises to be a play on words.

65. The *weird sisters* in "MacBeth" have been seen sweeping up the mess after a storm of hexes were scattered all over the yard.

66. Be thankful for those Middle English dishes, one of which is the *Cranberry Tales* all lumped together in a saucer waiting for the wife to finish her bath.

67. A bird's eye view of Shakespeare: "Hark no! gull, eagle nor dove above? Fie, what fowl o-puns the air waves-vulture venture forth towardst mine vision?"

68. The crowd stirred and held its plates as three cases of lima beans podded up in a black limousine to watch the grand opening of a can being purred into a hot pan spoof. (Topics like this will be the bane of life on this planet as we know it.*)

69. The nonuse of caps certainly resembles the style of E.E. Cummings, however, we're doubtful about the content: evelyn's eleven and if you'll wait for a year you'll understand why elvin can't be her twin brother because he is only twelve.

70. For this pun, we went to Texas and asked kite fliers Kyle and Kelly to mark a Langhorne field between them so that "never their twine shall meet."

71. A nation of Cyclops will only see half as many optometrists per person.

72.   If indeed the golden retriever is descended from, that would explain its resemblance to *Old Yeller.*

73.   How many times did Zane Grey write off into the sun set with a manuscript in his saddlebags?

74.   Mark Twain was wearing an Oklahoma land rush T-shirt when he arrived at the gold fields in California.

75.   Expect poetry on wheels when a sixteenth century Stanza delivers a verse di-Spencer to your residence.

76.   If it sits on the shelf for an extended period of time, salt residue will form under your copy of *Mutiny of the Bounty.*

77.   Rodrick Usher was too Poe to purchase fire insurance.

78.   Ezra Pound might have been put in charge of the weigh station for abstract thinking.

79.   Paging James Joyce: "Up to my neck in this Nick Nack Shop whittling wattles for Rick Bleed-soe. I quit to wait for Les Downes to knock on . . . wood you stop the reading and go to bed?" (Joyce was a twentieth writer known for his at times difficult prose style.*)

Look Around

1. The farthest reaching telescope on the planet has been invented. What do you see with it?

2. What are we doing on this planet?

3. How can you get so attached to a machine? (Some of them are equipped with attachments.*)

4. Imagine that you are the number two hundred, talk about relationships you have had with one hundred, ninety nine and two hundred, one.

5. Is there nourishment other than food?

6. Why do you hear when you listen to silence? (White noise? *)

7. Can you take the pulse of a street? (*Beats* sitting on the curb counting the cars per minute.*)

8. What is feeling good and healthy?

9. Should the Spilliards live in a town called Half-Empty?

10. What is the value of a point of reference? (The answer may be across the street from a brick building.*)

11. What is the reason for school? (You may have to study that one.*)

12. What shape will your answer take when you think about form?

13. Why are there never any fast aid stations for the slowest people in the race?

14. Can you see your life from a distance?

15. Have you noticed that even the smallest creatures have a will to survive?

16. As a planet, are we small? (We are and that is largely due to our point of view.*)

17. Be sure to sign in when you get to the top of Mount Register.

18. What do monsters look like? (What do you want them to look like? *)

19. Where does dust come from? (Dust is the leftover debris from an insect chatter.*)

20. Doe the menu at Rainbow Restaurant list the entire food spectrum?

21. Why is football so popular?

22. Is the air crowded?

23. For five bucks can you tell us what goes on at a rodeo?

24. Does wearing a hat change the way you feel?

25. How can you get lost on your way to observation class?

26. Will a full time comedian have the entire audience laughing?

27. How long is the gutter life of a wind-blown chewing gum wrapper?

28. "We didn't know there were sensitivities in that box," explained the delivery man. "It should have been stamped *fragil*."

29. We acknowledge the modesty of those administrators who have championed the Peter Principle.

30. However slow or fast, would you agree that most of us are improving?

31. If it's not too much of a bother, would you please tell us what you think about arrogance?

32. Some people don't want the bumps taken out of the road. (Some people need speed breaks.*)

     56. Since your life is the centerpiece, how do you like being in the middle of your surroundings?

     57. Have you planned for a floating feather to tickle your observation?

33. To make a long story short, try condensing your introduction/conclusion cycle.

34. A trendy bedbug was vacationing in the basement of the Coral Reef Shag Rug Company.

35. Why are all the plastic ducks sitting on the edge of Bathtub Arena? (Because they have front row tickets to see the water games.*)

36. What does a wink mean or is it simply a single blink?

37. Would a Ferris wheel override a merry-go-down?

38. Will a ring of keys unlock a round building?

39. Is there a national pot of beans to be found at the end of an economic rainbow?

40. Why do people dismiss the movement flashing in the corner of the eye?

41. Is the modern woman supposed to own a pair of Sadie Hawkins's track shoes?

42. The only function for this lamp is to create a circle in the dust on top of a bookshelf.

43. Somewhere in West Texas a steer ambles up to a water trough, lowers his head and takes a nice long drink. (Ah! *)

44. When someone mentions *medi*-tation, you might think in the middle of things.

45. Petrie tells us that his visit to the Dish House was the ultimate cultural experience.

46. Nurture the nature of who you are.

47. Have you noticed the leaping action that makes up the hot weather dance of grasshoppers?

48. Is it true that there are fruit trees growing on both sides of the path of least resistance?

49. Have you noticed that church architecture is usually arched skywards?

50. Now do as you are told and tell us if you are a conformist or a nonconformist.

51.   Why are the contents of a cartoon so soft and rounded and cozy and pleasing to the eye?

52.   Azure looking up on a clear spring day, how blue is the sky? (Blue enough to hide the stars.*)

53.   Most toy pickups are loaded with *do nots* and *can nots*. (The staff prefers peanuts and donuts.*)

54.   Tell us about the time your Aunt Mini Scule took you to see the Molecule Building.

55.   The designated area for finding a lost penny is now under the pillows of most couches.

56.   "Hey Madison Gardley, can we as a society depend on our institutions to reinforce conventional thinking?" asked a man who was good at posing questions. "I'll have to give you my answer later? I'm late for class."

57.   The doctor recommends that you loosen the tie, step outside and take a walk in the woods and call me in the morning. (Of course that isn't his real name.*)

58.   Willy Pound worked his foot with such intensity during his solo that the bass drum bolted. It rolled out the door and down the hill flattening six puns in rapid succession and finally came to a halt in front of the Fish Skinner's Cafe. "Beats me how it happened," Pound later weighed in his opinion.

59.   You are a pogo stick. Describe the kid next door who is always jumping up and down about something.

60.   Headlines: Pollution Lobotomizes Environment

61.   Morality maps indicate that the low roads have turned into major interstate highways.

62. Why would you allow any wolves into your personal fairytale that can huff and puff and pop your private little bubble?

63. A citizens' summit meeting was held at the Hotel Anywhere to determine how to caution the planet against the increasing number of daily distractions. (As soon as the football game is over, we'll ask the folks if they can handle this one.*)

64. What will you find when you open a box of information? (Probable instructions on what to do with the contents.*)

65. On the third shelf down, next to the bottom of the lectern is a stack of tickets for guilt trips.

66. Do you use ink or a quick blink when you want to make a memory copy of the scene?

67. We are such territorial creatures. How could we possibly allow something to cross that vertical line that connects our eyes to our feet?

68. Do not stick your hand into a wild leather glove. We now know that they are prone to sudden grips and slide easily into fits.

69. Have many of our solid, well-crafted and fundamental thinking patterns been replaced by inconsistent, synthetic whimsy?

70. Tell us Les-ter Moore, how many kitchen counters have you installed?

71. We know of a wolf who is handing out sock caps and if you're not sure, he'll show you how to pull the wool over your eyes. ("Things are never as they appear to be." —Sara Shakespeare?*)

72.   Most of the cities across this land have a cement stable that houses its Trojan horses.

73.   The latest cup and saucer poll is filled with people who support Catherine Irene's efforts to shake the coffee habit.

74.   People accept an anemic interpretation of events only when they have failed to formulate a more accurate and robust model that would expose all the imposters.

75.   An agricultural report taken from the Leprechaun News tells us that grain cereals harvested from fields containing crop symbols offer a highly nutritious breakfast. (Would you like some honey on your toast? *)

76.   For best overall actor in a day to day dramatic performance, the Oscar goes to John Q. Public.

77.   Did you hear about the drummer who changed his beat to satisfy the expectations of a difficult listener?

78.   When you're thinking about water, does the thought process seek its own level?

79.   You may recall that dim-witted day when Narcissus saw a mud turtle moving about below his reflection. (From Greek mythology, this young man fell in love with his own image in a pool of water.*)

80.   Three cleaning agents have been waiting at the Scrub-a-dub dock to catch a ride in a bathtub that is scheduled to float by.

81.   Everybody knew she was ahead of her time when the ice skater did three record breaking revolutions around the clock shaped rink.

82. A dirt spot on the flashlight can turn into any number of scampering creatures.

83. Part of his daily routine consists of making alternative plans. (And I'll take a paradox any day over two chickens.*)

84. Daylight Saving Time means you can stay outside longer making rainbows with water hoses.

85. "It's in the water, Lou," cautioned Napoleon to Elbe Alright. "Don't drink it!"

86. Would the height of architecture be a waterfall tumbling from atop the Sears Building in Chicago?

87. Optometry announces a new eye wear with a lens ground specifically to make the eye-contact comfort zone two point three seconds longer.

88. If you won't study science, at least be a part of the wave at a football game.

89. What can you conclude when you see the hands on your clock wearing gloves?

90. How long has that calendar been hanging in the same place on the wall?

91. From the crown of my puzzled brain, a random gust of wind tossed my hat down to a footnote of physics.

92. Some songs push the needle indicator out of the middle rang and into the danger point which threatens to upset hearing stability.

93. If you're not satisfied with your present level of development, step out of the dark room and buy a digital camera.

94. The three bends in a paper clip create an unfailingly simple system.

95. Are you outgoing or going out to find your place on the personality dial? (And she drives a late model Extrovert.*)

96. Who pays the property tax on both houses of congress?

97. One thing you can be certain about: it's the same scene every time you open the curtains or is it?

98. Do lines guide our vision?

99. Twin sisters were staring at each other between opposing mirrors. (We see it as a double take.*)

100. If music affects your heart rate and your heart pumps chemicals that affect your mood, better be careful what you listen to, dude.

101. Megan Camera landed the job not only because her smile ☺ had the fastest shutter speed: She was also quite *pixil*ating.

102. Quite often you'll find something dark, brooding, and lurking in the shadows waiting for the tailor to put the final stitches to a Dracula outfit.

103. "Folks, we can save you money," turns out to be nothing more than a mote of sound washed up by the radio waves.

104. We need someone to trim those white fern follicles that have sprouted on presidential ear lobes at Mount Rushmore.

105. Trevor Imatrion never blinks when people ask him to spell his last name.

106. All living things within the domain of Isabella Amour's cottage grew faster and lived longer than the flora and fauna in surrounding areas.

107. A basketball game will certainly beg the question: What is all the hoopla about? (We all need to keep a goal in mind.*)

108. NFL fans should know about the tiny toe rockets being used by kick-off specialists to blast the ball further down the field.

109. To most people, it's obvious that you are a parent. If you can't see that you must be a transparency.

110. Any medium will speak to you. Even a teapot will hold you in high e-steam once you learn to whistle back.

111. Do we need to give people extra time to meet to dialogue to a consensus as to the importance of the meeting?

112. We know about the books that occupy shelf space for the purpose of impressing clients with the owner's erudition.

113. Holly Graph was told to leave the round table meeting so that they could talk about more down to earth issues. (Such issues as "how to build a fence in one day" by one of King Arthur's retired knights.*)

114. Let's go fishing. Let's talk about all the red herrings that have been dragged across the trail to confuse the hounds.

115. Sporting is safe. The only questions the participants ever ask are: Who's on first or who caught the biggest fish? (And why have a row over sculling when we can go rappelling?*)

116. "How could you tell that the salesman was a fraud? "Well, he wanted to sell us some huge hinges that had once been attached to the Gateway to the West."

117. We took a survey to see if it was the real state of the art or a borderline impostor.

118. The ice cubes sat there frozen as hailstones pelted a refrigerator standing in the middle of a field.

119. When was the last time you were issued a summons of observation to notice something commonplace?

120. "It's nice to meet you too. What did you say your name was?" "Are your eyes so busy gathering data from a first impression that the ears are ignored?"

121. The first questions in the interview with D. A. and Toni were: "What was in the trunk of your car when you drove away from the Daytona 500? What did you take from the scene?" (Part of a retread?*) As a follow-up question we asked, "Where would be the least likely place to find a speed bump?" And the last question dealt with the qualifying time to be accepted in the human race.

122. Precisely as she was waking up, a button fell of Mozell's pajamas and landed next to the alarm clock.

123. Do we need nets at the periphery of our vision that can capture the movements that are leaping beyond the sweep of a glance?

124. One thing you can be certain about, it's the same scene every time you open the curtains or is it?

125. He is a different male who, when sliding his belt through the many loops to hold up his pants uses all eight.

126. Socrates said that the unexamined life wasn't worth living, but then he never had a beach ball or roller skates to play with.

127. How often do you mention dimensions in the course of your day? ("Hey Lucy, what's up?" *)

128. If you're looking back or reflecting on patterns that have a sense of rhyme in your life, remember that "objects in the mirror are closer than they appear."

129. Stockman Athos Talmidge attached a cell phone to the neck of his lead bull, Bill. The idea being that he, Athos could call the bull at any given time to determine the herd's location. On more than one occasion, a wit of a bull offered a description of the herd's whereabouts, adding, "Now does that ring a bell?"

130. Once upon a time "The Fingernails" cut several albums. They were managed by Silvio Hand and for a while were big on the charts. Today, it's hard to find any of their music that isn't full of pops and snaps and scratches. (A former fan filed this report while doing her nails.*)

131. The Yeast family never answers the question as to what time they usually hop out of bed because it always leads to the same old joke. (Early risers?*)

Metaphors

1.   Describe the fruit that you would pick from the professional tree.

2.   Is there a place for the human element on the periodic chart of PC's?

3.   Some of our deepest metaphors have come out of wells.

4.   A conformity tank will hold about forty pounds of peer pressure.

5.   If you're driving a late model short story, where do you plan to take it?

6.   Is language the clutch that allows us to mentally shift gears?

7.   Would you agree that books are like cars: They can shift gears?

8.   Will it test your mettle to have tedium hammered into a long thin line of patience? (Ted and the rest of 'em have waited a long time for this topic.*)

9.   Clean air may be getting rare: keep pumping that oxygen into the earth-arium.

10. A life jacket will come in handy when floating down a stream of consciousness.

11. Stitch some imagination into your magic carpet and see if it will fly.

12. A diocese of vines grew to enshrine Saint Peter Moss.

13. Will you be the first to know when the bubble is about to burst? ("Pop goes the weasel." *)

14. If the comedian is on a roll, you should see laugh tracts all over the humor carpet.

15. Are you advancing the film when you blink? (No, we're going through a small town, that all.*)

16. This book on greenhouses is filled with short stories about plants.

17. Do you enjoying riding the merry-go-round on the economic playground? (The wooden horses do have their ups and downs.*)

18. We need illustrata or layers of visual compliments to the rock solid ideas we're digging up.

19. In this neighborhood, there is puzzlement by the yards as to the fabric in our personal tapestry.

20. Have you noticed that there are always numbers resting atop the houses occupied by a geometry student?

21. Will the carpenter's wit be the insulation that fills the wise cracks in the wall?

22. Howard Basely sold his ticket to Grant Fielding who took a seat outside the culture hoping to catch a home run ball.

23. Nature is shifting gears into winter. Your clutch coat is in the closet.

24. Try watering your sentences if you want to grow more colorful paragraphs.

25. Rodney Lightener conducts the atmospheric disturbance band.

26. Are there some things you should know about that are not getting through your perception filter?

27. The House of Jobs will advise you to plug your skills into a profession that will not drain your voltage.

28. Since the earth is wrapped in a stellar blanket, is the needlework by physics?

29. A reasonable amount of rowing will take you across the river of moral dilemmas.

30. Most of us are kept quite busy trying to connect the dots.

31. If somebody is thinking inside the greenhouse, it means that words and ideas are likely to be cross pollinating.

32. My metaphor machine thinks it's ready for the Indianapolis 500 of fiction writing.

33. If your vocabulary is derived from a word spectrum, it should be colorful. (If you have read a lot.*)

34. Has conformity been stamped on the human envelope?

35. Do you remember when leaves from the Chinese gingko tree were known as a memory enhancer?

36. The municipality known as Green has photosynthesized a zip code. (We need to take a picture of the people who are spearheading the Green Movement.*)

37. A new wave of trends always seems to contain an undertow from the past. (A lot of people seem to enjoy surfing.*)

38. A healthy stock of words will always be grazing in the Land of Dictionary.

39. A spider ringmaster tells us that his web site is located inside a circus. (The trapeze is always a crowd pleaser.*)

40. Are you loaded with too many sandbags for your thinking to get off the ground?

41. Sonneteers have always dipped their pens into the well of romance.

42. You can always see better when you switch on the earth lamp; also known as the moon. (The light is dim in here. Is this a metaphor? *)

43. Are the rivers in your body free flowing?

44. If you want to grow music from your garden personality, you'll have to plant a C-major smile of seeds.

45. When stuck, the old phonograph stylus was an audio hiccup.

46. Do you recall sliding down the memory banks into the river of the past?

47. A metaphor-ectomy removes some of the figurative from a body of language.

48. An astro-turf manufacturer confessed that he had to graze in a lot of fields before he got his big break.

49. Drop a funny joke into the Pond Club and listen as the humor ripples out and over the audience.

50. A trainload of logic has had an emotional derailment.

51. The consensus has it that change is the meat and potatoes of the more advanced cultures.

52. His body language was edited by the size of the chair.

53. We can thank the farm belt for holding up the nation's pants.

54. Are the nuts and bolts of culture necessary to fasten a value system into place?

55. Do you have enough social finesse to leave a pleasant sampling of your personality with the people you meet?

56. Do you know how to breakdown such a rocky question as: How do deserts become filled with sand?

57. Pour a compliment of water over a thirsty personality and watch it grow.

58. An argument is a dry river gulch in the topography of human interaction. (Let's call Arizona Arroyo and find out.*)

59. The Scubans thought that Gabe Troust was far too super-fish-al to swim around in their deep conversational waters.

60. The night sky on a beach is a good place to see the Constellation Starfish.

61. Pamplona computer owners are advised to open their logic gates and let the Boolean bull stampede the bits and bytes throughout the circuitry.

62. The literary seamstress binds the story with a spindle of motifs.

63. Some people have a range of personality that is no less complicated that a springtime weather pattern.

64. A complete sentence is a balanced formula in the chemistry of English.

65. The candle that was once a fairy tale has now melted down into a mound of wax.

66. Imagery is the number one industry located in the northwest corner in the state of Mind.

67. If the Arrog ants are not checked, they can in short order be out of control and your flower bed will soon be reduced to weeds.

68. As projected, does your life contain all the color and adventure of an animated film?

69. The winds of change blew the money into a web of power lines woven by the George, the giant spider.

70. Black's Laws of Linguistics:
    1. Language misdemeanor—a cliché
    2. Language felony—refusal to read
    3. Language Court of Apples—recant or having to eat all those delicious words

71. The alphabet is the root structure to that mighty English oak tree.

72. Plant some seeds if you want your intelligence to grow.

73. Will you bake for us some analogy cookies with a sprinkling of puns on top?

74. Can the vicissitudes of a novel's main character be mapped according to the musical scale?

75. Alex remembered the wooden block being there. As to what happened to the left edge of it, his memory is chipped.

76. The Erg team is trained in the dynamics of clean, wholesome and vigorous mental flux.

77. The horn section from a stall of "Traffic" slammed into a Fender guitar jamming the start of the concert.

78. When the room gets too small, Dirk Neurante suffers from subatomic claustrophobia.

79. By definition evolution means change. Some caterpillars will fight into the night to keep from becoming a butterfly.

80. A thirty-eight caliber micro drama can spin through a space time bore. (Puns are more fun than guns.*)

81. The M. I. T. stockyard is where pallets of research are piled high and waiting to be processed. (The reference here is to Massachusetts Institute of Technology not something used to catch a baseball.*)

82. Notice that when you drive into your fifties, you start getting fewer seconds per minute at the local time station.

83. Luke Warmley lowered the bucket on several writers when he decided that too many topics are being pulled out of a cold water well.

84. What is the missing component when you ask a computer to write a poem about chemistry's Periodic Chart?

85. The Guppy Filtration Company admitted it is swimming upstream when it comes to cleaning the human aquarium.

86. The rust of the story deals with the fact that *alumn*us from the Metal Cutters College insist on having a reunion whenever their mettle begins *two weak*en. "The very idea," lamented one of the officers recently, "is getting to be a bit *numb*ing."

87. A petition tree sprouted thirty names during Barclay's run for circuit judge.

88. In the life experience register, how many people refuse to open the drawer for a little change?

89. Promul-gate, irri-gate, and insti-gate are words that fall apart when their accent pins fall from their hinges.

90. Geo-topical suggests a stratified approach to reading this material. With writing, reading and understanding, sometimes you have to dig.

91. Cynicism and sarcasm shakers can be used to sprinkle condiments over a forced compliment of a meal.

92. An aisle is the apostrophized distance you walk between two rows of good intentions.

93. Kites make an excellent metaphor. (However lofty they appear to be, you do control the strings.*)

94. Tarina Lighthouse, you'll have to turn on your beam and open your eyes if you want to know when your ship is coming in.

95. Two yellow throated metaphors have built a nest in the upper rafters of the convention hall for mainstream thinking.

96. Here is a picture of Mt. Eaton wearing the food chain inches below the neck and above the timberline.

97. Shockly was the spectator as his uncle sat there in the chair, both hands on both poles, generating energy through the armature.

98. A hose connected to a dictionary was use to pump words into a think tank.

99. The Topics Nebula is located outside the Milky Way of thinking.

100. When you're typing your stories hit the pun key to unlock a double meaning.

101. Does that type of stereo have a demographic bias built into its speakers?

102. The state of confusion has panhandles for getting a grip.

103. Some social gatherings need traffic lights to keep the flow of words running smoothly.

104. The steering committee driving this book has been advised to limit their parking time in front of the Division of Controversy.

105. Are there players in your private theatre production who are making too much noise? (Have them play the part of a mime.*)

106. From the garden of romance, we see honey-dos growing on the relationship vine.

107. Let's call them Wimbledon Morality Matches insofar as the little ball of right and wrong gets slammed back and forth. (Is that why Dennis likes tennis?*)

108. Some information is self-adhesive.

109. We are here to help you scale Mt. Metaphor.

110. If we could reduce a stadium to the size of a Petri dish, we could tackle various aspects of the football culture.

111. We need to crack that crystalline safe to see if there is a tetrahedonal combination that might store vast amounts of UHF information. (On this United Home Front, I need to sort the laundry.*)

112. If when trying to trying to use a metaphor to describe fire the figure of speech can get too close and yes, turn to ashes.

113. What's happening at the DNA Hilton? Some of the Chromo kids are splashing around in the gene pool.

114. How many reels of experience do you have in your film library?

115. The weight of the ocean compresses the sediments at the bottom into the pages of a limestone history. (This is a rock solid metaphor.*)

116. Has anybody ever been trampled by the bulls as they run through the street in front of the New York Stock Exchange?

117. A maritime watch will provide a new wave of seconds with each new minute.

118. A reverse metaphor ala the NBA way of thinking; if a ship doesn't plow through the sea there is nothing happening on the surface of the mind. (I can't think of anybody who has ever tried to write a reverse metaphor, but don't give up the ship.*)

119. Is a formula for conformity to be found in the top pocket of the cultural uniform?

120. We know the geologist can fly a mala-kite. Does he have a pick to mine an ore for a float trip? (I, me, mine and that leaves him all alone to sail down the river.*)

121. How many people are compounded with interest over their energy banks?

122. To ascend a mountain of thought, we need to draw a higher level of ideas into contour lines. (These lines connect areas of similar altitude on a geographic map.*)

123. The repairman rolled in and installed a disposable karma wheel. "Read the instructions," he cautioned, "this modal won't handle relationship trauma."

124. If your playground is a quarry, be aware of rock slides.

125. Would a retired cowboy put a saddle roof on his house?

126. An academic floor plan might include math, science or history as joists over laid with three quarter-inch language plywood.

127. A hiring freeze might defoliate a wallet tree.

128. You don't want to know what the crowd did to the pitcher for the New England Lobsters when the team ran out of steam.

129. Poets wade in up to their ears trying to accurately put the sound of a river into words.

130. Those cell blocks along Masterpiece Row that boast having captured the human spirit remain empty until the reader sees himself staring out from behind the bars.

131. With two in a canoe, puns can float quite swimmingly down a stream of poetry.

132. If overcast conditions are blocking your creativity keep in mind that you are allowed to write about clouds.

133. Any tree that towers above the others can become the alphabet arm that slams into the ribbon on the horizon typewriter. (This topic is absolutely obsolete and should be cut down and hauled off. *)

134. Turn on your blinkers if you want people to know your punning left or right onto Double Definition Road.

135. By the way, according to the Brits, there was that *unspeakable day* of the Slang Mutiny aboard the Queen's ship "Idiom" as seen live on the English Channel. (Had there been a camera present at the time we would have a slang shot as proof.*)

136. If you pull a small Midwestern town up by its roots, you might find a rich deposit of European soil.

137. In time, the warden's log became filled with deposits of rock cells replacing the wood cells at Petrify Prison.

138. If you are the branch that fell from a family tree of intelligent ancestors, perhaps you should test for the Mensa Club.

139. Will we have to sleep on it before that metaphorical sheet of ice thaws out and we can see what it means?

140. To create an atmosphere of protest try sliding the blue cold air curtain up against the opposite fabric of red warm air.

141. Beginning with the initial crest of two hundred basic words, there are contours of vocabulary complexity that expand outward from the central silence.

142. What kind of fence could you build with a five year subscription to Saturday Evening Post?

143. The Rutile Family beamed a reddish brown color. Their son Titanium had dioxided with honors and was being considered as a specimen for a human geology lab.

144. Static thinking will not generate enough of an idea to put a glow in a light bulb.

145. We took a foundling drop of detergent, applied water and suds it into a huge population of bubbles.

146. We've been carrying a golden acorn in our topics pocket for a long time waiting for a blue chip futures investment in a trees metaphor.

147. The candle has to wax humorous to light up the smile on a pumpkin face.

148. We recommend that you wrap your sentences in grammar if you want them to be illiteracy proof.

149. Before you feel an onslaught of cold comments coming your way try weather stripping your personality with fiber wit insulation.

150. The Dean of Hammer at the School of Hard Knocks usually knows when someone is at his door.

151. You'll need to dig up a bucket of epitomes, edit the dirt and arrange them according to size to bring out their best. (The best we can do is offer the reader an apology for this empty bucket of biology.*)

152. Your electric flow of thought will trickle south with little resistance. Try urging your Aurora to the lights of the Borealis North. (How much did you charge for this one? *)

153. Richard tells us that cherry stones are much too small for landscaping a walk around the orchard.

154. Your thinking will slowly get deeper the further out you wade toward the middle of a pond-erance.

155. If the conversation belt that holds up small talk is adjustable you won't be waisting your time.

156. Each time you close your eyes, you lower the curtain on the "Energy Players."(I usually go to sleep.*)

157. Step right up: ladders are being used in more and more metaphors.

158. We packed up the families of such words as *luminous, lullaby,* and *murmur* and headed into a wilderness to homestead some poetic imagery. (Yes, that is spatial.*)

159. A specific floral arrangement of notes is required before the potted madrigal will bloom.

160. You can double the stock value of language maps by investing in metaphors.

161. On second thought, let's take a few minutes to draw a circle around our daisies, then fold up the week, place it in a month long envelope and file it in a yearbook.

162. The last of the icicles are still hanging off the eves of our roof memories from the cold war.

163. In the spring, a variety of shades of green can be pulled down over the topographical window.

164. Was the odometer invented as a way of measuring the many strange things some people do per mile as they are walking down the highway?

165. The song played over and over like a gerbil in the wheel of his mind.

166. Into what mold will you cast your main character and will he/she be a hero or villain?

167. Sometimes you have to wrestle with a topic for a while before finally penning the central idea to the paper mat.

168. How many people carry a pocket full of pebbles with them to toss into the pool of daily events only to have the ripples go unnoticed?

169. Does a vampire take the inventory at the protoplasm warehouse?

170. Try cleaning the tips of your conceptual spark plugs if you want to ignite some metaphors.

171. Will you pause to ponder occasionally when doing the mental legwork up some abstract mountain?

172. Some people have stained glass dramas that are the windows to their souls.

173. He fell asleep at the potter's wheel and fashioned the bowl of his dreams.

174. That vast ocean of the subconscious mind is constantly sending ripples of information into your stream of consciousness. (This one exceeds the weight limit of the topic's bridge.*)

175. In sports, a baseball bat was used to drive home a point that diamonds are a girl's best friend.

176. When the dollar bill is no longer a vehicle with purchasing power, barter plugs will spark the economy.

177. Metaphors are the handrails up the spiral book staircase.

178. The net value of a verbal rapport pings back and forth, to and fro, until the ball is hammered and a twenty-one-point conclusion is reached.

179. Plastic ligaments can attach to and reinforce pipe elbows. (Let's ask Robert the Robot. *)

180. Spiritual hydraulics is for lifting moods.

181. Is there some confusion about when or if your life will need a transfusion?

182. A body of small talk has been known to reject such alien organs as quantum physics.

183. Will clichés settle at the bottom of a bucket that is filled with a watered down vocabulary?

184. So, the economy of humor is in a recession, which would explain why we receive dozens of applications from unemployed puns on a daily basis.

185. A herd of wild bullets were grazing in a field of targets.

186. Numerous unhatched grenades have been known to incubate at the bottom of a machine gun nest.

187. A meal ticket will take you through the doors of the Cafeteria Express.

188. This graveyard is filled with stumps from family trees. (Ask Willy-Nilly, he'll tell you about our methods for cutting down trees.*)

189. The typography of the human mind does contain a lot of hills and valleys.

190. A higher demand for new ideas snapped the branches of a neurology tree. Since original thinking is free, workers didn't charge anything for cleaning up the debris.

191. A roll of humor can insulate you from the vicissitudes of the weather. (Vic who?*)

192. Are quanta echoing through the canyons of an atom?

193. The burlap to riches account of Jack's climb up the corporate ladder was thrown into an editorial fabric softener and became a fairy tale about beans.

194. The nature of your ideas reflects your ability to navigate in an ocean of energy.

195. From the circus of science, physics has not made the leap through the metaphysical hoop.

196. Well, what do you know about that? Ancient information is rapidly becoming modern.

197. Petri Dish changed his name to Pierre Hendricks after closely examining some of his cultural contributions.

198. To deconstruct a bias use the claw of a hammer to loosen thinking that is nailed shut.

199. The Erg (mental electricity) team is trained in the dynamics of clean, wholesome and vigorous mental flux.

200. A word sluice might be constructed to channel your stream of thought into rows of prose.

201. They may not have been equally funny and yet the two jokes were balanced on the scales of humor.

202. The poultry belt seems to be holding up the pants of area farmers.

203. Green grows the gerunds as garden editors go into action pruning their sentences. (A letter arrived from the Green Nations today.*)

204. Yes, it is no less than *awesome* the many things that will enrich the sold from which a garden will grow.

205. For the essay police who were duty that morning, the lights began flashing early. The officer in the passenger seat took out his blow horn and issued a warning to the car they were following, "Pull over and show us you're writer's license." The young wordsmith was issued a citation for having one too many run-on sentences.

206. Folsom Prison cell division separates the mitochondria from the chloroplasts.

207. The four-lane genre of literature is for fast readers who want to view the text at a glance and avoid completely those dictionary pit stops.

208. Sustained creativity will gradually undermine the roof brain clatter and allow the future to leak in.

209. Do you have an information compost near your garden?

210. Listen to the stories flow rapidly from the mouth of the river.

211. Opening the door as to who you are depends on what your personality hinges.

212. "Let's go trolling. Let's float along the river under the trees. We'll stop long enough to check the trout lines. I wonder if they are catching on to the fact that you can go fishing for anything."

213. What does it yield? You simple grow more attractive when you spend more time in your electromagnetic field.

214. Liquid conformity was found in the canisters behind the Generic Office Building.

215. The Dictionary Corp of Engineers gets the call to flush out the word ways when there is an excessive sludge build-up from media treatment plants. (After wading through all the adjectives, we agree and we want their number.*)

216. In the eighteenth century, when a feather fell from your imaginary wings, it was converted into a writing instrument.

217. None of the Florida Keys are capable of unlocking the mystery the Bermuda Triangle.

218. Keep in mind that you are the tip of the iceberg that is afloat in the ocean of your mind.

219. Police are looking for a metaphor equipped with an atomic motor and stolen from a physics parking lot.

220. We've been listening to the music of a narrow band called "White light."

221. Honestly things will go much smoother for you if you'll shovel some truth pellets onto that slippery slope reality.

222. Would you damage the soft ware by cyber watering a bouquet of electronic flowers?

223. You might try tuning into the gap setting of your neural spark plugs on a more frequent basis.

224. Does your conceptual grid need a new filter?

225. Would it help to loosen your clogged thinking? Try inhaling the steam from spring water steeped in alphabet tea.

226. If you want your thinking to be razor sharp, hone your wit on a pun stone.

227. Try raising the mercury in that creative thermometer.

228. Boolean oars are used to paddle boatloads of information through electronic gates.
(*Boolean* has nothing to do with scaring you. The word is a form of algebra dealing with *logic* or yes/no gates in PC's.*)

229. Can you see flashlight beams being used as a support structure to a house of lights?

230. We are continually making deposits at the first national level of neural banking.

231. A calendar of events allows the news a clockwise exit through the drain at the bottom of a front page sink. (Hold the presses, we are metaphor heavy.*)

232. Didn't we fill up with ink before we started writing about this trip?

233. Dimitri is still wading around in a shallow pool of physics trying to understand tadpole north and south and the Wave Theory in between.

234. The Agri-editor walked his pen onto a pasture page, deleted every twentieth word and dragged them into the margin to be used as a vocabulary sample to test the richness of the prose. (The editor must be going through a prepositional phase.*)

235. R. Witfield soon learned that he would have to think fast if he wanted to score any points in the brain ball game.

236. As it turns out, the marriage of water and clay when molded into a flower pot held the longest, most colorful metaphor.

237. The two of them were quite a sight to see, dressed as human mistletoe. (Isn't mistletoe a parasite? *)

238. In a manner of speaking, a personality lights up when connected to a charisma pole.

239. They were flooded with adjectives describing the monsoons; is a metaphor that figuratively falls under and literally rolls off the umbrella of weather.

240. Out of a long line of red ants trekking through the Ganglia Gap, one in four stops to nibble at incoming information.

241. Would you be walking down a tele-path if you went looking for your sixth sense?

242. You'll need two hands to float the Memo River. This body of water flows around and down and circulates until quite late when it arrives at the mouth of our present reminisce.

243. Once you close your eyes does your vision make a u-turn back into inner space?

244. Therm overheated when his backpack became filled with mercury near the top of Temperature Hill.

245. The sentence was balanced. The metaphors had lift. The motifs were tight. The puns had been doubly checked. All the parts have passed a grammar test and the propeller compels us to take it for a spin. Let's see if it will fly.

246. A geometry of puns might consist of two different meanings intersecting at the same word.

247. Are you pining to be a poet? Our sources tell us that a Lexi-chaun can tell you where he has buried his bag of golden syllables.

248. Does it mean that your mental equipment is shrinking when there is only a one inch hammer in the tool box of your memory?

249. What would you expect to buy at a yard sale for community writers? A can of earth words for anybody fishing for a story line.

250. Through the lamp of your mental acumen, you have by now concluded that some books do more than others to illuminate a room.

251. The film industry is related to the family pharmaceutical in that it will sell you a bottle of movie pills.

252. A raindrop is trivial information that falls into that larger pool of intellect.

253. Metaphors are high octane thought propulsion. (Sometimes my car runs low on feul.*)

254. Most people will open their neural gates to the path of least resistance.

255. In this text, we don't use metaphors that injure the puns. Translation: Sometimes when the truth is shaped like a knife, make your point some other way.

256. Will a lace of leaves tighten the sole of a shoe tree?

257. The yellow arms swing across to block the road from traffic when too much rain allows the creek to flex its muscles.

258. A kitten brook can grow to the size of a cat river over whose bridge stalks the lion waters of a flood. (Nice *parallelism* . . . Nearly a hundred pages into the book and we finally found an opening for that word.*)

259. Yes, Joyce, you have a choice: You can either let the weeds grow or you can cultivate flowers in your little corner of this planetarium.

260. Air pumps are being hyped as the ultimate metaphor. (This entry is under too much pressure. Let's inflate an old inner tube and go swimming.*)

261. Most of us are aware that there is an outer circle. Did you know there is an inner circle? (Are you talking about one of the new Radials I just put on my car? *)

262. The wheels of passion keep spinning in the race of life. (This metaphor was the first over the finish line.*)

263. Shiloh steep out of her Toyota long enough to announce that she had written a new metaphor: *Will the traffic of fresh, new and creative thinking ever come to a standstill?* And then she hopped back into her car and drove off.

264. Of course the metaphor with atmosphere has many strata.

265. We, the human race, as diamonds in the rough, would be a valuable contribution to the cosmic gem lab. (Alas, a twenty-four caret topic rings the bell.*)

266. Most of the metaphors in this collection are swimming upstream to spawn puns.

Money

1. We'll give you five dollars if you can tell us what money is. (Inflation tells us that it'll cost you more than that.*)

2. If a money tree grew in your back yard, what would you do with its leaves?

3. If money did grow on trees, it would explain why we have so many wealthy birds perched in the top limbs.

4. "The guy on the phone wants to know how important money is to you."
    "Tell him I'll get in touch with him later. I'm late for work." (That's a value call.*)

5. Prices are consistently being monitored during their hike up an inflationary trail.

6. Is your electric bill overdue? Better write a check. We doubt that your credit card will neutralize a static charge.

7. Today we will learn a new way to spell $ucce$$.

8. Banks should be built on Primrose Lane. (Is that what is meant by a bank holiday?*)

9. An observant few know that it takes the penny hand one hundred seconds to go around the face of a silver dollar.

10. The Dow Jones Neverland must be out there somewhere afloat in a billion dollar ocean.

11. Walt wanted us to write a topic about his state of exaltation. We asked him what the capitol was and of course he replied, "Money."

12. How much money can you carry in an umbrella? (Will you have enough for a rainy day?*)

13. What do you hear when you apply a stethoscope to your checkbook? (In England it would be a series of pounds.*)

14. "I always leave a stack of money on the table for him to count when he gets moody," noted Penny Moore to her sister as they walk out the door.

15. Is time money? It is according to that one thousand dollar flexible band on your wrist.

16. They could not locate the Phantom of the Opera to refund the money from the recent rainout. (Was he taking in "The Rainman?" *)

17. Will monetary diet plan provide the short term rescue of a bankrupt or undernourished value system?

18. For what in the world of rhetoric is "innovative business venture" doublespeak? (Awkward if accurate.*)

19. Levi's eyes lit up when they plugged the money into his wall-et.

20. Since dime stores are no longer in existence, where can we buy a ten cent piece?

21. The businessman of the month was found to have a picket fence built around his brain. His nose was the mailbox with an accounts receivable ledger in it and the flag was up.

22. Dairy farmers are squeezing a lot of change out of registered cows that have been grazing in a field of dollar bills.

23. The time is twenty-seven cents past the O'dollar value of three.

24. "What in the whirl is that on the shelf over there?" "You're looking at a money vortex and we're down to our last one. Once seen they are easy to get caught up in.

25. Eat, ate eaten: Is satur-*ating* the market with a product the same as force feeding it to the public?

26. Some people have a DNA helix shaped like a dollar sign.

27. The tin man did squeak by and with his money made a sizable investment in Nestles. (Because the lubricant in the can he used was none other than chocolate.*)

28. Oleander Tumbler keeps all his money paint in a wall safe. (How much of it is oil based? *)

29. A stun gun is perched atop the electric door and shoots a beam of discounted prices through the gaze of an approaching customer.

30. Note the quality of information you can buy if you'll *pay* attention. (You'll find that a lot of it is free. *)

31. Agenda audits will be arranged for those people whose lives are too scattered for them to focus on saving metaphysical dollars.

32. "Okay," said the painter, "let's add a tad more green to that money tree to let the viewer know it's the season for investing."

33. Somebody tanned a note and left it on the treasury's desk suggesting that dollars be made of leather so they will last longer.

34. If a dollar bill is our flag, then a recession means it is flying at half mast.

35. Some of us paid in plenty for back-row tickets in the Social Security Auditorium.

36. Along with a crystal bull, he uses a money-scented candlelight for seeing into stock futures.

37. Philanthropic topics are all about giving yourself a chance to believe in you own creativity. (So sit down in your favorite chair-ity and think about.*)

38. Why would anybody drop a penny into the ground, bury and pour water over it, if they were able to work?

39. Wall Street offered a list of predictions for the New Year longer than a profit's beard.

40. Each leaf group is made up of three dollars: Some people are in big rash to catch investment poison ivy.

41. The scent of the dollar bill kept the money hounds pounding after the ever elusive lucre.

42. When the dollar bill no longer works as a vehicle of purchasing power, barter plugs will spark the economy.

43. Have you not seen the dollar signs that are detailed as totems on football helmets?

44. You can always tell when the nickel defense is beginning to weaken, the offense will be running ten dollar plays at them. (Does the *quarter*back call the plays?*)

45. He spent his life watering a money tree that had to be uprooted to make room for his casket.

46. Is your personal castle so constructed to offer a bird's eye view of the world? (Yes, I, Norgana can gaze out across the entire wingdom.*)

47. Do the canyons of New York City have money running through them?

48. Do you remember back in 2015 when business became our second language?

49. Piñata economics seems to be taking quite a few hits.

50. Future intensive care units will have plastic bags filled with liquid money for IV patients.

51. Rolling in dough? Where does it fit in the economic pie chart?

52. The penny has become nearly as small as is the image of Lincoln minted between the columns on the coin's flip side.

53. The idea is to stay well vex-cinated against the fever pitch of shopping that appears endemic during the holiday season. (How about saving your money at Christmas time? *)

54. Have you ever seen the clowns as they juggle their prices on Haggler Row?

55. Check the soles of your boots before hiking up the money trail.

56. The green needle that leather stitched your wallet always points toward magnetic money.

57. The broadcasting beehive drones on and on buzzing for the money, honey.

58. What nature of *vandal*-ism is it when you thrust a javelin through a money-making machine?

59. You will need a certificate of surgery from Uncle Bob's heart operation when you apply at the Time Bank for a five-year life extension note.

60. Your intuition should tell you which university to attend.

61. When hard times grabbed him by the seat of the pants and a quarter fell out, Ernie Dollar phrased the coin, "I am spent" when it landed on tails.

62. We offer a ten percent discount on all chess games if you can carry the set up to the checkout counter without thinking about money.

63. Is it I Ching (ancient Chinese *Book of Changes*) or ka-ching (cash register)?

64. Ira Foley has four hours and twenty minutes in his time wallet.

65. The Whoa Society attempts to slow those monetary stallions that stampede through the consumer valley.

66. You are advised to get some inside information before approaching the Tao Jones Stock exchange.

67. When Jack fell down and broke his crown, Jill immediately called to see if Nursery Rhyme Mutual would cover the damages.

Music

1. Explain your favorite kind of music.

2. The birds know when a musician is winging it.

3. Is it possible to cook beats in a kettle drum? (Only if you serve them with chicken legs.*)

4. Why do people have such varying tastes in music? (Sounds like there is a lot on the menu. *)

5. A musical scale will weigh a variety of songs. (We conclude that heavy metal has its' own scale.*)

6. Music may be food for the soul however, Mr. Nottingham did not say "troubled chef." He said "treble clef."

7. Mulligan tells us that he has added a delicious stew of music to his harmonics menu.

8. Beatrice Earnshaw had the dance hall floor stamped with sheet music.

9. He keeps his sheet music in bird cages when he wants to write songs about flying.

10. Toob plays the didjeridoo for the Australian Outback Band.

11. The Elastic Recording Co wants you to be more flexible with your repertoire of music.

12. Three musicians were fretting about nuggets to be found in the river bottom of Tin Pan Alley.

13. Which of the seven birds of the musical scale is the leader? (The one who can hit the highest note.*)

14. We should pass an ordinance that requires noise at some point to become music.

15. The humdrum can be broken when selected words are strummed into a song.

16. Valerie Counter will be leading the guests in the vanilla fudge polka.

17. Can the footprints of a song be seen in the sand? (If it is being sung by the Beach Boys.*)

18. Thor, vacationing from mythology, found a hammer hidden in a folk song.

19. Some people have speech patterns that lend a musical quality to their words.

20. Words with the proper composure are usually picked for song lyrics.

21. Do you have a compact disc of "The Wind's Greatest Hits?"

22. Would your life be turned off without music?

23. When the Buffalo Bill Symphony played, you could almost hear the hooves pounding the drums.

24. Can guitars fly? You'll know there is music in the air when you find a player who can turn the strings into wings.

25. He plays the frugal in the Tennessee Tight Wad Band.

26. If notes leak from an unused musical instrument, will it cause the strings to lose their pitch?

27. Would a song about sunshine leave a shadow of its notes on the ground?

28. *Do* fell out of tune with the chromatic scale. He however went on to start a band called "Solfeggio."

29. People from miles around heard the tunes after someone at the aviary took a Disney pen and sketched wings onto the musical notes.

30. Wrap your notes with fiber sharps and flats one half step tighter to insulate against frozen music.

31. Would music written on a balloon be given much air time? (Not if it is a pop song.*)

32. Why not use a rope if you were demonstrating the function of a sound wave in western music?

33. When air borne musical notes perch on the arch of a rainbow, you have coloratura.

34. The Clouds were instrumental in releasing some rain music. (Yes, they are playing tonight at the drop-in.*)

35. Is music audible medicine?

36. Some musical instruments required special entryways called tuba doors. (Would a lyre played by a troubadour qualify?*)

37. "Opus the door and listen in."
    "To open the door is to turn the house inside out?"

38. A symphony of splashes occurs when you observe a major Salmon route leading into the Northern Pacific: you then get an idea where fish are covered on the musical scale.

39. Music was heard cascading down the Niagara Symphony Cataract. (The volume of water was the important thing. *)

40. What would a bumper sticker on the fender of a car hauling guitars say?

41. Would it take two John Keats to write the lyrics for the music of the caged bird?

42. Informally, they bounce over lyrics at sing-a-longs. Formally, they don a gown for a night of ball room dancing.

43. The bee buzzed through a clover leaf pattern, its wings working 192 beats per second or a hair above a Middle C vibration level. The hive was in tune and took its cue from the queen as a *honey do.*

44. After Maris dipped her bucket into the stream of conscious she was more than surprised to find several dream minnows swimming about in it.

45. Joe Banmore's instrument cracked due to the temperature contrasts of the lyrics in "Oh Susanna."

46. Willy Pickens has the guitar notes to a new song in his *cord*uroy coat.

47. Rail shipping cars now include built-in panels inked with sheet music for traveling folk musicians.

48. A three-way conductor system allows orchestra music to be wired into and thus control the tempo of a train. (If this was happening live and on stage (coach) we would have tickets to that concert? *)

49. Many musicians have it within their talents the power to heal.

50. Slide your fingers down the strings of an acoustical metaphor and notice the tone of the sentence change.

51. Is the chord chart the alphabet of music?

52. You can provide the life that pulses through the notes of a musical instrument.

53. Insulate your thought processes with rolls of music from a weather-resistant symphony.

54. The violin is the most frequently used vehicle for transporting emotions. If it doesn't move you, apparently you are quite content where you are sitting.

55. If puns are a play on words then metaphors should be a musical instrument.

56. While perched upon the acoustical instrument the bird wondered if he would need a guitar peck.

57. If you want music to be the root system to consciousness, plant some high frequency seeds to grow the three B's. (We're back or is it Bach, Brahms and Beethoven? *)

58. A cardinal was perched on the violin bow in the orchestra pit of neighborhood sounds. (I read about this in the "Aviary Gazette."*)

59. Is there a rock 'n roll warehouse for discarded music?

60. We should listen to musical notes that correspond to the response time between whippoorwills during a crescent moon.

61. What would be the pulse of the drum set during your favorite song?

62. Can the high notes cross the bridge of a guitar into bass land?

63. Bugs wired into insect trails found beneath tree bark were discovered to conduct the entire range of wood instruments into the intercellular symphony. (Wood you repeat that? *) If you slide an electronic bug under its bark, you can listen to the beat of the tree. (That's better.*)

64. We never knew how much a song can weigh upon a person's mind until we started using a musical scale.

65. The Atlantic organ will hit a wave of wet notes should its heavy metal band expand during the summer heat.

66. Are various instruments choreographing musical notes? (Better yet, make a note to dance at the next concert.*)

67. Art Deco, we want a picture of your Aunt Jessie kneading a circle of dough into a song about apple pi.

68. At Roy's Chord Delivery you'll find the notes in your pants and coats: from there you put the song together any way that suits you.

69. A trio of songs in a Kingston Topic: "Tom Dooley" was a "Worried Man" when his "MTA" sister handed him a sandwich for his last meal beneath a white oak tree.

70. What kind of music plays in your mind throughout the day?

71. A musical instrument equipped with the String Theory of the universe might require a quantum set of headphones for listening.

72. The analyst told the musical theorist that he, the patient, was high strung.

73. We were flooded with notes when the sound of rain reached a crescendo.

74. "*Oh, Karina,* as I listen to and feel the power of the instrument, I know that it is truly the ancient voice of the gods connecting us to the wisdom of the earth, "confessed Guy Smitten.

75. "Not every good boy deserves fudge," commented Dina Dissonance as she pulled a flat knife through some terrible sounding brownies.

76. Is a finely tuned ear a musical prism that can bend a song into a spectrum of notes?

77. After Major Muse found a key in B-minor he hummed over to unlock his voice box. He lifted out a tune, placed it in a breve case and carried it to the end of Harmony Street.

78. Is noise to music what weeds are to the garden?

79. A tiny little *Mu* rebelled and left the Sousa Instrument Company to captain a much sounder shipping firm.

    Would ringing it twice be an act of rebellion?

80. Do three dog nights call for four log mornings?

81. What takes place in the space that inaudibly unfolds between two musical octaves?

82. At some point in their careers most music instructors took their morning coffee with a hummingbird perched on the lip of the cup. (If magic were a song, our conductor's wand would set many of these topics to music.*)

83. Who are your favorite musicians? Why?

84. Ray Ann, whose guitar likes to wear her brown vest while she rests, will usually find a note in one of the pockets the next day.

85. Does music insulate us?

86. Feel like dancing? Wrap some music around the soul of your shoe.

Musings

1. **Write dialogue between:**

   - a stick shift and the clutch.

   - Swiss cheese and a cow.

   - the moon and the earth.

   - a pen and a notebook.

   - Frankenstein's monster and Dracula.

   - a square and a circle.

   - a canoe and a river.

   - a handsaw and a board.

   - a coin and a dollar bill.

   - Saturday night and Sunday morning.

Describe:

   - Batman in the army.

   - a giraffe driving a golf cart.

   - Paul Revere, the mailman.

- a cardboard water tower. (Would you see leeks grow out of it? *)

- and write your observations concerning insects.

- a Friday called off.

- no more seasons.

- the *Rise and Fall of the Gravity Empire.*

- *t*he pa *i* nting of a dog.

- anybody eating turnips. (Beats me why anyone would want to eat a turnip. *)

- skateboarding on a foam rubber pond.

- the fall season for trees. (Yes, the dogs will always have a few things to say about their bark and that leaves us with a quiet tree.*)

- fashion. (I saw a Humphrey Vogue-art suit hanging in my aunt's closet.*)

- what an awesome person you are. (Shakespeare is quoted as saying that greatness is thrust upon some people.*)

- a serum that will transform you into Dracula. (Please write something we can sink our teeth into.*)

- a world without money. (We'll give you credit for almost anything.*)

- your thoughts and reactions when in the passenger seat and moving one hundred mph. (Are you living in the fast lane? *)

- what it is like to be a genius. (You may have to think about this one.*)

- an illusion. (This topic is not what it appears to be.*)

- the last two minutes on the ocean-liner Titanic.

- your life as a park ranger.

- one of your ideas that your friends consider bizarre.

- movement that gathers your attention. (Action!*)

2. What will you be like as an adult? (We like most adults.*)

3. What one topic occupies your mind the most?

4. What happens in this classroom at two am?

5. Is there life after high school?

6. What is the first thing that you remember? (Playing crib-bage.*)

7. You are a drop of water and the temperature is approaching thirty-two degrees. Now What?

8. What will you grow in your life's garden?

9. Here's the problem: You are sinking in the ocean with cement overshoes and the only way to save yourself will be to tell us what SCUBA stands for.

10. Would you rather work or go to school? (Why not work at going to school? *)

11. Is going to school an easy life? (Or will you have to study that one? *)

12. Would you be thirteen again? Why or why not?

13. What would you do to prevent a third World War?

14. You are on the Hispanic menu. Write dialogue between yourself and the other parts of a taco before you become someone's lunch.

15. As pizza dough are you just *flat* tired of your job?

16. Are you driven to find a substitute for the car?

17. If your brain was a car would you need a license to think?

18. Would you like to take a float trip in a helium balloon?

19. Do you avoid walking under ladders?

20. Are you obsessed with technology?

21. What would you do without the world of technology? (I would get on the internet and find out how to buy a horse.*)

22. The draft once meant military enlistment or should I close the door on that subject?

23. A celebrity stopped to give you the hitchhiker a ride. Tell us about this brush with fame.

24. What kind of person is your journal becoming? (Was your last entry all about personification?*)

25. What are the advantages of living in a small town?

26. How would a modern day Little Red Riding Hood story line go?

27. Of Snow White and the Seven Dwarfs, pick your favorite dwarf and tell something about his life. (Make it a short story.*)

28. What do you think about when you eat an ice cream cone?

29. Where would you rather be instead of here? (Are you there instead of here?*)

30. "My house is tumbling through the air. When will it stop?"
"When the pants are dry."
"Why?"
"Because it is a small green plastic house from a Monopoly Game that fell out of a pocket in a clothes dryer."

31. Is a beauty salon in the crosshairs of your ambitions?

32. How would you like to have 100,000 more words in your vocabulary? (I would buy stock in Expresso coffee.*)

33. You are flying a balloon across the continent. Describe your trip. (Whatever the destination, you shouldn't *poke* along and try to be punctual.*)

34. You must pick a profession. Which one will you choose and why?

35. Compose a story on the origin of Santa Claus. (Would you prefer his sister, Santa Catalina? *)

36. What is the one request you would make of the Wizard of Oz?

37. "Strata" is performing at tonight's *rock* concert. What kind of music do you expect to hear?

38. What do you think about when you are alone? (Should we leave the room?*)

39. We still don't know the real reason why the chicken crossed the road.

40. What do you care the most about?

41. What would your life be like without your parents?

42. Wouldn't it be a dull world if all our questions were answered?

43. Gone are the days when you'd see a leap of frogs sitting on the banks of the Pond-ike River waving to the minors as they float by enroute to the gold fields.

44. Writing can be as easy as a having a talk with your aunt Edith. (Is she discussing a plot with you? *)

45. Was the paper well written? You be the judge. Carrie completed her research paper on ground beef, slipped the assignment into a notebook and left the house with plenty of time to get to class. She stopped long enough to pet the neighborhood dog Ralph who fastened his teeth to her research paper and ate it.

46. What would have happened in grade school if you had adjusted your thinking cap to be about two sizes larger?

47. The Carvelli Family was sitting around Roman-iscing about last summer's vacation in Italy.

48. The Sand Band will always go against the grain when playing ocean amplified music.

49. Penning verses to a lady? In the eighteen century, if you happen to be waxing poetic, you could use a drop of poetry to seal the envelope.

50. A man was thinking about evil recently when he stumped his toe on the way up the stairs. (Thinking empowers it.*)

51. Once a week we drive to the summit of Scenary Mountain and we always return with a trunk load of inspiration.

52. Is it true that you are taught to ask questions at the Socrates Training Camp?

53. Did you feel a rush of cool air when you opened the air-onautics textbook?

54. Would a borderline genius have one foot in the land of observation and the other in the land of creativity?

55. Were there two aardvarks aboard the ark?

56. Where would you expect to find an electronic monster named Google-zilla?

57. You'll get a phone call from the *cell*s if your health is not what it should be.

58. "Will a well developed imagination defy the law of gravity?"

59. "Yes, if you have an airplane flying over the Metropolitan Mind Complex."

60. Do you know of anybody who lives in a bubble? (Yes, and they do like to take float trips? *)

61. Hinton Altus claims that a picture of a walleye fish stares back at him when he lies in bed at night.

62. The Rocky Mountain bridge players need you to drive the snack wagon across the Great Kitchen.

63. Absolutely, telephone companies as we once knew them will soon be obsolete.

64. If you happen to make water noises when you sleep, we recommend that you wear a snorkel.

65. A pocket full of bells will no longer get you in the door at the telephone company.

66. If you take note of the weather shouldn't you be able to find the corresponding keys on a piano?

67. This is no laughing matter. Some people have a serious thinking problem.

68. Now that he was safely ensconced in his cell-ophane tree house, how was he to contact anyone who had trouble following him up the stairs?

69. The only way you are going to put that canoe in the attic is thorough the Upstairs Shuttle Service.

70. Finally, after lobbying days on end for six months, a national Johnny Appleseed day has come to fruition.

71. Rebuilt concepts are for the daring few who can handle the thought.

72. Headlines: Imploded Restaurant Bites the Dust

73. As his ship made its way through the fog, Captain Barge, an eighteenth century pilot might have been the first to see the need for the Erie Canal.

74. Memories . . . once you see a kite, you can fly it as often as you want to.

75. A herd of sea horses were trapped at the O K Coral Reef.

76. If you are *serious* about sealing some of the cracks in that drafty old house, try using some comic strip tape. And by the way:

    Have you noticed that in the comic strip "Geometry" all the characters have sixty—seven degree noses?

77. To locate an upbeat spring day is to connect a weathervane to an electrocardiogram.

78. We stenciled seventh inning stretch on a beach ball and bounced it to the crowd.

79. Did the dolphin make a loud deposit in the beach bank when it went down the repossessed slide on porpoise? (Yes, the i-rate of interest went up five per cent.*)

80. We need a word to describe the liquid that comes out of the water faucet. Wet a minute, I think I know the answer.

81. Describe the scenario between kitchen colonels who are about to start a range war over tap water.

82. My aunt did crochet a muzzle loader that uses cotton balls for ammunition.

83. The Dale Carnegie course on *How to Win Friends and Influence People* includes a recording of "The Ballad of Jed Clampett."

84. We had that tire pumped up in thirty seconds flat.

85. Should we tie a rain-bow around Thor's neck for the next weather dance?

86. Would an anti-trust law require you to be suspicious of the people you meet?

87. After your personal and iambic only metric feet have splashed around in a word puddle, you should be inspired to write a poem.

88. Did they frisk your mind for a concealed vocabulary? (Yes and the only words to describe it have been confiscated.*)

89. Does the warden of your personal self bar you from ever being impressed by anything?

90. Someday the circle of humanity will display a twenty-four care-it diamond ring.

91. Picture the possibilities of thinking with images as opposed to words.

92. Have you ever seen an information cemetery? (*She wrote her own epitaph* will be at the bottom of SB's grave marker.*)

93. The human mind is to the computer what Victorian Falls is to a garden hose.

94. What is the membership count in the Association for Information Recall?

95. Should a microscopic pen be used to describe the personal lives of electrons complete with a subatomic background?

96. In the Friday night topics game, the puns are leading the metaphors. (And the similes are the cheerleaders.*)

97. If you can compare prices, you can contrast events and in so doing detail the forces that color your experience. That's Dynamic! (Are they having a two day sale on dye-chotomies? Should we wait for the dictionary man to arrive? *)

98. You might think that a 2000 year old tree would be well *read.*

99. Where is your communication comfort zone?

100. If morality is nine on the scale of ten, then its square root would be the three times you have done the right thing.

101. "Haveyoulookedintohowmuchamirrorofthesizewillcost?" "Yes, and we were also told that it would start working the moment we hung it on the wall, if not before."

102. What would the computer generated image of a mirror reflect?

103. The world is a spectacular place when seen from the top of Feel Good Mountain.

104. Follow your own ball of twine: mine has a knot in it. ~

105. Do you think that a gerbil running in a wheel will ever inspire a song? (He might make a new circle of friends.*)

106. What does it mean when three clouds of smoke rise above a specific teepee in a Cherokee camp?

107. Would you use clay to retread a potter's wheel?

108. stet > How did a Mason jar lid found under a partly burnt mattress located in a remote shack south of Hot Springs get a dent in it? (By errant typesetting? *)

109. Does a picture of Spain's Rock of Gibraltar belong in a dark room, a geology lab, an insurance office or a rappelling camp? (Excuse me for turning on the lights but dark rooms are now obsolete.*)

110. A highly fluid mind invites the expression "deep in thought."

111. Hey Al, could you repeat the question? My mind was elsewhere doing some *super fishing*.

112. Check with your band leader as to where specific instruments will take you. You may want to combine wood, string, and percussion, depending on the extent of your imagination.

113. Dictionaries, unlike calculators, are something you can *look up* to.

114. If you have the right plan, long distance float trips on the Cellaphonic River are free.

115. Bells can be tintinnabulatingly self ringing. (Excellent sound to a colorful word.*)

116. By definition all that a rock has to do is keeps a clichés distance from a hard place.

117. The Ti Ming approach to life management places you where and with whom you should be at the optimum opportunity to achieve maximum results. (Bingo!*)

118. Have you received a card recently from your sympathetic nervous system telling you to get more exercise?

119. Somewhere in the valley below Big Rock Candy Mountain little boys and girls get around on roller skates with cookie wheels. (Do they live in a gingerbread house?*)

120. The best way to leave a massage on your answering machine is to say appropriate things that rub people the right way.

121. Would a float trip on the Cartoon River inspire a thought bubble?

122. If the canoe overturns while you're floating the Cartoon River, will you be soaking wet with pixels? (Yes, if you read about it in the Sunday paper.*)

123. Will a fairly sharp ax-iom be all that you need to split the difference between fact and rumor? (An axiom is a universally recognized truth.*)

124. Never under estimate the opposable thumb. It has taken us down many hiways.

125. This uncorked thought bubble shows a band master on horseback trotting down the Main Street of Champagne, Musica.

126. Does the earth create tides in the moon's Sea of Tranquility?

127. Synesthetically speaking, what color is your name or what does classical music look like? (The dictionary man reports that this is "one sense evoking the sensation of another."*)

128. The length and width of your interest is in direct proportion to your attention span.

129. How would you like to help us find a lost gold mind?

130. Dustin Broomley has been known to sweep on the job.

131. All we get from people who drive by is a lot of vacant stares at a yard where once there was a house sale.

132. How much horse power is required to generate one idea? (Are you thinking about the races? *)

133. Would a dull routine of a life inform a person that time is in the cockpit of a Boring 747?

134. If you want to be simpatico with the cows, try chewing gum while you're in the field.

135. A small amount of mettle is enough is enough to forge a psychological wedge between two people.

136. If you want to draw interesting people into your personal orbit, write letters to them from a launching pad.

137. Why does the Grim Reaper carry a bag of sunflower seeds in his pocket?

138. This week the subcommittee on table omit-tees will discuss how some food particles always manage to get the brush off.

139. Al Chism owns a statue called "The Beach" and he attests that it's the best example he has ever seen of ocean sculpting.

140. Does it alter the quality of the music when you can see the instrument being played?

141. Would a dam qualify as a breaker box for switching off a current?

142. Would anything that attracts attention be magnetic?

143. How will you know if Frank and Earnest are telling the truth?

144. How many of you have ever been through Thick n'Thin, a town with a growing population?

145. What day of the week would you estimate Thor's hat size to be by glancing at a thunder*head*?

146. If you are laying out an ad page should you position winter clothing photos next to stories that detail cold weather, snow falls, etc.?

147. Is someone who continues to give you false information re-lie-able?

148. Sometimes, you do need the information behind the pause between the two glances.

149. Two thumbs up: You had to hitchhike to Anywhere, USA to participate in the fifth annual thumb wrestling contest and you won it.

150. Prehensile utensils are for eating while hanging upside down. (Some readers will leave that word hanging.*)

151. Why not fax your next electric bill to those inventors who decided that electricity could be sent through wires, then sold as a commodity to the people?

152. How can you take the oldest rock pun there is for granite?

153. When does order seem to be overwhelmed by chaos? (When they give you a hamburger without fries?*)

154. Most events occur in cycles. So when two of these lines of energy coincide, look close and you'll find an elf wearing an acorn cap for a helmet and peddling a bi-cycle. (Different . . . *)

155. Are you an interesting person? Can you segue through five topics in as many minutes all the while accentuating the positive with mild guffaws that tie the last with the first into a tidy morality tale? (No!*)

156. How would you describe your stay at the No-Tell Motel?

157. Cattle nap, bull doze, sleep with your head on a caterpillar. (Pardon the fragment, the machine isn't warmed up yet.*)

158. Beyond a shadow of a doubt . . . he was absolutely certain that a doubt would under no circumstance cast a shadow. A devout Doubtist will always cast a shadow on certain eternity. Sun Prosecution waited until high noon to ask the six foot Don Doubtful a seven foot question.

159. If your thinking is philosophical, do you have some extra terrestrials you can put on the plate when you *phil up* my *soup bowl*?

160. The graffiti scratched at the bottom of a lighthouse might read "watch out above!"

161. Is fog a water ghost?

162. A poultry-geist is making a rather ghastly attempt to impersonate a turkey.

163. Destiny is (Are you ready?) the rigorous and robust unwrapping of your personal roadmap.

164. The No-Bell Prize for silence goes to anybody who will listen.

165. Plate glass oceanic's: The condensation outline on the window bore a close resemblance to the Marianna Trench. (If your sink is that deep, you'll never find the dishes.*)

166. How fragile is a sense of right or wrong that dissipates in the shadow of a contrary position?

167. We can feel good about the fact that the Neural Shopping Mall is the backbone industry throughout the nation's heartland.

168. If a tree falls in the lake will fish sticks wash up on the shore?

169. Let's *talk* about whether or not it takes an air gun to "shoot the breeze."

170. Are you going in the wrong direction if you're trying to locate Memory lane?

171. Phil believes that leaves have chloro-feelings as long as they remain connected to a limb.

172. A convocation of whacky weed eaters was having a swinging time at the Overgrown Emporium last night. A pun weed that was the first to be cut down spun an interesting question: "Did Stephanie Teflon know all the chords?"

173. Arctic navigators might have used a round black device attached to a fishing line called the "nose of the polar bear" for sniffing out magnetic north. (Why in the world don't you have more geography topics?*)

174. We get an ample supply of shaved ice from a huge bearded snowman.

175. Would alpha and Los Vegas be the beginning of a gambling spree?

176. The only way we'll get to know the real you is to *focus* on the essential I.

177. Why are writers never referred to as author-ities?

178. *Hallo*, Y'know, sometimes it takes a circle of light around a full moon to harvest the forage and fill up the silos.

179. Contrary to the fumes and rumors and noise from a lot of good ol' boys, nearly all the mufflers on this scrap heap died from exhaustion. (Report was bolted in by the Rusty Madewell Recycling Center.*)

180. Headlines: Lemming Takes Swimming Lessons (The little rodents are known for following each other over the edge of a cliff into a watery grave.*)

181. A hobby horse is what you'll need when you retire if you intend to ride off into the sunset.

182. Did the Union Pacific need training wheels in the early days of railroad?

Nature

1. Do you understand the value of trees?

2. Is it easier for a bird to fly downhill?

3. You are an insect. What do you do when winter puts the sting on you?

4. Write about a frog's existence in the winter time. (Hop to it.*)

5. Last night you as a reporter attended a city hall meeting of bees.
   Did they be-hive themselves?
   Was the queen in charge? (Do they still need pollen-teer bees to do field work.*)
   When your work was finished, did you spend the night in a suite?

6. Write about your favorite *season*. (Take your thyme.*)

7. Are bald eagles ever seen at an aviary salon?

8. Where would you go if you were a cloud? (I'd be a drifter.*)

9. Explain the flight pattern of a butterfly. (Should the flutterbys use turn signals? *)

10. Describe a tadpole to someone who is wading around to see one. (Be careful where you step. *)

11. Two sparrows are sitting on a telephone line outside your window. Translate their chirps into English. (One of them flew over to the side of the house to do some eves-dropping.*)

12. Isn't that some kind of *land*light that is swinging from the wing of a *tern* as he walks down the beach?

13. How would your life change is water was scarce? (Somebody is certain to note that it will be dry story.*)

14. You are a river. How do you decide what's current? (Shouldn't this be in float-tation marks.*)

15. You are a grape. What is it like hanging around in the vineyard?

16. You are the fog. Describe your occupation. (Don't get lost.*)

17. Headlines: Landslide Victory for Aztec Muddaubers over the Incan Wasps

18. Do crickets have to get a job in a rock and roll band before somebody will listen to them? (Hey Buddy, we know you're working hard. Will you be home for the holidays? *)

19. The wind will amplify the individual interests in the leaves on a tree.

20. Homogenized leaves are for the picky insects.

21. Do birds practice human calls? (The myna bird might impress you in a major way and yes, Carlene, we know it's only a starling.*)

22.   The insect community has rejected the name *litterbug*. (They'll pick up on it some other time.*)

23.   At the *Eat*on Hall ant meeting, it was mentioned that "something is sticking its nose into our business."

24.   The Watermelon Recreation Hall is where a melon collie came to relax and unwind and gnaw on a rind.

25.   Headlines: Earth Rejects Landfill (Did someone throw the newspaper in the trash? *)

26.   Cultivate your intelligence if you want it to grow.

27.   A praying mantis is always accompanied by his walking stick when it makes the spring trerk into the rain forest.

28.   One plant asked another after proposing a lifetime of faithful pollination: "You don't spore, do you?"

29.   An elderly praying mantis uses a walking stick when his work is finished at the branch office.

30.   The Insect Insight Report tells us that the small creatures impulse as strong a survival command code as do humans.

31.   Put an X in the 'a' square if you agree that nature is geometric.

32.   Are small creatures guided by information emanating from an invisible control source?

33.   Canoeists can now listen to a Rapid City broadcast of Soft Water Sounds. Simple turn up the volume when you want to see the V in the current.

34. Nature becomes both pro-fuse and profuse when warm temperatures and rain virtually ignite the plant life.

35. Tell us Skylar: How did you get over Bluella Ocean; learn how to fly or date someone further inland or arrive at the conclusion that the two of you were on completely different wave lengths?

36. In the rain forest, you'll find an Atlas oak trunk that can support the weight of a planet in ecological limbo.

37. Would the charred remains be a carbon copy of the original forest? (The machine will make as many copies of a tree . . . until we run out of paper.*)

38. Nature usually maps her hiking trails tele-*path*-ically. (Are you thinking I should pick up this pine cone? *)

39. When constructing an aviary (bird sanctuary), have it nestled in a woodland area. The blueprints should include two wings, a plumage closet and a whet stone for sharpening their beaks. (A worm farm would be nice.*)

40. The electric insect is always buzzing about looking for that outlet in a wall of heat.

41. Two birds overhead were heard sorting out a situation:
"We drew straws to see who would build the nest this spring."
"That must have been quite a picture."
"Yes, he drew the short one and when all was said and done, it was hung on a support twig in the living room."

42. To many trees, spring means re-lief.

43. "Somebody has been talking to this tree."
"How can you tell?"

"Do you see the way the leaves form the outline of an ear?"

44. After Gill Fishman was recruited by the Oceania Police Squid, he became one of the many tentacles who were required to wear an ink blue uniform.

45. When the Pebble family grows weary of life in the main stream, they check into the Hotel Bedrock to view the Current channel.
"There's the Minnow. That means *Gilligan's Island* will be on in about three hours."
"To be followed by a '60s music special hosted by "The Drifters.""
"And there's a school of fish. I wonder what today's lesson is. Look, they're playing a game of chess on that algae-covered green board."
"Hey, here's an old "Star Trek" movie. So that's what the captain's logue looks like."
"Yeah and chalkmate. It's all over."

46. The vulture will circle its prey for pi days until a line forms down the middle of the geo-carcass and the radius begins to decompose. (Please, no jokes on decomposition.*)

47. The Punfinch wanted you to know that if you *purch*-ase this bird feeder and take it home and hang it on your front porch, his relatives will not have a place to sit.

48. "And she's dating a moth," complained the monarch Beverly Butterfly regarding her daughter Mary. "Of all the ridiculous things, I mean, just look at those wings and the antennae! He should wear a cap. And his legs . . . he should wear pants if he hasn't eaten them. And does he still flit about under street lights during the warmest months of the year, oh, dear? Mary, put on a cap before you leave."

Oblique

1. "The *Boomerang* never rings," complained the kangaroo as he folded up his new cell phone and shoved it into his pocket. "Nobody ever returns my calls. Is there something wrong with this thing?"

2. A recording of a barking dog erased the recording of someone breaking into the house.

3. Clearly, he must be looking through a defective telescope if traces of Nigel's imagination are left on the lens.

4. Were there two aardvarks aboard the ark?

5. Tell the cleaning lady to check the chisel cabinets for saw dust when she works the lumberjack camp.

6. Three blind mice were singing "Que Sera Sera" in a grain elevator. (Or " . . . wheat will be will be." *)

7. Penguins in tuxedos were playing volleyball on the beach. (This year's game is informal.*)

8. They call it the cutting edge or would you like to go dancing with my scissors? (Are they as sharp as you are? *)

9. Haven't you heard how simple it is? Place the noise pump near the problem area: set the volume control for the desired level of silence and wait.

10. The four Moss-keteers were hired to sandblast the lichen from the noses at Mount Rushmore.

11. When you do research in the Alfalfa Field Library, you cut the kind of hay that can be published.

12. R. Gyles is going to write something so funny it'll knock your socks off providing you walk on your sense of humor.

13. A bowl of rainwater invited the local birds to a beak-in. (Did they have a wren for a guest speaker? *)

14. Terry Ann asks, "To rain or not to rain? The land is dry."

15. Caleb Cursive was more than helpful:
    "You'll need to click the top if you want to open my granddad's ink pen collection."

16. Isn't it a real hoot having the new owl eyes, bedroom wall covering?

17. For that dusted on lawn look, Landon sprinkled a bag of powdered chlorophyll over his front yard.

18. At the intersection of echoes between two houses being built, the Smithsonian should want to know why there is located a dollhouse.

19. Anachronism: Did you know that George Washington slept with his dentures in a plastic bag? (The bag must have been quite crowded.*)

20. "What was that noise?"
    "The bark came from a dogwood tree."

21. The man who was selling a new spin on the gyroscope fell off the ground.

22.   Is it an accident that the turn signals in your car move up or down to indicate left or right?

23.   The man accused of being boring has bolted wooden wings to his rocking chair. (The chair's already been used once, so someone from the pun playground needs to say; "Keep rocking." *)

24.   Descendents of Uncle Sam rally each year to throw tea bags into what used to be the prime minister's bathtub.

25.   If the sun gets stuck and we need to keep pushing on toward evening, who do we call that has the necessary heavy equipment?

26.   Did creatures that hibernate teach people how to go underground?

27.   When the satellite dish cracked, movies leaked all over the yard.

28.   Put a lemonade stand next to your driveway for any ideas that stop in the need of direction. (Put the stand next to Stonehenge and the sign will read "Fluids for Druids." *)

29.   Would the nose on the Statue of Liberty know anything about what is blowing in the wind?

30.   Barkley O' Arbor who thrives in a thicket outside of Boltimore did managed to lower his branches long enough to note that "it strikes me how lightning has such free reign in this area." (Rick from inside the thicket tells us that it was a split decision among the other elms as to whether or not BO'R did the right thing.*)

31.   If you write about yourself, are you from Pencil-vain-ia?

32. Some pens cannot write on a wall or horizontally so the writer is left with no other choice but to write off the wall items.

33. If you keep hearing the same old sounds, you might be trapped in an echo.

34. Does thirteen act as a pivot point on the way to green? (If so, let's change pivot to divot and be on our way to the golf course.*)

35. We can hear from your applause that the hands-on approach is the only one to take.

36. Turning up the volume will not help you to hear the call letters to a silent radio station.

37. Will the light bulb that you painted on your mailbox turn on when it's a good idea to check your mail?

38. Motorcycles come and go.

39. Since you can't clean the air with a broom, try a vacuum cleaner. (That's an idea that will take your breath away.*)

40. The House of Gadgets received an application patent for a board stretcher.

41. As opposed to homes will we someday see *domes* on the range?

42. What does a retired guillotine salesman do in his spare time? (He has a sharp mind for business. Let's say he's the head of a department store.*)

43. If you hang the picture of a snowy landscape on the wall will it lower the temperature in the room?

44. Did the canal locks keep Panama safe from the pirates?

45. With a Swiss time piece, the accent is on time while you're under water.

46. Erin's circle of friends is constantly in orbit.

47. According to the owner: "These donkeys do not buck. They are docile and as advertised the ride will cost you a dollar." (The owner M. Yule Rider knitted all their straw hats.*)

48. Tie your horse to that hay and come on in. (Hey ho, you do know that "mares eat oats and does eat oats . . . ."*)

49. Caves provide an excellent back-up source of night energy.

50. If your curiosity runs at least a mile deep in places you'll wonder how the Grand Canyon was really carved out.

51. Does color determine the efficiency of a heater? Gaston has never seen a white stove

52. What are the effects of work erosion on human hands? (Ask a wood cutter from Callous-thornia.*)

53. As soon as we hear from the Roman Canning Co, we'll have chariot races on the lid of a fruit jar. (Is Appliticus the driver?*)

54. "I am telling you that for 104.3 seconds she was sitting on my radio and tuning it with her toes." (She has found her station in life.*)

55. A neon fish is on its way to school below the hydroelectric dam.

56. For reasons that nobody seems to understand, the Salem witchcraft trial has been cancelled.

57. Bank on it, the museum of natural history has a river running through it. (Can somebody float me a loam? *)

58. We decided not to include the empty observatory in the Point of View category.

59. Musical roughage calls for you to listen to the William Tell Overture while munching apple slices.

60. With 432 scarfs in his closet, is Merlin Sturges ever in danger of becoming a fashion statement? (We'll ask Polly and Ester, the spinster twins who leave next door.*)

61. You'll need to get soaking wet if you plan to write a poem about seven geese splashing down in a lake.

62. The "Jungle Voice" reports that Tarzan has been appointed chairman of primal scream therapy at the Swing Center for Behavioral Research located on the corner of Firth and Vine. (Lower your voice. We're in the same room.*)

63. An animated fly swatter was patented by Toads of Pond, Incorporated.

64. Can you imagine puppets with no visible strings attached?

65. Kirow joined a group of Knilites who were headed for the cliffs on which were etched the latest in hieroglyphs.

66. Our wager will amount to little more than peanuts that the elephant will remember how to spell *proboscis.*

67.   Warning to all marine life
         Boat is made of glass
            Go around

68.   Shouldn't you be thinking about tricycle insurance for your child?

69.   A late model Mercedes was found stabbed by an exclamation mark. The wound was two inches below the sticker price.

70.   The air sack has an air clasp that fits snugly over the non-reference of an air hook. (All such sacks should be thusly secured from air thieves.*)

71.   A windmill will run out of oats in the horse latitudes. (A geographic reference to thirty-five degrees north and south that has little if any wind.*)

72.   What kind of tree would you want nearby should you decide to shower in the middle of the forest? (Toiletries? Beats me. What about a sassafras tea? *)

73.   Lionel's L-shaped vision helps him to see around corners.

74.   Does Perry's scuba scope help him to see above the water?

75.   Is today's journalism cushion filled with soft news? (Is that the reporter's intent when he has decides to *sit on a story?* *)

76.   To plant the idea of a geome-tree, start with a square root.

77.   One parent wouldn't hear of it: the other wouldn't stand for it. So of course, their son wore his shoes on his ears.

78.   Willy Smothers was fired from his job as pitchman for a line of heat resistance cleaning products.

79. Let's try rolling up the carpet of a quiet street and sending it to any urban area that has an open pint of traffic jam.

80. A slightly puckered seersucker suit had a lemon rind in one of the back pockets.

81. A child's rope swing has been located one hundred, twenty feet in the air attached to a branch of a giant redwood tree.

82. Can you trade the building's condition for something more traditional?

83. Are you allowed to ask questions if you live on a ship inside a bottle?

84. Will a Phillip's screwdriver fix out of proportion? (Let's ask Phillip.*)

85. What happens to the short sleeves of August? When the business of summer closes we hang them in the weather closet.

86. Be careful how you wire your house unless you want the room to rotate when you plug in your fan.

87. The truth is you can't study for a polygraph test.

88. Kim Komando, how can I down load mental images that can be instantly and accurately converted into on screen words?

89. Spread a twenty pound bag of ground up marble into your soil if you want to grow some garden statuary.

90. Medieval kings of England sat on satin cushions designed to be inflated by whoever would be heir to the throne.

91. The dentist told three jokes about nitrous oxide before extracting his patient's tooth.

92. Burmese mudfish are packed in Aloe crates and imported to American salons. From there, they are slapped onto the sagging jowls of octogenarian customers. (What do they do with the crates? *)

93. How would you describe the sound made when warm water fractures an ice cube? (That would be a perfect question for a pop test.*)

94. For the average male, seventy-five years will max out the wallet size, plastic, birth certificate that gives you credit for being born.

95. Sunflower plants will add much more to the garden of your personality than will a persimmon tree.

96. When he stepped on a book about scales to check his weight, his thinking immediately went to page one hundred sixty.

97. According to our resident unicorn, a true cornucopia is loud enough to be heard throughout the land. (The big word is located in the horn section of the Plentiful Orchestra.*)

98. Eight businessmen and three secretaries extended their lunch hour to observe the antics of a Tasmanian dancer as he skipped across on some hot lava rocks.

99. Have you ever noticed the filament flickering and voltage dripping from an electric candlelight? (Now that's a wicked idea.*)

100. If part of the steeplechase takes the equestrian over a Calvin Klein billboard, will it leave the rider panting? (Interesting question.*)

101. The hot air balloon must be cactus shaped if it is to be propelled by the prickly heat of the Southwestern desert.

102. Crew members who wore banana-colored bandanas peeled off a seventy percent increase in their daily fish catch.

103. The paint gun that was used to rob a siding company was found pointing down in the up-holstered liner of a recliner.

104. Some of the creatures that escaped from Pandora's Box have built nests in some most unusual places.

105. The Pilgrims would pause to rest near Plymouth Rock which should have been located under a tree full of roosting turkeys during the fourth week in the November fields. (Shoot that by me again.*)

     During the fourth week in the November fields, Pilgrims did pause to rest on a rock located below a tree occupied by roasting turkeys. (That's better.*)

106. Rumor has it that if you will wrap a grapevine around a bottle of wine, it'll enhance the flavor of the gossip.

107. "Hey, running person, pull over and fill up the relief tank at the new Endorphin Pump Station located on the Second Wind Turnoff," yelled the trainer.

108. Flying machines tend to leave noise blankets all over the terrain.

109. Remember to check the bulletin board to see if the pun gun is hiring or firing.

110. Did you pipe some jungle music into a freezer to defrost that compartment?

111. Was it pushed for time? Not at all. The butterfly cleared its throat and flitted in for a landing atop the caterpillar blade where it could kick back and do a slow flap.

112. If a Munchkin is a small person, then a napkin is a small person wiping his chin before going to bed.

113. Would an electronic cricket installed in your phone rub two wires together when you have a call in the middle of the night?

114. We know of several phones that are available for calling down to and receiving updates on all cellular functions as reported through the external membranes. (My neighbor Mito Chondria keeps me posted on all the latest events.*)

115. Can you turn on a feather bound volume of bird sounds?

116. Should you want to freeze your age, put your birthday cake in the coldest part of the refrigerator.

117. "Charley Beaufort tell me," Windy finally got her husband's attention, "on a scale of one to ten where will you put this box full of breezes that I bought at a yard sale?"

118. A *dah* might be a fifty yard dash in the telegraph line.

119. "Hey, Arroyo, have an Arizona T-shirt with a cactus flower in front in case you need needles to stitch a few repairs," suggested Jamie Sanger. (This topic once had a creek running through it. *)

120. Are all the citizens wearing happy T-shirts in Shangri-la?

121. Your clothes might feel better if you would toss those imaginary illnesses into a psycho-somatic washing machine.

122. Our TV antennae can now receive the metal recycling channel.

123. An antique rifle is usually aimed at the past.

124. Should you wave the magic wand if you want a *Harry Potter* book to appear from nowhere?

125. Would noise be considered a virus to silence software?

126. To clean the lodge after a Saturday night dance, we usually send out a Hoover echo and it comes back filled with stray notes.

127. If you put a trumpet mute next to your ear, will you hear wave after wave of horn sounds? (We see that Shelly is trying it and she is tapping her foot.*)

128. An old Union Pacific cattle guard was melted down and pounded into shoes for horses in *training*.

129. The teacher deliberately took the beam out of her lighthouse lesson plans hoping that some of her students would lose themselves in their studies.

130. As he drove past the Breakfast Menu, the wind blew the cornflakes from a cereal bowl sign painted on the truck.

131. What kind of chemical reaction would we get if we inserted a heating element at the bottom of the periodic table?

132. Royce E. Harmon was a favorite in laundry mats where he would pull a song out of his pocket about loose change and sing it to start the machines.

133. Shouldn't there be a medium *sized* poster of Louis *Pasteur* sipping a cup of warm milk on the wall at Barnes and Nobles?

134. The Guns Galore Tournament for big game hunters was about to start when a moose was seen on the loose and running across the surface of the billiard table.

135. Will a rung out cloud leave behind a vapor ladder?

136. Hey, two hundred years is long enough. We need a group of concerned people who will scale that mountain and update the P's at the top of Pike's Peak."

137. The last time Belinda Waverly combed a beach, her imagination became stuck in a washed up hairnet.

138. Pink Floyd's 70s single, "Run..." might have been inspired by the tumbling bass rhythm of jogging shoes in a clothes dryer.

139. Helicopters were heard broadcasting the sounds of a waterfall over the forest fire.

140. Shouldn't they play Bob Dylan's "Blowing in the Wind" at kite festivals?

141. If storms had legs, would they would leave behind a lot of running water.

142. If you want to eves drop on the sound of water, you'll have to stand next to the side of the house during a rain storm.

143. Have you ever listened to a Singer sewing machine? (do ... ra ... me ... fa ... so ... *)

144. Why would Mort Winger keep his feather bound volume of bird sounds on the banister of his front porch?

145. Since glass is melted sand, you should never feel deserted when looking out the living room window toward the beach.

146. We fed calcium's atomic number into a neuro-optical capacitor to convince the eyes they could see into a rock.

147. Does Jim feel more secure since he had three lines of rubies inlaid on the clasp of his seat belt?

148. Would you call it honey extract or does Winnie the Pooh lose if he expects Big Foot to help him with that honey jar that's stuck on his nose?

149. The pun relating to timbre has fallen on deaf ears, so if the tree falls and nobody hears it, will it make any noise?

150. A camouflaged metal stove out in the wilderness will serve as a warming device in advance of deer hunters.

151. A new shipment of plastic, pins, props, dyes, anything applicators, something sound-a-likes and left handed camera angles has arrived at Contrived Supplies, Unlimited.

152. Would you question why sixteen people would line up at the court house on the same morning to change their middle names?

153. A bevy of retirees thought it would grow on them if they inverted a Burma Shave sign to use as a bridge table.

154. You should install better yet, paper your bedroom wall with castle's if you want to gaze out across the landscape of your dreams.

155. If you chisel a likeness of the sun into a piece of wood, will it season quicker?

156. Cows milling merrily always do a face east four bells after a group moo. (Herds do seem to do a lot of synchronized grazing.*)

157. He was so upset with the monthly psycho kinesis bill that he floated it across the room and into the fireplace.

158. What kind of fence could you build with a five year subscription to "Saturday Evening Post?"

159. We repair stuffed marsupials. (And you will not need deep pockets.*)

160. Will wearing your blue collar shirt to bed convert a good night sleep into labor?

161. A stack of finish lines is waiting for the track meet to begin.

162. One movie critic agreed: the other disagreed with the story about the opposable thumb.

163. Geologists were scratch testing a chunk of limestone when they found a fossilized mosquito.

164. To demonstrate her writing prowess, she penned a vivid paragraph describing the movement of a bulldozer as it arranged six-ton blocks of granite into a circle.

165. He owns the sound rights to a ten-acre farm that is fenced in with guitar strings.

166. The sticker price on their friendship took a beating when two car dealers ran into each other on the street.

167. Will snow falling on your keyboard inspire winter poetry?

168. To avoid damaging the products, pack those spurs with jingles from a tambourine before shipping.

169. If you talk at length about agriculture, you'll spend a bale of time picking the hayseeds out of the conversation.

170. We would like to think that an ankh pen is the best instrument to use while taking notes on Egyptology.

171. Fahren especially likes the thermometer that starts working the minute you buy it.

172. A fairy tale company is credited with installing the extra padding you see on Pandora's box.

173. Anybody who is familiar with the west coast of California should be able to tell you where to find Lena the cat.

174. The purring sound that emanates from a list of cat names can lower your blood pressure.

175. Have a seat. We're looking at some rare footage of an Aztec soccer game shot from the ankle strap of a coach's sandal.

176. Athletic Supporters worn by Sumo wrestlers should be cut in strips and used to reinforce the nets on hot air balloons. (Effective only in the sumo time.*)

177. Do you roll snake eyes when you see an absurdity and check your thermometer as to what degree it should be tolerated.

178. If the track is next to a greenhouse, Phillip Hill's horse Chloro might beat out the roan mare and win the Color Preakness.

179. A late model Spitfire ran low on fuel and had to pull into an oxygen station.

180. Sixteen tons of square dancing were leathered into that oak floor last night. (Country music does have some sole.*)

181. Does a light plant begin as a bulb?

182. "The only club in which he claims a membership is Primates."

183. You did know that detachable coat tails can prevent static cling. (Shouldn't this be in coat-ations?*)

184. Use the sundial to call Helios twenty-four hour hotline and order some warmer weather.

185. Will the fire be difficult to start if you are using newsprint featuring river stories?

186. "You let your phone run out of rings," said the repairman as he opened the canister and began filling up the circuitry.

187. Be sure to put a jacket on that book if you're going out for a walk.

188. Are there contour lines that indicate levels of noise on a sound map?

189. If the noon nose of a biplane has been blown off the runway hopefully it will land in a field of four o' clocks.

190. Cutting edge fiber optics shows us an arc of color fusing the vision with the imagination.

191. Madam Tussaud's wax museum features a likeness of Hans Christian Anderson dressed in tales.

192. How did the four presidents at Mount Rushmore manage to turn to stone?

193. To the Finnish, Thor Heyerdahl, a whale of an explorer, painted a water spout on the rudder of his faithful balsa boat, the Tantika.

194. The weight of the ocean has caused a leak in the Atlantis water tower.

195. Would you find central heating circulating throughout the lower chamber of the Nautilus?

196. Divination: Of the ten paper airplanes dropped from atop a paper mill, one plane dived into the trunk of a tree that was marked to be cut for pulp.

197. Don't come gliding up to my desk riding on the dorsal side of a dolphin and tell me your here because you are poor and you need a job. (Somebody wrote this entry on purpose.*)

198. A news story that reported the Olympic scandal involving antigravity athletic supporters never got off the ground.

199. Most aluminum tires work their best rotation when rolling with a rubber car.

200. A box of clown noses sits on a coffee in the lobby of the Jocularity Building.

201. A chain saw was hung in effigy from a cedar limb located outside the headquarters for tree lovers on South Maple.

202. A late-breaking tidal wave muddied the news when it inundated the pressroom at the Atlanta Herald.

203. A clothes hanger bent into a divining rod went straight for the raincoat.

204. When the iron cooled faster than the blacksmith could pound, the fire poker pointed the way to a card game.

205. What would a ventriloquist dummy moonlight as? (The word of mouth tells us he is a public spokesperson for Manikins Anonymous?*)

206. Do you inhale an oxygen pill? (Ask your doctor.*)

207. Many rappellers enjoy scaling Mount Zero. Upon reaching the apex most of the mountain climbers agree that there is nothing to it.

208. The spokesperson for the company tells us that it has constructed a unicycle for Siamese twins.

209. Fans from the Motor City who followed Mitch Ryder and the Detroit Wheels would show their adulation by throwing their belts on stage.

210. The hottest news in town is published in iceberg font. (We don't know what that is unless it floats across the middle of the page.*)

211. The errant son of the Barter family is known as Leon Loan.

212. The pontoon boats were disassembled, flipped on their sides, and used for flood control.

213. Are the blue pixels that make up cartoon water saturated with humor?

214. A right-handed spatula was for sale after the man of the house declared that he had become ambidextrous and couldn't use it anymore.

215. A sun powered ship would depend on solar sails to keep the vessel moving in the right/light direction.

216. Clothiers over look the cotton bricks that align the banks of the English Channel.

217. The Greyhound bus turned off on a side road to follow a rabbit.

218. A smoke screen will slide comfortable over a stained glass window that depicts a flame.

219. The wheelbarrow was filled with extant science books. (If the texts were no longer in use, should we suspend the laws of physics?*)

220. Would a bag of caulking keep your house from hyperventilating?

221. A parachute was used as a bed sheet in case the sleeper should dream he was falling.

222. The amount of scaffolding you claim you need for making a mountain out of a mole hill is greatly exaggerated.

223. How much do you want for the washboard design on the front of the soil resistant T-shirt?

224. A husky distance to the north of Prudhoe Bay, Alaska is an area designated the Potter's Field for Freon free refrigerators.

225. The post office now requires a stampede of buffalo stamps to mail a package containing a Remington rifle.

226. Hatfield's grandson placed the vaporization chamber of a still on stilts and used it to steady a telescope aimed to chart the phases of the moon. (We are still feudin' over what this one means. My neighbor tells us it has something to do with lune-atic.*)

227. A vile of Egyptian wrinkle cream leaked down the head of the Sphinx making the face look a thousand years younger.

228. A scroll of résumés was slipped into canisters then stored in dry ice to freeze hiring.

229. The leftover side of a menu featuring food for thought lists both sides of an argument sandwiched into a compromise.

230. Some books are offensive and need to be stored at freezing temperatures.

231. A family tree might be rolled into a scroll then tucked into a pocket inside its coat-of-arms.

232. A person sitting in a doctor's office was heard to comment that there were seventy-two seconds in that last minute.

233. A telegraph office hired a woodpecker to extract the bugs from the dead air.

234. The treble clef that introduces the musical staff is shaped like a can opener.

235. Bell-shaped glasses are for people who look for the phone to ring.

236. Air must be pumped into the base of a rubber tree plant on a frequent basis if you want it to produce regulation size basketballs.

237. Antler-shaped limbs rammed continuously against the corner of a building that housed the gaming trophies of one Barry D. Bonner.

238. Thirty to three hundred motorcyclists gather on an infrequent basis at Radio Station RIVV to ink tune their mufflers for drum tattoos. (The dictionary man is convinced that a tattoo is also a drum signal sent to summon soldiers to war.*)

239. Morris Larson decided that if/when his mind became addled or saddle sore from writing horse storys, he would retire his keyboard to a grassy website. Plus:

    The IRS wants to know if Morris plans to write off his horse stories into the nontaxable sunset.

240. A map to the city named Recovery might be called a picture of health.

241. Fancy postage should keep all the buffalo stamps inside the field and busy grazing.

242. We need October fireflies with a proven off-on beam consistency to man the lighthouse search for a red ant armada.

243. The same calipers used to carry a block of ice can be used to pull the throttle on any machine that needs to pick up steam.

244. What would a cave repair kit consist of? (We'll deposit the simplest answer we know of which is dripping water.*)

245. Did the Panama Canal un-*lock* twentieth century ocean travel?

246. The inspiration for this song came from the lid of a pickle jar that spun to a stop on a Formica counter top.

247. A furniture factory uses an iambic ink pentameter to measure five-foot sections of trees fallen to fashion school desks.

248. Ice cycles hanging from the awnings at the cryogenic headquarters take ninety-eight point six seconds longer to start melting.

249. Barn swallows were seen perched on the tail-gate of a wagon that rolls on candy wheels.

250. Perception fluid can be poured into the optical cylinder slightly below the swivel joint.

251. A pattern resembling a log cabin can be traced in the marble block supporting the right foot of the Lincoln Memorial.

252. When he's in the mood for floating, he drops his hat into the river to locate a size seven current.

253. If your goal is to get in pictures, be careful how you frame your house.

254. After a windy night, Bo-trice Taney noticed husks on her bedroom floor inches below the coconut trees that were stitched into the curtains.

255. No one knows why or what they were hiding when the Intrigue Company stopped making trap doors. (I'm not going to fall for this one.*)

256. The song "Over the Rainbow" is a spectrum of musical notes that can be photographed in the blink of an eye.

257. When profits soared on Burlington stocks, plastic surgeons were brought in to readjust the smiles on their male manikins.

258. You cannot *escape* the fact that if you send a ray of light through a prism you will see colors.

259. Shouldn't the snowman that was standing on the Astroturf with a football under his arm be running from "The Spring Thaws?" (Is that a regulation team?*)

260. Around sunrise, Capricorn the goat escaped from his Zodiac, found a chicken pin and punctured our plastic lion.

261. Our secretary Norah Southerland placed a magnet below the shelf drawer to help keep the filings properly aligned. (So, it is no axi-dent that she is so organized.*)

262. An insecurity guard was assigned to an empty vault.

263. We called in a paragraph inspection team to make sure there were no toxic definitions hidden in the walls behind some of the words.

264. While in their prime at Greenwich, England, Marie, Dean and Ann perfected the geographical coordination system by playing tic-tac-toe at the base of the Royal Observatory.

265. The latest electric coin to be minted should bear the likeness of Nicola Tesla.

266. Should your flashlight ring in the middle of the night turn it on to see who is calling you?

267. A properly mixed gravity drink will leave the glass in a smooth even flow.

268. The old oak tree had an elevator that would ring when you reached the thirty-second story of its development.

269. Water that evaporates can be absorbed into the Periodic Chart of Elements.

270. If a long division problem is well over your head, toss a grapnel up and over the top line and pull yourself up to a new level of over-standing.

271. Eckles Calhoun doesn't like to carry a wooden chair with him when he goes for a stroll. Furthermore, he knows that in time he'll sit down and think about it and realize that he can walk away from the chair.

272. In terms of billiard sales, he had knocked in the eight ball by age twenty-one. (In terms of pool, things are going swimmingly.*)

273. Would dream pipes carry the night imagery into full blown daylight events?

274. "Is this the anti-septic department?"
     "Yes."
     "Tell your supervisor that Teria is Back and we need to know if there has been any changes in her personality that we should know about."

Other World

1. Talk to us about the dialogue you have recently had with a Martian. (His last name was Terry, Planet Terry.*)

2. As an astronaut looking back on planet Earth, what are your thoughts? ("Whatever is, is right."-A. Pope; "Essay on Man." *)

3. You are a meteor. Describe your fall to earth.

4. Describe living a day on the moon. (Only a lunatic would try it.*)

5. When informed our younger brother Lunice Moon that he was about to be eclipsed, his face turned blue and he started to wheeze and act as if he wanted to spin out of orbit.

6. Offer a commentary on the life of a comet. (Haley tells us that it's a long tale.*)

7. Let's talk about women in space. You are marooned on Mars. Describe. (I once knew a *Maureen*.*)

8. Your luggage awaits you at the depot between Nebula and Nucleus. Where do you go from there?

9. "I missed the coordination points and landed in a storage unit full of rotten yams," reported the alien through his cell-ar phone.

10. Somewhere in the year 2062, a hybrid carrot is being pealed by a raccoon with contact lens. (In time, this picture might lose its appeal.*)

11. A sign on the wall at the comet station on Jupiter reads: "A number system no longer applies beyond the border of Neptune."

12. Would an interstellar note tell us that we are looking in the wrong direction and that the human mind has always been the next frontier?

13. What if beings from other realms have been camouflaged on this planet for centuries?

14. A few people can see the plot of ground that makes up planet earth.

15. Your application to leave this planet must be accompanied by a sample of your imagination.

16. To mention a fourth or fifth dimension seems to engender a noticeable tension.

17. Bill and Millie May Galaxy were at their spiral's end: "One of our sons seems to think that the entire world revolves around him."

18. A Persius plumber managed to tilt the southern lip of the Big Dipper at such an angle as to create a meteor shower.

19. Here's a room with a view and once you have opened the quantum curtains, look out!

20. The planetary phone system makes no apogees when it boome-rings a message out that is usually flashed back within a light year.

21. The human race, as diamonds in the rough, would be a valuable contribution to the cosmic gem lab.

22. When a scorpion crawled across the zodiac, eleven constellations yielded the right of way.

23. "Ca' moan! Something is making a lot of noise down by the creek and we gotta see what it is," yelled Mona as she grabbed her hat, coat and a flash light and tore out the door.

24. Have you ever seen a lunar ellipsis . . . ?

Personification

1. The last six times we personified Sunday, that individual was wearing tinted glasses.

2. Nickolas Astor not only wanted to be personified, he wanted a star by his name. (Interesting.*)

3. Aunt Chovie has a whole string of fish stories to tell.

4. Funny stories were heard sipping from the River Mirth.

5. Most tires have been around long enough to know when the bag in the road has a brick in it.

6. Doesn't it open up all kinds of possibilities when a white room refuses a window?

7. Can you use a card catalogue to look up outdated and defunct systems?

8. Even though we trimmed its hedge, my yard refused to be personified.

9. A radical brick caused the entire structure to fall.

10. Did *arrive* get here before the rest of them?

11. Can coins refuse to be fused into a shrine?

12. Envelope flaps have been glued to secrecy.

13. What kind of shoes should a progress report be wearing before it takes its first steps?

14. He's waiting for his house to clear its throat before installing the intercom.

15. *Double speak* is like a hot air balloon that's grounded by the weight of its own exaggerated sense of importance.

16. Satellite to earth: "It's a new day and I am beaming and now if you'll excuse me, the sun is up and I have some rounds to make."

17. Big Ben has gonged: "Unsold clock and watches are no longer required to fix their arms at a pre-designated time." (Was this topic written at ten minutes till two? *)

18. Grumble wheat was sprouting from exhausted soil. (Even the livestock realize the need to fertilize.*)

19. Do towering evergreen trees ever pine for water?

20. A pachyderm who was working for peanuts, took some worn out jeans from his trunk, put them on and tightened the belt. (The ground will shake if our local elephant ever falls on hard times.*)

21. Stomach noises were vying to see which could cause the most embarrassment.

22. Keep your eyes on the dancing typewriter keys as they spell out choreography.

23. Chaos was wearing the mask of organization. (Didn't Shakespeare note that nothing is ever as it appears? *)

24. Lavania Flowenthal was one of the first people to chart the digestive tract of a volcano which included the molten overlays.

25. A male hormone was leaning against an hourglass waiting for his voice to change.

26. Madison Square Garden presents the Forest Show and the Waterfall Act of the Century.

27. Slice your bread with this ax-iom: even the tastiest of sandwiches has to work hard to get quality ingredients.

28. A cliché crossed the picket line of the striking Grammar Union carrying a sign: "We speak for the people."

29. The river pulled itself up and out of the limestone bedrock, stretched its tributaries, splashed some water in its face, then went about the course of the day.

30. "Are you new to this shoe?" asked the aglet of the grommet.

31. Trini Tangerine and his Citrus Fruit Band won the vitamin C award for his pe-alto voice combined with a plucking of some juicy chords.

32. Two many times we have seen the guns blazing in a dual between the puns and the metaphors. (And you can see it all tacked to the main office bullet-in board.*)

33. A symbols guard patrols at night to interpret what you hear.

34. Dr. Igneus put his fingertips on the volcano's ridge, checked the magma pressure and ordered ten tons of calcium to be dropped down the gullet to neutralize the lava burn. (The missing pun is in tablet form. Can you find it? *)

35. "We always lose our chlorophyll this time of the year," stated Fademan the Leaf to a local branch of the Color Preservation Society.

36. Are there always limbs attached when you're trying to be a-*loof*?

37. "Honey don't," was the response after the queen announced that the hive was downsizing and that thousands of workers would be laid off.

38. Maurice and Tonie Monotone stopped by the office speaker system to get some sound advice on how to become a metaphor.

39. Should it ring a bell when you go fifteen rounds while boxing with your shadow?

40. Is it conversation or conservation when twin brothers are reunited during a debate over environmentalism? Are they punctual or nuptial twin sisters who are watching the Lakers which causes them to be late for their own weddings? (After the ceremony, I'll take my dog for a walk.*)

41. Peri-helion is applying for metaphor status and yes, it can be punned (pairs). Question is, will it point us closer to our destination at Sun Publications? (If we get the point.*)

42. The moonlight is the surrogate sun at night.

43. Ora Orion stepped out of the meteor shower, finished her Milky Way, grabbed the comet, tore off part of its tail then went to clean some sun spots.

44. Are two metal clothes hangers that chime together exchanging information as to which family members have the most hang-ups?

45. We'll have to personify that big deep blue Leviathan of water. There are no other jobs available.

46. If we need a cliché violation, we can write "whatever floats your boat." (Guilty!*)

47. Nature is much better at personifying people than we are skilled at personifying nature.

48. A worry stone is a concerned mineral.

49. A rush of cold air reached out with a pinprick touch that made the skin reel. (Brrrr! *)

50. A ruse is a rose that has been convinced it should drop its petals.

51. How about color, nutrition, and music as co-partners in the human energy system?

52. In this day and time how often does the flow of words become anemic and expire from chronic interruptitus?

53. Willy Rushing called to say that he was on his way and that we shouldn't *personify* without him.

54. A nervous tic was seen in the eye of that timeless edifice, the Sphinx. (. . . and the nose is still missing.*)

55. Some of the vultures took the day off, telling the rest to *carrion*.

56. "A, U! Herb Alchemy, where are you going toting that armload of goldenrod?" asked the poster chairman for the Periodic Table of Elements. (A U, tell me, who is going to know the chemical symbol for gold? *)

57. Puns are words that have altered their voices and appearances.

58. The metal post *read* about the approaching rainstorm and would eventually translate a few drops into rust.

59. Are weather forecasts being sent through the wires that span the earth's two poles?

60. A botany lure was stuck in a tree that was spawning fish sticks.

61. Headlines: Talent Scout Ambushed by Mean Mediocres (On the average, most readers should know what *mean* means.*)

62. Tomorrow's dialogue is working its way into the evening script.

63. Can a candle with a dim flame be called superficial, tallow or a half-wick?

64. The wind strummed the field into waves of wheat music.

65. Wilderness Hardware has a spring sale on food chains.

66. The Oscar for a lifetime achievement of best metaphors goes to water.

67. Rust had welded the nut to the bolt.

68. Are we right or wrong in saying that we are manacled by dualism?

69. A honey bee was setting on a lily pad resting its drone and sipping a glass of nectar.

70. The original fonts for print behavior, Pica and Elite, walked hand and hand out of an arche—type-writer. (An archetype is the original model from which others are patterned.*)

71. He understands that he is a part of the architecture, however, during the rainy season this gargoyle wants out of his job as a water spout.

72. Two larches stood, leaning and yearning for someone to notice their manner of framing a lake scene.

73. Ion Asterisk is the character who can best symbolize a static pop.

74. Does the speed of light ever slow down long enough to think about the speed of darkness?

75. A plane tends to broadcast a line of growls across the sky.

76. If we personified *rules and regulations* there would be a large number of things *he* would not be allowed to do.

77. Do empty highways suggest, "The Road Not Taken?"

78. Even the sun has its ups and downs.

Poetry

1. What else can we say?
    The world changes in the light of day.

2. When the sun shines longer, the days get stronger.

3. Old red wagons should be retired with the proper background setting.

4. Poetry di-verse-ifies.

5. A headline from the kite festival on the moon starts with a quote: "We need a windmill." (And a red flag goes up here because a quote should never start a headline at least on this planet. *)

6. Poetry always calls for a cup subtle-ty.

7. Do you treasure those twilight celebrations that manage to slip into our thinking?

8. Leave it to the wind to choreograph the dry dance when you have a pageantry of clothes pinned to the line.

9. Dory has a clothesline with pictures of clothes pinned to it in her back lawn.

10. For three days now, the wind has been moving a picture of Frank Lloyd Wright along the Arkansas Tech shoreline. (Your topic is not architecturally sound in its reference

to a college in west central Ark. which doesn't have a shoreline.*)

11. Is the wilderness menu for hungry eyes?

12. Sometimes, the dark ticking of the clock creates tension and invokes suspense. (Suppose the plot involves two missing *noias*.*)

13. Notice the water beads that are strung across the tractor seat as they disappear into the air.

14. A leaf tumbled down the limb stairway to the ground.

15. Can you feel the imagery of winter rain, wind blown and coating trees with ice?

16. Can cans roll, high kick or dance down to their gutter jobs?

17. Waves of eerie music pounded the moss on a rock wall. (I'm starting to take a lichen to this one.*)

18. For several minutes, Reggie Croaka, the secretary of the frog seminar, took notes on his lily pad as to the value of observing the upcoming and coming leap year.

19. Ice cubes were melting their way to the bottom of the glass.

20. A huddle of toes were plotting against a cold floor.

21. Sitting, rocking on a buoy, lost in the expanse of the ocean: at night I swim out of the picture to get some rest.

22. A pond painted on a screen several days ago is now a puddle on the floor.

23. Even though their home rusted to the ground three days ago, the Ferrites still want to remain within the scientific community. (The family wants the public to know that they are an iron compound.*)

24. The wind choreographed the shadows while the sun looked on.

25. Do you know the sound that whiffs over the surface of the mud as a hippopotamus lifts his right hoof?

26. On a sunny day, the sky funnel drips blue.

27. A recent snowfall creates a crisp, clean and pristine world.

28. Cele B. Rat-lif practices the art of constant amusement.

29. Matches are always going on strike. (Unions tend to get people fired up.*)

30. My margin release has been arrested. (And it was charged with guilt by association with an old typewriter.*)

31. The ten foot doughnut sign in front of the bakery was glazed with sleet.

32. The two sounds raced up the hill to see which ear would be the first to hear them.

33. How about a blue cellophane sky folding your imagination over the horizon?

34. Roll a red ball with *heat* stenciled on it into a cold room and feel the temperature go up.

35. Chicken crates are used to hold down the tarp that protects Stonehenge from scientists. (Sounds like something is being covered up.*)

36. The vending machines are taking a coffee break.

37. If your lunch breaks are too short, try sprinkling some thyme on a slice of life sandwich.

38. What would be the outcome if King Cotton was the presiding judge in a case against a polyester shirt? (Will synthetics win over your sympathy? *)

39. Hurry! The twisted pulp vitamin C dash to the Immunity Center is on.

40. Can those narrow bands of sunlight that fall between the curtains be rolled up and saved?

41. Stream-ers of paper flow through the valleys in the confetti hills of celebration.

42. A hot summer day of weeds was waiting for a passing car to whip some air their way.

43. A bolt of fabric was held at needlepoint.

44. When you get to the end of the maze you'll find that you're in a cornfield. (That is a pun popping good idea.*)

45. When the fog lifts where will our discussion on dissipation go? (At least you were there to precipitate.*)

46. Waves of inspiration rippled across the lake front, up and into a poetry line.

47. Will silence dehydrate a melody-fed brook?

48.   Does the playground of the imagination feature a spangle slide that twinkles into fantasy?

49.   A nervous tic detonated a frown.

50.   Isn't your flashlight searching to reunite with the big beacon?

51.   What do you think about the sound prints left by the breeze? (The leaves floated the story to the ground.*)

52.   Have you experienced the persimmon pleasure of learning to be patient?

53.   Headlines: Daffodil City Populated with Bees (And all the pollen-teers are up to their nec-tors in flowers.*)

54.   She laughed so hard she disappeared. (Some of the humor in this book is invisible.*)

55.   A blend of night sounds wafted down to the dew point.

56.   A city skyline was etched in cement.

57.   Olivia Octavia and Iamb Pentameter enjoy nothing more than mixing their poetic feet in a rousing dance.

58.   Flying machines tend to drop sound nets over the terrain.

59.   Be careful when working with shadows: the better the idea, the quicker the shadow disappears.

60.   Will the use protractors help you to measure the ice-sosceles snowflakes that land in your hand?

61.   Take a cartoon rope ladder and fling it skyward. Now climb until you know "what's up?"

62. Sometimes an emphatic wind breezes through the circle of chimes that hang at the end of our conversations. (We'll have to talk later. We are running out of chime.*)

63. That's not a window shade. That is one long rolled-up shadow.

64. Only the people looking up saw the piano shaped cloud or heard the notes falling as rain.

65. We see dust motes as nanoseconds floating across the space of a day. (Or are they remnants from insect ramblings? *)

66. We're still looking for that poet who can extract a cool breeze from the language of summer.

67. Can you warm you hands on the shadow cast by a fire?

68. Has your imagination ever been absorbed into a bluish transparent sky?

69. What can you see when you are writing in the dork? (The pun is deliberate so let's shine the light on dark.*)

70. When sound waves lob a vibration toward, then in and around the hair that curls below your ears, what do you hear? (I'm listening to the "The Barber of Seville." *)

71. A fall wind caused the knuckles in a tree branch to snap and point the way to winter. (Fist, excuse me, first, it's hot then it's cold. *)

72. How many of you noticed the leaf that came to life, turned green then flitted across the top of a compost to escape the rake?

73. Things that haunt the earth can be pulled upward to undergo a clear blue sky transformation into a harmless wisp of a cloud.

74. Some insects can do a ninety-degree pivot. (For sure the wasp police are on the job in case of a traffic violation.*)

75. The panorama of the hillside features trees whose leaves rhyme in different color schemes.

76. Do whales nibble at the toes of the Italian boot?

77. This bucket is galvanized for sensitivity in order to catch and hold only the rain producing pitter sounds.

78. The sun came out of a blooming ar-*ray* of flowers.

79. To recall the greener days of spring is to experience a chloroplast blast from the past that blossoms into memory.

80. They found a chair sitting in the middle of the forest with a note handing from an arm: "This oak tree is ahead of its time." (Not all trees grow up to be chairs.*)

81. The ocean stories that rolled up on the white sandy beach were lifted up into a moon beam.

82. Durwood patiently pumped the billows into the dark underbelly of a night log hoping to ignite a spark that will burn into the light of day.

83. Anything that floats through the air is designed to answer a follow-up question.

84. Words would perch on the ink tank to fuel up before migrating to the paper lands.

85. Waves of inspiration rippled across the lake front and into a poetry line.

86. The wind ripped the month of March right off the calendar.

87. As the sun went down, it moved the shadow of the window across the floor and up the wall where it framed a table lamp.

88. A shadow always seems to be in the background of our daily events quietly tapping its foot in rhythm.

89. The fireplace fizzles, crackles, and mumbles through the wood that is burning down into ashes. The sounds become a sleeping bag of popcorn that is munched into a dream movie.

90. Can you feel the silence that fills in the space between two people?

91. The description does flow from a teabag full of adjectives when you dip it into a paragraph of hot water.

92. Have you heard what it takes to purchase a golden earring?

93. How can you sleep with the wind raging and the rain pounding unless, by and by, there is a lull in the storm?

94. If you like to wade into rumors, here is one that flows: Murmurs can be heard when water plunges over a rock and consumes itself.

95. Yes, the advertisement for butterfly coaches fluttered by unnoticed.

96. A tranquility wave will be the quickest to absorb the loudest notes of noise.

97. A quiver full of gravity arrows might be used for shooting stars.

98. If the cast calls for a shadow who will play the part?

99. After an inflationary trip around Churchill Down, Penny, the winning horse tells it straight, "Your thoughts are now worth two bits."

100. You would need volume control to turn up the silence.

101. Are you game for hiking up the foothills of a compromise? (We had *meditation* in this entry but after further review the ball did break the plane of the goal line. Touchdown!*)

102. The leaf that gets the most out of what's current will do a Z slide into the fall compost.

103. Who can micro-manage the motes or the sweep of Friday's dust rag?

104. Can you see the seconds evaporating from the river of time?

105. Doesn't writer's block mean you are stuck on a rock in a river with several ideas swirling about you?

106. As we began to sink entire schools of word fish were deflected from our trance then there was silence.

107. A harp-arium can ripple fish back to swimmingly good health.

108. Some of our staffers often use a broom shaped flashlight for sweeping away the dusk.

109. Is it possible that the upward push of a tree might create an angle where the point meets the sky?

110. Plug in the waterfall lamp and watch the light cascade out and over the shade then tumble down and around and fill the room with waves.

111. Cyrus T. Driftley makes it a point to pause in the afternoon to monitor a cloud that has been under-looked by the crowd.

112. The wine bottles were melted down into the shape of a grape.

113. Taurus the bull was too busy grazing to think about the future. He did not see the signs of the cow leaving him to jump over the moon.

114. Tiny beams emanate from the headlights of nocturnal creatures. They stare into the night dim or bright according to their level of fright.

115. Do you ever wonder how a conductor's wand can produce an arc of spangles that is decoded into music and color?

116. When the silence is broken, get some volume control glue, go to a quiet room and put the pieces back together.

117. Meet Isabelle Alonier. Her best friend is the voice in the answering machine that tells her she has no messages.

118. Feeling particularly generic one clear day, the sky writer churned out the word *cloud*.

119. Can you envision the silhouette of a condensation rivulet as it streams down the window? (Let's talk about a drop of water? *)

120. Waves were pounding out "High Tide" on Steinway's ivory-coast.

121. Do roses stitched into a quilt or a flowerbed might need a sheet of plastic covering in cold weather?

122. For what would ten minutes of golden dawn sell on the poetry market? (Of comparable value would be a clear blue sky.*)

123. His patience dripped from a pail that once held fresh water drawn from the well of humanity.

124. Spring chimed in with a melody of green that quickly filled the empty spaces between tree branches.

125. The sound of a *mellow d* rises from the phonetic alphabet to introduce a new dawn.

126. The day before the Clouds moved out, young Stratus, in a moment of thought evaporation, looked around and wondered how long it would be before they were mist.

127. Do people with monopoly *eyes* have to control what they see? (The exception is the train rolling down Reading Railroad.*)

128. The genealogy of a breeze was blowing through its family tree.

129. Do you think the moon might disagree that most shadows are quite down to earth?

130. Your ears can't help you decode the color wave lengths.

131. Is a shadow a record of a day in progress?

132. Doesn't it make sense that by vacillating (back and forth) between clouds and sunshine a creative spark is produced? (Doesn't vacillate mean to rub something on your back when the weather changes?*)

133. A wave of information loses its vitality the farther it travels from that initial splash of truth.

134. From the weather kitchen, another batch of Cold Snaps will be served on a wintry platter.

135. For three days and nights, a rhinoceros of a hurricane gnawed away at the southwest corner of the African continent.

136. We all know the person who uses the cushion provided by an information cocoon to keep people and events at a distance.

137. He developed the visual capacity to pull distant objects in for a close-up scan of surface detail.

138. A wave of inspiration crested, broke and fell across the contours of the beach.

139. The drawbridge went up to allow passage of a boat loaded with moats en route to Castle Marina.

140. "Some down time," pitched Ava Wave to her cycle of friends, "All we have to do this morning is carry the notes from some local bird songs."

141. Have you been on a tangent flavored spree lately? As mentioned in the *Vitamin C Book of Experience* that is the only way to see your plans reach fruition.

142. If indeed we do have a stream of consciousness, have you been *thinking* about filling up your new aquarium? (The guppies would like an answer.*)

143. Pour your mind into a goldfish bowl if you want the nightmares to turn into sea horses.

144. Would a carpenter's instrument be tuned to a ten penny hammer tone?

145. As a wolverine pulled tenaciously at your pant legs, you gathered your wits about you and they all agreed it was time to head for higher ground.

146. The thought process is as subtle as are the color tones in the leaves during the fall season.

147. Southerners might use a cotton pot holder to close the door on summer heat.

148. The prickly beat of prairie heat was pulled skyward by the afternoon sun.

149. A silence brigade was organized to put out a loud noise.

150. When you finish your story about paper snowflakes: when it finally melts down into a plot and all the elements fall into place, send it into the Puddle Press.

151. The mid-morning sun etched a silhouette of the well house into a melt line of frost. (Jack left about ten o'clock a m.*)

152. The one thousand words used to describe a picture of the fog will dissipate to one hundred, eight words by late morning.

153. She knows how to switch on the flower-escent lamp post when she wants to see the fragrant roses.

154. When growing three inch mirrors from the vine, the agri-reflectorist must keep a close eye on the weather vane.

155. When you hear the music while scaling a mountain you'll know the crescendo indicates the highest point to which you can climb.

156. "Does it take a psychological broom to sweep the clouds away?" (<You used this as opposed to this?>*) "Those blue drop eyes could sweep the clouds from the skies."

157. You'll need metric feet when stepping into that formal dance of poetry.

158. Should any member of a single minded band of birds opt to feather in a contra flap, the rest of the flock wings off key?

159. As determined by the couture in Paris, the only apparel Rita Water Drop could possible wear in public as winter vogue is the snowflake coat.

160. Since an ice cube floats, it'll never be used as the bottom line in a warmly worded poem.

161. The poet burns to pen a trenchant definition of fire that gets close to describing the flame.

162. Does the scansion or rime scheme in cyber poetry consist of one, two, one, two?

163. The gravity bell rings when fall is in the air.

164. "If he doesn't start feeding us more than a little bird seed," complained the Cardinal, "I'm going to tell his readers that most of us are now moonlighting at a furniture store called Chirp-endales."

165. Would you ship your imagination in a kite box?

166. Note the condensation flowing down Window Valley into the River Sill.

167. Clever isn't it; to grow a four leaf clover next to a sham-*rock*? (As luck would have it, we flirt with the poetic.*)

168. Do clouds exist to awaken the imagination?

169. If you choose to see land mines buried in your cultural field . . . Boom! . . .others see flowers that are ready to bloom.

170. When the parks poet hears his belt beeper, she knows that somewhere on Scenic Mountain, imagery is either being ignored, is lost or in trouble.

Point of View

Describe:

- the perfect top-ic on which to write. (How about a marble desk? *)

- romance in a burning building. (Is there something about an old flame? *)

- having something under your saddle that annoys the horse as you gallop along through the snow.

- free-falling from an airplane. (A free fall clearance sale? *)

- a description. (Feel free to use adjectives.*)

- your grandparents.

- one round in the ring with a professional fighter. life on an iceberg. (You should have an ample supply of frigid air. Why would you need a refrigerator? *)

- a moment at the beach gazing at a constellation of starfish.

- one minute of swimming at Lake Full-of-Water with the current temperature at fifteen degrees.

- your future mate. (To what extent are you describing yourself? *)

- a day in your life as a homeless person. (Busking for handouts.*)

- a day in the life of your cell phone. a day without electronics.

1. What does it take to become a good writer? (Writing! *)

2. Tell your views on any movie.

3. What will be in your personal state of the nation speech?

4. What would you prefer to study in school?

5. What do you think about the world of computers?

6. Do you have a password on that cyberspace suit?

7. Have you ever Googled the question: How human are computers?

8. What does Pink Floyd's "The Wall" mean?

9. Write a letter to your children explaining war. (We'll let a carrier dove deliver it.*)

10. Do men or women make the best soldiers? (We might start a war with this one.*)

11. What do you think it would be like to be a teacher?

12. Do you consider yourself lucky?

13. What was it like being *The Invisible Man* for a few days? (Talk about transparency.*)

14. How was your life as a beach comber? Did you get sand in your hair?

15. You are a Los Angeles psychiatrist. Describe an exceptional patient.

16. Was it exciting being Germany's Red Baron for a day? (Did you have to be well read? *)

17. Is a nail important? (If you are a hammer.*)

18. You are in the Ringling Bros. Circus. What is your talent? (Thinking in circles as opposed to linear.*)

19. If/When you have children will you raise them as you have been raised?

20. What is prejudice? (I made up my mind on this one a long time ago.*)

21. Why is football so popular? (Would you prefer to let someone else tackle that one?*)

22. You have ten minutes of early morning FM time. What do you want to broadcast to the world? (Wake up! *)

23. "I had the words to complete the poem. They were on the tip of my wings. By the time I landed they were gone."

24. Is it possible that we all have wings and that we have opted not to use them?

25. Are you extroverted or introverted? (Outgoing or self-contained: Taken together they might be a revolving door.*)

26. You are a blade of grass or a flower during a drought. How will you feel when the rain comes down? What will you

say to the trees and the squirrels? (Luella, get out your umbrella.*)

27. Have you been *ostracized* in school? Your friends won't speak to you. Describe. (Isn't that a tall, fast, land bird found in Australia?*)

28. What do you hope to learn by writing a journal? (Read it after twenty years and let us know your thoughts.*)

29. You are the King Tut Display. Explain your latest thoughts as you wrap up a dynasty.

30. You are a totem pole in old Tucson. Are things stacking up the way you want them to?

31. You are the referee in a basketball game. Describe. (Whistle while you work.*)

32. Are you easy to surprise? (When someone hands me a boo!-quet of roses.*)

33. Humor me; tell me, what is humor?

34. Are you self-centered?

35. Will you respond by saying, "**I** don't think so?"

36. Why is it considered important that you attend school?

37. Is it more important to think or to feel?

38. How do you feel about the idea that you should never stop learning?

39. Discuss open minds versus closed minds. (Open minds certainly get more business.*)

40. Apart from with your eyes, how do you see people?

41. What do you *think* about people who are judgmental?

42. If you were a book, how would you read the person who looking down at you?

43. Do your experiences make up the pages to your life's book?

44. Why are some people seemingly more talented than others? (Why are some people willing to work harder than others? *)

45. Why is it important to be good to yourself?

46. Do people who feel good about themselves feel the same way about the world?

47. Do you have more patience than a doctor?

48. Have you ever experienced jealousy?

49. Should you be doing something to change the things with which you disagree?

50. Do people have a right to be ill-tempered or to experience negative drama?

51. How would your friends describe your temperament?

52. Why do some people have a low self-image? (Do they need a raise.*)

53. How successful are pity parties?

54. The photographs in "National Geographic" are quite capable of inviting the reader in for a brief visit over bagels and tea.

55.   A highly popular rope disappeared into the sky. Did it hang the moon?

56.   A beeline will take you right straight to the nectar in the flower. (We have been asked to repeat the announcement that pollen-teer bees are now doing field work.*)

57.   Shouldn't we get pumped about interconnections? Without air we wouldn't need basketballs. (That was a three point topic.*)

58.   Is this grist for a theological mill: I haven't the slightest idea what I'm supposed to be doing here? (So pretend that you are an angel and wing it.*)

59.   Is there anything we can prejudge before we get there? (Is this a good way to arrive at conclusions? *)

60.   The couch would yell "hustle!" and his alumnus would get out of bed and get ready for work.

61.   Isn't it peculiar to function through a system of opposites? Are we stuck in a binary bog? (It is, isn't it?*)

62.   A wedding cake is a marriage of several ingredients. (Did you plan to marry your high school sweetheart?*)

63.   To what degree do you want an education? We have plenty of libraries.

64.   We never thought we would find a quart jar that could reflect on its gaze of being a pint. (Sounds like you opened a door.*)

65.   Why is the *different* person often described as being weird or crazy?

66.   Will a haircut, a suit and tie and patent leather shoes help you to find the pearl in the oyster?

67.   The electric razor was plugged into the wall of the 1950s. (This kind of information certainly grows on you. *)

68.   Since we are all determined to find a ghost, let's go haunting for an old and atmospheric ante bellum house. (Say hell-o to my aunt.*)

69.   Any group that can *hold* a meeting should do so before things get out of hand.

70.   Do you agree that the vast majority of people cannot control power and the few who can do not want it? Where are you in the scheme of things?

71.   A diamond cutter should be aware of white light pivot points.

72.   What qualifies something to be placed on the top of the refrigerator?

73.   Pandora's Box is locked from the inside out. (Does this mean that all our pesty little problems are from within? *)

74.   A thunderstorm played backwards is a clear spring day.

75.   A joke construction crew became riveted to a woman walking down the sidewalk and the punch line collapsed.

76.   We are listening if anybody can tell us the real reason Van Gogh cut off part of his earlobe?

77.   "Sudden death" in football overtime certainly sounds like the National Gladiator League.

78. If prisons were modeled after the Egyptian pyramids, we would redefine cell block.

79. Look out! There's a u-turn straight ahead and you're still thinking linear.

80. Two equal sides of a triangle produced a rare isosceles that can now be seen at the Geometric Zoo.

81. We asked the owner of a shark tooth necklace if he understood the term *mega-byte*.

82. Clusters of question marks are all too often left hanging in the academic vineyard.

83. We'll have a lively conversation if you can fire off three questions about what interests me the most.

84. The loser will eventually win when Yin and Yang are playing chess.

85. You'll find a beacon of hindsight will quickly weaken.

86. The chicken soup is heating too fast. I won't be feeling ill for several more hours.

87. "You can't have the apes pacing in front of the bars and wearing head phones if you want to sell this property," warned the G. O. Real Estate Co. "What's more," the agent continued, "we'll never be able to flip this animal park if you continue to house three elephants."

88. The seasons have a way of turning the leaves to the pages of a tree.

89. What is it like living in a mailbox? (When the red flag goes up, it means it's time to go out for a while.*)

90. The man looked up from his reverie, confused and attentive. He heard birds close by, shrill and sharp or was it his breath pushing down a column of nostril? (Domus tells us that the old bearded man was about to make a prediction.*)

91. Since we have two eyes, are we taking pictures with a digital camera?

92. What do you think about the person who claims that he is *awake* and is constantly taking pictures without the aid of a camera?

93. Somewhere, nobody knows where, is a casket with an inner lining of silken pockets stitched to hold thirty secrets.

94. "I don't like the grass in this pasture."
"What's wrong with the glass in this picture?"
"The price of gas may determine the future." (We have a triumvirate in these three sentences. Are you sure this won't be a has-sle? *)

95. How much class does it take to be aware of such distinctions as blue-collar freshman, bourgeois sophomore or aristocratic seniors?

96. Several blocks of information were stacked into a city story.

97. Paris from three miles in the air resembles a stucco wall.

98. "My niece Ashley F. L. Light will never have the purity of beam that emanates from her mother Laser."

99. What would you do with a handful of white pebbles? (Hide them in a white room.*)

100. How many of you can see why we talk about quantum bifocals?

101. Hunters should always carry a cell phone in case they get a turkey caller.

102. While piloting the Goodyear Blimp, Captain Ant gazed through binoculars at the Orange Bowl.

103. Is it a watered illusion to believe that the man standing on his front porch is wearing a hanging potted plant for a hat?

104. "What is this rocky old road having for supper tonight?"
"From the way he's eating up my tires, I'd say he's having a tread meal."
"Well, we could park the car and get some exercise."

105. The new body-heated portable furnace is in effect an exercise program.

106. What message are you sending when you tell someone that you have a lot to be modest about? (Well Amy, it's big of both you and us. In other words, we're talking about an ambiguous statement.*)

107. The vulture will circle its prey for pi days until a line forms down the middle of the geo-carcass and the radius begins to decompose. (Please, no jokes on decomposition.*)

108. Your body consists of two boards and some old clothes and you're stuck in the middle of a field? What are the crows saying about you?

109. "In the back of my mind," observed Aerial Spanner, "I know there is a screen that I view on a daily basis."

110. Surge-ant Electricity, you are now in charge of the fifth roll from the Copper Wire.

Psychology

1. Do you go with the flow of the highs and lows in your personal weather?

2. If you're obsessed with the past, your thinking is counterclockwise.

3. No, it doesn't take much mettle to forge a psychological wedge between two people.

4. Does repast include a constant diet of memories?

5. Some personalities seem to be constantly inflated by word pressure tanks.

6. My mind's eye was reflected from a shard of memory broken from the window to the past. (Yes, it sounds like you need to replace that window pane.*)

7. The lobby register tells us that all the rooms are completely booked in the Past Hotel.

8. Thirty minutes of Bleach Channel four should scrub the major TV networks back to their original broadcast standards.

9. Are there too many bumps in the road for you? Contact the Humor Co. They will fill you in on the latest in psychological shock absorbers.

10. Through eye contact you can see either the unfathomable depth of the ocean's soul or the shallow trickle of a small stream.

11. The clarity of yesterday's film is directly proportional to today's level of awareness.

12. Is there gold somewhere in the human mind? (Depends on how deep you dig. Most people are too busy rooting for the San Francisco '49ers.*)

13. "I have a cave on my mind. Would you like to explore it?" flirted Tyron Troglodyte.

14. An emotional roller coaster can be found at both ends of the Midway.

15. Pavlov, a physiologist who experimented with training through conditioning, wants to know if you are getting enough positive reinforcement in your life. (Isn't anybody going to ask how he kept *his* hair so shiny looking? *)

16. In the future there will be "Dorian Grey" mirrors that are digitally equipped to reflect you true personality.

17. Some humans are magnets capable of erasing certain vital areas of rational thinking in other people. (If you know what *rappel* means you can send such people over a cliff with only a rope to hang onto.*)

18. When comes the time to view your personal film keep in mind that you were the producer, director and main character.

19. Sometimes we get the feeling for vertical exercise when emotions run high.

20.   Horace and Mona use only state of the art methods when it comes to regulating a large body of chemicals in their private business.

21.   Will a refund on your electrical bill be enough to jump start your emotional battery?

22.   Most people who are adept at *dodging bullets* are in effect verbal stunt men.

23.   Does anybody know the chemical breakdown of the fuel that moves an emotional roller coaster?

24.   What does a human magnetic center attract? (People with mettle? *)

25.   "Hear ye! Hear ye!" yelled the town crier, "We have air wave pollution problems."

26.   Mood swings were found in the playground of the emotions.

27.   What would the needle in a self-conscious meter register before an audience at Madison Square Garden? (Why did I plant so many rows? *)

28.   Eight out of ten is the octane level of optimism.

29.   A caution sign on sponges warns against soaking up the pessimism of a rainy day.

30.   Relationship poker calls for knowing when to hold your verbal words and when to pay the ace of compliments.

31.   Would you like a transparency of your ego? (I'll have to wait and see.*)

32. If people would stop thinking thorny thoughts, maybe the briars would cease to grow in the wilderness of their minds. (This little stretch of underbrush won the Metaphor of the Year Award.*)

33. Where is your personality located on the mood control dial?

34. We recommend a bulldozer of a mind if you want to push back a thick undergrowth of distracting messages.

35. He's concerned that if you put a sample of his thinking process under a microscope you would find traces of paranoia.

36. Sometimes a teacher's job is to put a plus sign in the corner of a student's security deposit slip.

37. Is an introvert or shy person someone whose laugh strings have been tied? If that's the case, all we need to do to set this shy person free is to recruit two of the field hands from the comedy farm.

38. Are comedians born in the land of comedy?

39. A psychiatric beep is heard whenever the coyote past catches up with the roadrunner present.

40. Having read their personal copies of *The Book of Life*, some people seem to prefer discourse that is listed in the pain index.

41. How often does a tall tale go over the head of the average person?

42. If you look inside the human brochure you'll find a variety of light shows scheduled for Independence Day.

43. We have all met those psychological surgeons who feel qualified to diagnose the problem then perform a *criticism* on vulnerable people.

44. Since you are in charge of your personal script, how often do you edit your behavior?

45. How would you like a ring with the sun for a setting?

46. "I honestly don't feel like buying a mood ring," she responded emphatically.

47. Does NASCAR intellect tell us that your mind is constantly racing?

48. We sat there in the middle of a wilderness trying to determine which path-ology would lead us back to civilization.

49. C.G. Jung might have been considered a press agent for dreams. (Since we chose to avoid Freud, we'll do the same with his student. Besides many readers may be too young to remember C.G.*)

Pun Intended

1. We found a paragraph that some writer had deadpanned and left lying on the floor. The main body of the text had been completely riddled with puns. The fingernails had been filed. The here was gone. Ligamints were chocolated. The nose denied the obvious. The fete had partied. The eyes had had it with pummel vision. The hips hopped. The back returned. The arms won the races. The humor bone was serious and to top it all off, there was an allusion to the Mad Hatter. We removed several cynicals from the opinion page and sent what was laffed down to the main orifice to see if they had an opening. (This little exercise, though playing rather loose with the language will get you in shape for what follows.*)

2. When you can balance two different meanings of the same word on the tip of your nose, you will be sent a stamp copy of the *SBR* Seal of Good Punning.

3. Miss Three, it's time you went out and met-a Four.

4. Even the trail of a duck has a web site.

5. The queen sat three feet away from the king. (And so it goes with rulers.*)

6. If you refuse to wear the latest summer fashions, does that tell us that you are close minded?

7.   Do cows ever think about Persian poets when they are standing in the middle of a field of fescue? (Nice setup . . . we have *Rumi* for all creatures in this *nation.**)

8.   Do you donate time when you volunteer to work in a donut shop?

9.   The Celerys although once removed still managed to stalk the family reunion.

10.   If there is too much information in this modern world, pull the plug and, clockwise, it will go down the bath tube.

11.   She is so nimble with a thimble and yet the super stitcher will not sew on thirteen buttons is a row.

12.   On a scale of one to ten, how fast are you at cleaning fish?

13.   Head-lines: Study Finds Worry to be Useless

14.   Where do you keep the clippers for pruning a pun tree? (In the pantry.*)

15.   Loaded with sensitivity concerning his new toupee, the man aimed a hair-trigger response at any statement made about it.

16.   By rapidly sliding an ivory pawn across a screen door, you will produce a sound exactly like an elephant snorting Tuska Loosa.

17.   Does Milk of Amnesia mean you forget where the cows are?

18.   We called him a dunderhead for serving lemon harangue pie at the local gear stripper's car auction. (For the last time what are you are driving at with this point? *)

19. "Surely you joust," fenced the pun.
"Are we dueling or is there jest one of us to make a point?" questioned the counter pun.

20. Are you in shape to run in the human race?

21. A comma in the storm gave us time to seek shelter.

22. My cell phone rung as I was starting up the ladder.

23. A character in a novel was confused after being left out of the plot of a cemetery scene.

24. A joke told during a fun-eral dealt with having a grave sense of humor. (Mort is obviously serious about his humor.*)

25. The South Sea allergy will flair when Pollen-esia is in the air.

26. Time will usually provide some answers unless of course it's tick-talking to the walls.

27. UPI checkmate: A bishop witnessed a rookie cop from Queens breaking into a pawn shop on King Street last knight.

28. Last Monday somebody slammed the lady mud wrestler with a pun when they told her to clean up her act.

29. Botch tape is for the little mistakes we make.

30. Would "The Anthology of Blockbusting Humor" explain how the pyramids were built?

31. Anna Pestic invented a slide rule for writing poetry only to discover her metric feet were stepping on mathematical toes.

32. Miasma tells me to start fuming when a menu begins to leak mustard gas.

33. "Have you thought of a name yet? We need an appellation for the longest hiking trail in the country?"

34. "Not true" denied a superstitious stilt maker who was found walking on wood after hearing that his business was out of step with the times.

35. Condiments are now found in department stores for people with no taste.

36. Somebody was pressed for time when they wrote this headline: Irony Steamed at Being Appliance

37. A little girl commented to her octogenarian aunt while at the beach: "The ocean waved to me."

38. Will homespun corn humor find a husk of a joke without a kernel of response?

39. A distracted writer might be sentenced to a restricted alphabet.

40. Anyone who plays the pun drums will understand the clanging of cymbolism.

41. Somebody punctured Perry's spare pun and now he has to decide on either a retread or retirement.

42. Get out of their way! The bulrushes are stampeding through the mar-egos of Spanish-speaking gardeners.

43. Had the Wingley Brothers invested in pillows, their *flying young men* might have been found down in a feather factory.

44. Run over to the bookstore and buy the hard-backed edition of *The Existential Armadillo.*

45. Why would a hair brush designer bristle at a bald joke?

46. A modern school for hard knocks is being constructed at the bottom of a quarry.

47. Would an egotistical magnet make such a statement as, "Buy me that copper coat and feel how attractive I can be?"

48. Headlines: Commencement exercises leave some people bent out of shape

49. Is there a filing system at your finger tips?

50. What might you sip from a suction cup? (Wine from the finest grips.*)

51. "Look at that crowd. They're eating this up. Who are we talking about? The Spoons. They are scooping up all the awards with music that begins with a tuning fork."

52. When a joke construction crew became riveted to a woman walking down the sidewalk, their punch line collapsed.

53. "Carry On," pronounced the high vulture as he wielded a knife and fork and waited for the cartoonist to begin.

54. How long is Coffee Street? That depends on how many sips you take.

55. The auto—bee-ography was Dewey Nector's life story based on his droning in a now dry honeycomb.

56. Sacred cows will hold a meeting on Wall Street to determine if they should take stock in the Dow-Jones trading.

57. Nobody takes the time to reflect on the size of the mirror in the living room.

58. Is coffee grounds for a divorce settlement?

59. A clarinet can become a percussion instrument. (Would the song be a hit? *)

60. Santa Claustrophobia was found stuck in Chimney.

61. "How can anybody see living in a cave?" opined the salamander.

62. A lumber company is looking for boarders.

63. Adventure films are stored in a closet on cliff hangers.

64. A milk can that is supporting a mailbox churns for the good ol' days.

65. A wayward wrecking ball crashed the party at the Law Offices of Brick and Mortar.

66. Tripping over illegal duplication of money might be known as counter-feet.

67. Since nobody has seen an Australian moot, it's pointless to discuss how they colonize a field of inquiry.

68. Can a not-so-spaced out imagination be trained to qualify for the one hundred meteors in the fantasy Olympics?

69. To get a picture of health, you'll need a camera with enough pixel power for vitamins and minerals.

70. A skilled lyre player can be brought in to handle chronic mendacity before the patient is hooked up to a defibrillator.

71. The dialogue at Point Barrow, I'll ask ya, will be between two principal speakers, Frigid Floe and Ike Berger. (And the subject will be Alaska?*)

72. During a party, we placed a blasting cap on a coat tree then detonated the coats to charity.

73. *Shame on* you for thinking that only a visionary optometrist can see into the future.

74. An eggplant will hatch hundreds of tiny workers who will find immediate employment at the chicken plant.

75. Her agents distributed manila envelopes depicting Penelope Vanilla as the people's choice for dessert during halftime at the Ice Cream Bowl.

76. Yes, the Earl of Sandwich has decided to raise the Pillsbury Doughboy.

77. A kiro-tractor was brought in to seed some relief from the pain of erosion.

78. Can you clean electricity with a wire brush?

79. Would somebody help the athlete find a guitar string for stitching together a three piece head band? (And if we set a new stylus we'll know it was the right size needle. *)

80. Have you seen the tad-pole that was taken to determine how many puns have been written about pond life?

81. The horse's owner should use a pitchfork to determine the frequency with which the old mare should eat.

82. A fictitious Percy Shelly-Edison might have said to his wife: "You are the filament of my life."

83.　Rhonda Raison wrote the logo that put a new wrinkle in the world of *fiber* optics.

84.　Do most wild enamals that are known for their protective coating live at the mouth of the river?

85.　If you want to draw interesting people into your personal orbit, write letters to them on a launching pad.

86.　According to the latest Gallup Poll, people who ride their trusty broncos too fast usually run out of luck when the horse throws a shoe.

87.　Major Bessemer from Anvil believes that pound for pound his town can blast the competition right out of the furnace when it comes to forging heavy metal bands.

88.　For purposes of animation, Warner Brothers should sell spark plugs in their car tune up kits.

89.　If you want assault without a battery charge, slip a container of sodium chloride into an empty flashlight and turn it on.

90.　Wasn't it Zeus who asked the Mt. Olympus legal team how many cases per jury? Apollo replied that it was one case per jury and on that day, it was the air headed Orpheus and his lyre.

91.　Since people are upward to ninety percent water, you can safely conclude that they run in streams, seek their own levels, form car pools, and drop in when least expected.

92.　In the South where farming runs in the family, scientists have developed a new breed of genetically-engineered cotton to be used in making denim foot wear.

93. A sled made of frozen teabags garnered for its sipper the Lipton Cup for a smooth performance down a slope that was too steep.

94. Some future university will outline its course syllabus on a chakra board.

95. What does Puget Sound like?

96. Several crates of rep-tiles have arrived and will be used to cover the swamp floor.

97. Is-a-bell that has mood swings in the belfry likely to have its clapper removed?

98. This group of rockers plays your mind like a musical instrument and to prove it the front man wears a guitar strap around his head.

99. This path isn't exciting enough, nor is it the way a mun Dane would take to get home. (We've been to Norway before.*)

100. We knew the rock specimens containing fossilized poison ivy would pass the scratch test.

101. Is it a redone dent to repair or damage the same fender twice?

102. Size nine hubcaps are recommended for shade tree mechanics.

103. Would a carrousel of golf be playing a game of rounders?

104. The coldwater tap will usually flush the leaves from the toile-try.

105. Have a can of Calisthenics. It's brewed from side straddle hops.

106. "We thought the number was frozen," they admelted when professors were persuaded to open the doors at the H_2O Waters Center for Convinsation Studies.

107. Envelopes will accomplish their threefold mission if they follow the instructions to the letter.

108. Should a writer be ailing while sitting at a bar waiting to be published?

109. Honk! If you are hungry for another pint-o-traffic jam.

110. I see. You climb the pun tree to get a closer look at the cones that turn words into such a double scoop of a tree-t.

111. Eye suppose potato chirps would grow if you planted birdseed.

112. The boys from Burma have built a log cabin barbershop for shaving pine trees.

113. We took a pole to see how many anglers were taping their fishing sessions and then playing them back reel to reel. (When you get to the end of the tape, throw the topic away. It's obsolete.*)

114. Is it am-big-uous of us or too small to ask if you are lost or found?

115. If you listen to lizard rap, you'll be reminded of the night an iguana's tale was cut short outside a local retail outlet.

116. "On the other hand," appealed the orange to the juicer, "you take me for palm granite."

117. Sonny Summer and his cloud burst team of fair weather friends were cooking up a storm when it struck them that the crowds were doing the thunder clap.

118. "I predict," said the giant to David, "that I'll have your bed after you die in battle tomorrow. Mine is as hard as a rock and gives me a headache."
"That is one big fabricated story," answered the young sling master, "Now go lieth elsewhere."

119. "According to that account, the fund is frozen. To reach our goal the money will come from a slush fund," reported chairman Gordon, during the ad hockey session. "I'll slide the puck forward for Pele's opinion." (To slide you some information about the skaters, these are former hockey players.*)

120. "You don't know where the field is? I'll tell you," rallied the old man. "And you're hearing it from someone who's in the nine inning of his life. It's right next to the gem-nasium. When you see that twenty-four caret diamond you'll understand how the game was won. Durwood Ruby managed to belt a home run jewel and it was all over for boys from Turquoise."

121. Captain Ira Gates sat his ice tea down on the table and stepped down from his back porch onto the grass. He shaded his eyes with his right hand and estimated that he could see about three binocular's distance from his present position. He smile and headed for the garden. Once there, the captain opened the metal door that was his last name and locked it behind him for piracy reasons. He smiled. The captain was obviously pleased with what he saw. He reached for the tilling tool that was reclining next to the fence and nodded to the left as if a crew was present. Tool in hand, he approached a row of beans and with a voice of discovery that only a ship master could muster yelled "Land Hoe!"

122. She left the Pun Center saying only that she was hungry and that she wanted to be serenaded. She never came back and for three weeks we had no idea where to look. Finally a local eatery reported that a woman fitting her description was sipping soup at a rapid pace and getting ready to order desert. Did we care to identify her? We were there faster than Uri Gellar could bend a spoon and despite several minutes of observation, the question still lingered as to who this woman was. And then she tipped us off by ordering cello for desert. We emptied our water glasses in tribute to her wit and then returned the serenaded woman to the Pun Center at Hilarity Memorial.

123. What kind of mathematics were they talking about at the Moose Lodge last night?

124. Who knows? If you open the trunk of an elephant you might learn all about the pachyderm's snout.

125. We sent in one of our best rock hounds to sniff out the exact location of a limestone fissure. (Pun setup: Who is to blame if he doesn't find it?*).

126. We heard that chattel ignited the range war that was fought at Knob Hill between the Cookson and Broyles clans.

127. Levi and Tate are being held for questioning concerning the illegal raising of a fifty ton rock block fund.

128. Let's make a decision about that in-deciduous porcupine.

129. The truth is Menda City is never where people tell you it is on the map.

130. Say Pam, if you're up to it, let's do some Rand McNeedle work and crochet a map of Croatia.

131. On Halloween night, a blood thirsty Dracula was seen in pursuit of some hemo-goblins.

132. We found this advertisement in the "Daily Clock:" Try the new fifteen second commercial spot remover. It is guaranteed to work or your time will be cheerfully refunded.

133. "Hey," Roy shouted out to the station owner, "that flat you lent me has turned into a well rounded tire."

134. *What it boils down to* is the burned-out residue of a cliché. (Is this what we have *at the end of the day? *)

135. That rotating rooster atop the house took one good look at his red face and realized it was all in vane or vain or vein.

136. When a hobby horse rocks back and forth, it generates more bucks for the owner.

137. Does it weak-end the system to have to work on Saturday and Sunday?

138. For the party tonight, we'll rotate a leg of lamb on a spit slightly below the Ball and Socket Joint.

139. Through the mathematics of housekeeping, Desi Whipple has learned how to divide her time between multiple rooms and when she is finished, the house is minus any dirt or dust. In addition, she never works overtime.

140. What kind of bored does one need for endless channel surfing?

141. Would it take a box of wood chirps to fuel the late-model Firebird? (Kudos! A double pun.*)

142. The other football team was given a twenty-one point advantage, so we recruited a sports carpenter, put a helmet on his head, and told him to level the playing field.

143. We are all still laughing at the inspiration date on a can of puns.

144. Who gives a hoot what sound an awl makes as it chisels a big bird into a stump.

145. The howitzer is a short cannon of a breed with a high trajectory that attacks at medium speed with an open muzzle. (Yes, the dog wants out.*)

146. A hair follicle walking out the door of the Barber Shop Prison heard the warden say, "Grow home."

147. "Hey Michael, what's up?" Asked an unknown enquirer: "You rowed the boat ashore and delivered the angel food cake. From this angle I can see Sara Phim and a whole host of coco-nuts are busy slicing it. So cherub."

148. We need someone who will catar-*act* in a play on water words. (A *cat*-aract is a waterfall with nine lives.*)

149. Fort Tuitous was named after Grat, the general who, on a tip, took a handful of puns and outwitted an entire stag-nation of clichés.

150. We think that Prometheus learned how to steal fire from the gods by reading about it in a book of matches?

151. Attach a worm to a question mark and think well below the surface if you want more than a super fish-al answer.

152. When Reese O'Pelican decided to run for mayor of Verbo-City, Punsylvania, he quickly stockpiled the leaflets

from a double entendre tree; leaflets that would freefall from his plane during the campaign. (Champaign? Anyone.*)

153. Does do-masticate-d mean that you have not only learned to live in a house, you can also chew with your mouth closed?

154. Suffix (Suffolk) is an Affix County on the east end of many English words, bordering on the North (I) Sea.

155. If it is stressful dealing with more than two of anything, quite possibly your life is full of *tri*-bulation.

156. Would a bird watcher need a meadow detector to find a buried lark-spur?

157. Superimpose the image of a whale spout next to Old Faithful and sea the change as onlookers begin to blubber.

158. Remember how drought affected their drinking pool in the Garden of Eden? Was that Eve Vaporation?

159. When you a-lube to something, you reduce the friction between the parts that otherwise wouldn't be mentioned. (Nice allusion.*)

160. Where are the stadium waves that celebrate when the tide recedes and exposes a starfish?

161. The man didn't understand the joke attached to the bulletin board until someone shot him with a double action pun gun.

162. On a scale of indecision, what is your weight (eight) length of time?

163. How long should you practice before the medicine ball game starts?

164. Will a rung-out cloud leave behind a vapor ladder?

165. Two *Mag*-azine poles plus the Inter-*net* will tell you that any business located between North and South Streets is sure to attract the most qualified employees. (Note that their uniforms never need to be ironed and should we mention the steel shoes they are required to wear?*)

166. John Wayne, fire fighter: "Fuel take my canteen and pour some water on my first two words; then take my horse and pull the reins in. We'll put an end to this conflagration before that word gets any bigger."

167. On a Thorsday we picked him out of a lineup of possible suspects who might have violated a noise ordinance on a clear spring day.

168. Do you play dominoes because you like to make ends meet?

169. Now that you've grown more sophisticated, how do you intend to harvest it?

170. If memory serves, they were too tired to gamble so a discarded group of poker players left a full house to meet at the Reminisce Restaurant.

171. If you sink a rope with a brick attached into a lake, is that a form of depth perception?

172. "Say, Jasper, no wonder you're sitting in front of the fireplace all alone: You're burning one of those iso-lation logs."

173. Will a weeping willow be properly nourished in the back yard of a funeral home?

174. We recommend clogs when stepping off a length of board feet in a lumber yard.

175. If housing were available through the Treasury Department, would it have been preoccupied with money?

176. Rock hounds lead us to a rock shelf where we found the fossilized remains of a prehistoric sniff box.

177. The president of the seminar must have washed a ton of geodes before he crystallized his decision to cut the meeting in half and go home.

178. Money gives him an 1849 Gold Rush.

179. When the month of December passes into January the least we can do is offer a Yule-ology.

180. You are taking a big chance-llor when you start telling jokes about sacred cows.

181. Two centuries ago, the horns were *hollow*ed out and filled with gun powder to defend out sacred cows.

182. When puns are on a roll, they see snake eyes as a grand dice-ment.

183. Does the setting sun foreshadow a tree?

184. A cata-log on politics tells us that the most popular tree is not always the one to vote for.

185. A haberdasher is a special breed of canine that sports a Superdog cape when pitted against brand names such as Greyhounds and Whippets. (The dasher also sells clothes.*)

186. Does a scholarship bear any likeness to a floating library?

187. "You're putting us on," pleaded Synthetic sisters, Polly and Esther, who were aghast at the fact that there was a wrinkle in their plans to go see "The Seersucker Blues."

188. "Ah, yes, we are pyrites and we want all your gold, all of it, right now," yelled the bewhiskered high seize thief in a piercing tone that would have left a hole in your ear. "We have gold, sir and it will stay with us because you and your entire crew are imposters, so be gone," replied the captain. (*Pyrite* is fool's gold. The thieves were pirates.*)

189. A maxi-stir would require a much bigger ladle than a mini-stir.

190. A downsizing company must be on a people diet.

191. The lady who works in sales is involved in a pillowcase whereby she claims to be the mattress of the company's president.

192. In Ireland, a rung of rocks lets you climb a fence in *stile*.

193. A pontoon sergeant took a group of greenhorns through waves of training until they landed on the beach as marines.

194. A box of bouncing chocolate-coated screen savers for computers will cost a mint.

195. What kind of wild creature lives in a fir tree?

196. A cache of checks was buried in the loam of a riverbank.

197. When the society for doing pointless things held its big auto race, a number of people were spinning their wheels.

198. We thought we were on a roll while searching for Tobacco Road. Now, having taken the Zig exit off Zag Street, our plans have gone up in smoke.

199. The joker's final guffaw would be an epi-taph laugh which took him beyond a grave sense of humor.

200. The stage production of "Apple" might call for an en-core.

201. The piano teacher turned the sheet music upside down looking for his keys.

202. What does it smack of when an experienced cook is hired to operate the microwave oven?

203. Not only did they imply that Orin was way out of orbit, a few people told him it was sheer lunacy to think that he could teach people how to hang the moon.

204. Will Rogers, the geologist, never met a meta-morphic that he didn't like.

205. Outside their barber camp, lumberjacks use a brush to comb the woods for fir trees.

206. Geof decided to play golf in the fog. At some point in the confusion of the micro rain he hit the ball backward and completely mist the green.

207. "No—no, you read the letter wrong letter," reported the fireman.
    "The Plode Building was once used to manufacture balloons and now it needs to come down. To make it a thing of the past, the job will call for an X number of dynamite sticks. We'll have to find another way to inflate these old balloons."

208. They were both young rock hounds who first met in the geology lab and that's where they began their carbon-fourteen dating.

209. When wondering how fast the cold air causes the mercury to plummet, ask for the tamp-erature?

210. Police were alarmed that afternoon to find a clock soaking in hemlock. The officers referred to it as P.M.icide or the killing of time.

211. You will never see a sidewalk buckle on the Washington D.C. beltway.

212. Several members of those warring clans, the Hatfields and the McCoys should have been locked in castle dungeons for reinventing feud-alism.

213. We had not the slightest idea what was to be seen in that single drop of water. Was it a micro Ness that we had unlocked, that had worked its way down and onto the science fiction screen? Unless, after thinking about what we did, there is a story about a squid . . . .

214. Pre-reading your kitchen stories before serving them to hungry students will help you better understand what's on their plates.

215. Does the cereal number on a box of breakfast food tell you the servings per package?

216. A tightly wound spring on a shade tree can cause the tree to roll its leaves down with the advent of cold weather.

217. How do the English weigh a sport that uses a pound of dogs to run down a one ounce fox?

218. To sub-due the grass is to cut it before the sun goes down and the humidity condenses.

219. You can have a whey-le of a good time churning out these buttered topics until the cows come home.

220. During their crouton anniversary, the vegetarian romantic sent his wife a bouquet of cauli-flowers.

221. The brochure describes a polar golf course for people who are driven to be on top of the world with their game. (Are you sure?*)

222. A customer who felt as if she had been Pompeiied fired back, "You pumiced me a soap bar that heals skin eruptions!" (Was her name Lavena Moltandorf? *)

223. When viewed by three people, a twelve-inch cause tripled the value of its effect at a yard sale.

224. If cotton is grown on plantations, then beans are packed into in-*can*-tations.

225. After a lifetime of bumpy rides Edsel was finally convinced to undergo shock treatments.

226. Here is a picture of a lemon aid stand taken minutes before its assets were frozen and it was squeezed out of business.

227. If the chocolate bell on top of the clock awakens a craving for sweets, it is only a false alarm.

228. If goats can butt heads so can the Los Angeles Rams.

229. The temple of the monarch butterfly rests on caterpillars.

230. To open a circle of hotels, you would need a ring of mar-quees.

231. Sweet dreams? Two lines of pra-lines were cross-stitched into a pillow.

232. Look at all those hungry ducks waddling around for something to eat. What must go through your mind each month when the bills come in?

233. Shelby Shaker was issued a salt-ation for being too far across the table from her fellow pepper shaker.

234. Lyle Scalpal never questioned his decision as he stood there poring over the picture of a subcutaneous incision.

235. Lumbar cutters from the Lower Thorax region often complain of financial lumbago: the result of interest rates charged by questionable Savings and Loins.

236. General Doe ordered his buck sergeant to "put the red terminal on the left ear and the black terminal on the right ear" and then he yelled, "Charge!" (Did he have a horse named Batterly? *)

237. What kind of funeral can be transmitted when a solar flare blows station 94.2 from Wednesday into Thursday, leaving nothing save dead air?

238. The Orphean lyre soothed the Twelve Labradors of Hercules.

239. About six stories up that redwood tree, you'll find Paul Bunyan's initials carved into the bark.

240. How are two by meta-fours treated in this world when they are used to construct observation towers? (We'll ask someone with an elevated point of view.*)

241. Dualism should be defined as a couple men with pistols who can't count past two.

242. Let's exercise our rights to frame a picture of health.

243. How much candle light does it take before a writer can wax poetic?

244. Has anyone explored the possibility that as long as the spelunker is wearing concave glasses he doesn't need a light?

245. Should piano keys unlock the door to good music?

246. A late breaking tidal wave muddied the news when it inundated the pressroom at the Atlanta Herald.

247. To truly understand the paperback version of *A Tree*, go through the book leaf by leaf.

248. A member of the Cavalry High School band caught his dog Rin Tin Tin chewing on a trom-*bone*.

249. Ann Tanna clearly understood the frequency with which men tuned their attention to her.

250. Only the nozzle nose the gas station time for an elephant who stops in to fill up his trunk with peanuts.

251. Jose Centavas came to this country because he only had one penny to his name.

252. The shish kabob metaphor makes a point that can be driven through anything put on the table to digest.

253. Chaos would be an appropriate capitol to the state of confusion.

254. Did you read the epitaph that specifically addressed the undertaker?
"You drove me to my grave."

255. The paint was flaking and peeling and the wood was rotting. To avoid a brush with the law and possible house arrest, the owner opted to buy the materials and paint and go to work.

256. Should you get canned for sipping green *te*-dium in the Coca-Cola break room you would be a party of one.

257. Two line baggers for the Sanitation Soldiers were penalized for excessive trash talk.

258. Computer wizards have planned a cursory trip to the Disney World web site to update Mous-kateering skills.

259. We will take off our hat to any horse-ologist at this year's Kentucky Derby who will step up and tell us what a Preakness is.

260. The Constitutional Fitness Center is for people who want to exercise their rights.

261. How much time does it take to explain to a child the difference between a wave in his hair and a big block of salt? The same amount of time (stay with me) is required for the cow to turn around and walk back to the barn.

262. What kind of whine do sour grapes make?

263. Athletes have a much lower im-pulse rate than non-athletes.

264. The latest fly-on-the-wall report gives us the latest buzz on search and destroy swat teams.

265. The late medieval sound would be lute notes issuing from bells installed in state-of the art trouba-doors.

266. Arkle B. Leash stacked the wood from a dogwood tree next to a kennel.

267. The race was so close that officials decided there should be a runoff to determine who would be elected winner of this year's marathon.

268. The name of the introductory story in the book *Lift your Spirits* is "The Elevator Control Panel." (So, what's up with that topic? *)

269. Here's an idea: If you can string enough neurons between two poles you might in Milton's words "trip the light fantastic."

270. Have a wrench-shaped dog biscuit for the many times that pet of yours decides to bolt and run.

271. Lariat, the greenhorn, was taught that calf roping hangs on your sense of timing.

272. When your name is Bentley Carvelo and you are being followed by a verb, a direct object and numerous phrases and clauses, you are subject to everything.

273. A joke about avocadoes will ripen with age.

274. He'll let Liam control the amount of gas that we need to inflate this balloon and raise it off the ground.

275. The film is a western and is called "Duck Tape." It covers a series of peaceful approaches whereby you should stick to your guns unless you prefer to feel ripped off.

276. The tactile Midas discovered that gold was ductile or could be compounded.

277. Jen Sing found her songs replete with a new invigoration after returning to her roots.

278. When a teacher presents a new idea, shouldn't the pupils in the classroom dilate?

279. Hickory dickory dry dock is where old wooden ships clock-in to rot.

280. Depending on what you drive to the "Theatre in the Round," a play on wheels is definitely a sa-tire.

281. He was cited for irreverence after being heard (ear) throttling (riv) the motor of, then stealing (errant) a car.

282. Marriage to an old bachelor is often pushing the envelope unless there is a Sadie Hawkins stamp on it. (I do agree with that.*)

283. How big would your water bill be if you were connected to a Roman Aqua Duck?

284. Bernice Upton is certain that the earth's atmosphere can be thought of as a meteor shower curtain.

285. How do we arrive at yellow journalism? At least once a week, certain staffers at the Quilting Bee are assigned to pen news that is fabricated.

286. Should a nihilist go to Egypt in search of a belief system?

287. "He embarrassed her," commented the judge after the prosecuting attorney assured his client that he had come to court. (You should know what a barrister is before we call the next witness.*)

288. Station L.A.R.M. ran a public service announcement calling for more Laramie lawyers to be alarmed by the long arm of the law.

289. How do you play the part of a passenger in a production directed by a stage coach?

290. Would a mechanic agree that a U-joint is a place where self centered people meet to talk about their cars?

291. If your thinking is tired, lose the retreads and get new wheels. (We are on a roll.*)

292. Should you plant the negatives for seeds if you want to crop pictures of corn? (If the kernel has a digital camera this topic can be made much more corn-temporary.*)

293. At any given Manner's Salon, they strip the rough edges from a patron's personality with a less-than-fashionable eti-*quette.*

294. Seconds before the gourmet cook began his first show, someone yelled from the wings: "Break an egg!"

295. The earth rotates on an air pocket located one size below the Van Allen Belt line as a part of the Blue Jeans planetary system.

296. The last of the alphabet soup drifted into a cloud formation at the bottom of a flying saucer.

297. Is it by degrees that we warm-up to the idea of higher education?

298. The joke about teasing a balding man came right off the top of your head and was only funnier than mine by a hair.

299. To liqui-date is to sell your exercise machine and plan to meet your boyfriend at the swimming pool.

300. You'll find Elasti-City to have between twenty and two hundred inhabitants and is located on a stretch of road south of the Playtex spur.

301. In the south, if you want to extend a glowing greeting to your circle of friends, simply say "Halo."

302. Some people have ideas flowing through their minds faster than you can synapse you fingers.

303. After two-hours with the binoculars and birds, she concluded that time flies.

304. The cinnamon role model is now on display at the good citizen bakery.

305. Nero the Crab performed a gig that certainly steamed the patrons at the Roman Red Lobster Sauna.

306. We found a reminder note fastened to the back side of a Mensa membership card.

307. "His trip to Sandmelto opened a window of opportunity" is a glass metaphor you should be able to see right through.

308. The next time you see a *reflector* on a tree please pause to think about when that oak was little more than a sprout.

309. Pico Iceburg's lecture on Cubism was clearly over the heads of four fifths of his students. The remaining fifth claimed that they had *caught his drift.*

310. Your well watered illusions might lead you to believe that the man standing on his front porch was wearing a hanging potted plant for a hat.

311. If you're addressing the sharp witted males in the audience, start your speech with "Ladies and pun-gents . . . ."

312. Cotton will crop up when the outskirts of Fashion Town are in vogue.

313. Many descendents of the Knights of the Round Table tend a farm outside Bath, England, where they occupy their days teaching young men to fence-a-lot.

314. A wild life employment agency has two mocking birds wearing finch toast shirts loafing near the main lobby.

315. To prevent shrinkage, put your size eight polar ice cap in the freezer over night.

316. Could an old bass-e-net be used to catch fish fry? (Fries are the spawn. Now we can move on.*)

317. We would all breathe easier if you would close that fumi-gate and keep the pests out.

318. A new personality till will only function if you are open to a little change.

319. State of the art thinking isn't always a capitol idea.

320. "Get cirrus!" stormed a cumulus thunderhead after being approached by a wayward alto-stratus drift of water vapor.

321. Didn't it take the public about half a century to warm-up to the idea of an incubator?

322. Evidently plants with the aid of light can take pictures of certain chemical compounds synthesizing. (If this one takes too long to develop, move on to the next one.*)

323. Most people would agree that there is much more to being a roll model that eating pastries in a bikini.

324. Yeast-terday, we punctured the Pillsbury uprising. (That would explain the holes in the donuts.*)

325. Take a stroll down Freedom Road if you need to see how your constitution is holding up.

326. Twins Cory and Dory flank their parents in the Hall Family portrait that hangs in the vestibule.

327. When Mel T. Hotcomb misses his honey, he can bee found behiving in his brood chamber.

328. How big does that make you for ostra-sizing an ostrich when not measuring up to the danger it faces? (One might feel like sticking one's head in the sand.*)

329. Let's read some rhyme polishings that were rubbed off the inner layer of imagery during poetry millings.

330. Fans who take tackle boxes to the football games are prepared to de-bait some of the questionable penalties.

331. Would a Dow Jones *bond* fire bring investors closer together?

332. We suggest that you use gloves when mud gripping in case the bottom falls out of the pond.

333. If the debate becomes overheated, will it kill any information germane to the reason for meeting?

334. Answers about ancestry, books listing breeds and seminars in strain are all apart of a long line of study required for a pe-digree.

335. When compliments season the discussion, the meal about which you are speaking becomes a palatial delight. (Yes, and in good taste.*)

336. Vexed, Len opted for optics and concaved into the family demands that he focus on a specific *occu*-pation.

337. Does the un*utter*able mean that the very idea of milking a cow makes you speechless?

338. The town crier was asked to relieve one of the mourners whose duties it was to show the customary signs of grief at a funeral.

339. The officer pulled the book mobile over and cited the driver for speed reading.

340. Would thermo-mentoring be learning by degrees?

341. Even though there seems to be a lot of dirty laundry in the news media, do we really need the *spin cycle*?

342. Getting your ducks-in-a-row boat will still be lily padding your pond story with clichés.

343. When Mercury climbed Thermometer Mountain, he discovered the uppermost degrees were known as Fahren Heights.

344. Will a metal detector help you locate the missing elements to your chosen field?

345. The relief that follows when an officer tears up the ticket might be called ex-citation.

346. Does being tackful have you setting on a carpet while the fish listen to you politely coax a green skunk lure from a metal box?

347. Miss Leadman, from Graphite, Pennsylvania, you have won the pencil contest for your ability to write what's wrong around the world.

348. Where else would Ann and Teric place an old painting of two such pieces of furniture; why, of course, under the cherry tree. And who was selected to occupy one of the chairs; an old man with his Irish Sitter standing next to him. (Some questions answer themselves.*)

349. Should a felon receive a sentence of three consecutive lifetimes in prison, the Hindu might view this as re-incarceration.

350. Gene and Eric Genesis work for the Narcissus Furniture Pool delivering picture mirrors from a van-ity.

351. Would you find clay pots inside a dome on the range?

352. Was it too daunting a feet to finish a twenty-five K run?

353. Should you put socks on the metric feet of a winter poem?

354. Will they sell you a cowboy hat that is a six eight cylinder? If and only if you're driving a Bronco.

355. We picked a stall and then our teeth with a straw and then listened to the cattle milling through an entire cycle of pedias at the Barn-tanica. (Whatever a pedia is, if we open that door the horses will get out.*)

356. The Conda Family elected Anna to put the squeeze on early stock returns in Salivator, Panama.

357. Will it take about an acre to grow an average yield of medi-okra?

358. When a fish seeks asylum in a net, has it gone in seine?

359. Did somebody pun-cture this flat pun?

360. Call it consolidation, liquidation, and when stopping for fuel, gas-tation.

361. You could always count on Pat Tern to show you one, two, three or four unpredictable flights of fancy.

362. If antique tools spin you around Ted E. Leck, you'll be in awe over augers that are dated.

363. An intern from the pun lab asked if a Rockette, a dancing female rock, was someone waiting for her career to tale off.

364. A bass drum without the skin beats nothing.

365. With the dawn, the particle sun arrived at the front door.

366. Connie, Gene and Al were all smiles when Amy and Bill steeped out onto the sim-patico with some saccharin to sweeten all that talk about tea.

367. According to Mayor Chuckles, "When we try to tell people why we prefer to live in Pun Town, a plane and simple explanation seems to go right over their heads."

368. With the weight of the world on his shoulders, do you think Atlas had an *axe*-is to grind?

369. Some people seem to think that the only tool available that will control the increasing powerful pun is a pun-dulum.

370. We have removed from a chunk of limestone what is quite fossi-bly the skeletal remains of an ancient laughing fish.

371. Your mind will have to move much faster down the Humor Highway if you want to see the pun billboard before the sun goes down.

372. How do you relace yourself from those negative responses to a broken shoe string?

Romance

1. Will there be cyber marriages in the future? The couple will live at a website. Nobody will ever be *out of line*. You'll have plenty of memory for anniversaries and if there is ever any key-board-om, try typing in the problem to down load some solutions.

2. Emma Diately is ready. She wants her boyfriend to propose marriage today, this morning, now!
   "Mercy!" Galore muttered to himself, "On the other hand, there is time aplenty," and he was off to play golf in San Clemente. "I mean why rush into anything?" (Should she be teed off? *)

3. The young man walked across the room to the chair his girlfriend occupied. He leaned over, lifted a long strand of hair and said in a soft voice, "I've got to start whispering romantic things into your ears."

4. The couple was gazing at a rose when the trolley started that would transport their relationship into the upper reaches of a spiritual romance.

5. We dated. She was my queen. I fell to my knees and asked her to marry me and was knighted.

6. To seal his engagement, the pitcher for the Remington Gemstones gave his girlfriend a picture of the baseball field with the diamond at the bottom.

7.   In the alphabet of romance, some letters are cursively designed to hold a long stem rose.

8.   Romance (on) (a) roll: The man under the awning began fawning as Dawn was yawning.

9.   "The Parlance of Romance" is available in fine dictionaries everywhere.

10. Romancing the ellipsis: "Dorothy, you know there is nothing in the world I wouldn't do for you dot, dot, dot."

11. The heart surgeon after trying in vein to express his heart felt feelings to his wife ended the letter thus; fibrillatingly, yours.

12. She keeps stringing me along and it's beginning to wear a bit thin. (Hey, Clyde, look to see if your romantic shoe is untied.*)

13. This gem of a woman was called Sapphire and she kindled a flame that drew me up into a deep blue sky of passion.

14. 14. Can you guess what would Argyle keeps in a sock with a knot tied in it? (Is it a rough draft of the speech he made the day he proposed marriage? *)

15. The poet frustrated over his inability to express what he felt for Eve, at last pronounced his heart imprisoned within a rib cage.

16. If there is static in your relationship, then move the dial forward to Romance.

17. Georgia met Rick and as soon as he understood her line of thinking, they were immediately geometric. (Did they co-sign the marriage certificate? *)

18. Two wires decided to add some splice to their lives only to become coaxial in the transmission of their feelings.

19. The book was called *Atom* and the pages were all blank except for one in the center which contained the nucleus of a plot.

20. Chess masters at romance work hard to avoid being stale-mated.

21. Morley Raines writes notes to his wife then slips them under her windshield wipers.

22. Laugh it up into the rafters. After all, laughter is what she is after.

23. Why would young single adults want to meet thrice a year at a dance hall called "The Box?"

24. How many layers of talk does it take to insulate a relationship?

25. Would a ribbon around a bouquet of flowers be the tie that binds?

26. The (h)ours roll into minutes when we spend some time together.

27. Mr. Flood and Mary Rainey inun*dated* for two years before being carried away by the high water mark of romance.

28. Yesterday, Ester and her boyfriend, Chester, were sitting in the moonlight sipping lemonade. (Today, we know that she was getting ready to ask him for a bank *lune.**)

29. Even if they lose a day, most couples are encouraged to visit the international dateline before getting married.

30. Waymon Femur and his girlfriend Tibia raised a glass of milk in a toast to calcify their relationship before tomorrow's bone-fire. (A bon mot would be fitting here.*)

31. After dating for over two months, Auggie Metropolis, his mayorial medallion swinging from his neck, proposed to May Towne that they *rezone their lives together.* May Towne, who hefted a heavy gavel, decided she had reached the end of her single city limits and henceforth allowed Auggie to be annexed into her life.

Sign of the Times

1. You can improve the world by being your bright cheerful self . . . . ☺

2. What kind of films are your friends making? (How do they project themselves on a daily basis? *)

3. Somebody in this class is going to be famous. Who will it be and for what? (Jessie tells us that she is already quite skilled at weaving straw hats for donkeys.*)

4. What would we find in the shoe box under your bed?

5. To you, what is the ideal marrying age?

6. What would you put on a class black board? (A pun on the word *choc*-colate? *)

7. How can a whale sell out his waterspout? (Hey, the big mammal must have had a blast.*)

8. Simon says, "Write something simple."

9. We are here to tell you that spray on cobwebs will hang freely from the ozone ceiling.

10. For those of you interested in power, plan a trip to Niagara Falls.

11. For your information, it now takes an unbroken series of twenty-three guffaws to earn a court jester's certificate. (A *guffaw* is smile that breaks out into a laugh.*)

12. Tell me Toby, why would anybody want to use an in-cuba-tor to keep their cigars warm?

13. How many porcelains died in their native fields-spar to make the ceramic coat your sink is wearing?

14. The *wren* looked up from his favorite tree limb and *sigh*ed, "Yet, another loud piercing noise coming over the hill to warn people to take cover because it's going to be a cold winter."

15. During daylight saving time, more people have more time to stroll through the fields where pennies still grow.

16. The professor of political science was politely informed that he was not allowed to express his views within the context of this book. (And yet, we all need an allowance.*)

17. "Who put this tack on my throne?"

18. Is your T-shirt big enough to play a game of size sixteen tag with me?

19. Have you learn the merits of packing that *Boy Scout Handbook* with you when hiking?

20. For snipe hunters, there is a new law soon to be in effect limiting the number you can catch and take home.

21. Headlines: Government Agency Unplugs Movie Industry

22. Some people would be better off packing an arsenal of gun jokes when comes the time for the big hunt. (We do post the better jokes on a bullet-in board.*)

23. Two midnights ago, as Drayton K. Hula arrived home from work he wondered how much it would cost to bury a fully clothed vampire in a wooden tomb.

24. An ex-ray of the city respiratory system reveals that people breathe a lot easier when you lower the taxes.

25. Investigations are now centered around a prairie dog community and their underground publication.

26. If we said that golfer Greenley Goforth was on a roll, we would be on par with a pun.

27. If there is enough nuclear energy behind all the talk, it usually leads to a mushroom of controversy.

28. A Red Cross blood mobile was hijacked to Transylvania.

29. A "to be continued" sign was seen on the front door of the funeral parlor.

30. The definition of the fight or flight mechanism might be etched with charcoal on a cave wall somewhere near Spain.

31. A long time ago Ronda warmed up to the idea that if she wears a muffler around her neck while crossing the street she won't feel so exhausted.

32. If he tells the truth, we'll have to take a chance that nobody will believe him.

33. A hand-operated adding machine was found washed up by a wave of technology.

34. Tyler Teenager was text messaging while driving up Mount Olympus when he got bopped in the head with a discus.

35.   Not so long ago, a lot of people were claiming to be a nonconformist.

36.   Was it ever asked of the pet rocks of the 1960's why they now occupy their time in the tank behind commodes?

37.   When he reached for and missed the golf ball gearshift knob, it caused the driver to swerve off the road.

38.   Whoa! Should you be practicing your mental isometrics by pushing against outdated thinking patterns? (If that doesn't work try the status quo.*)

39.   Plants tend to lean in the direction of light.

40.   Shouldn't there be a warning sign in front of an en*counter* with useless information?

41.   Most economists agree that they are experts.

42.   Headlines: Spontaneous Combustion Sued by Match Industry

43.   "Such a moving commercial," noted the robot after seeing an advertising for a wheelbarrow.

44.   "A snake! Kill it!" is the typical overreaction of anybody who might have been working in their garden when this topic was being written. (Have you ever wondered why they don't stick around to discuss the latest issue of the "The Rattler?*)

45.   The world consciousness needs a raise. (Yes, let's expand our resources.*)

46.   The sign said: No dragon flies may land here between the hours 1-5 p m

After reading the sign one particular dragonfly was overheard saying that he was being forced to take a fly by night job just to make ends meet.

47. If this is all too much to think about, go buy a diversion. (Hey, this is much better than video games.*)

48. By all accounts limestone footstools became the rage one weekend following the Paleolithic Era.

49. The twentieth century has emptied a lot of saddles.

50. When did taboos and awkward situations become geographical and result in such cliches as: "Let's not go there."

51. Should you be walking down the street and meet a person with the same color laundry basket on his head as is on yours, call it rapport.

52. Ray, sir, why don't you dispose of that blade and shave your head with a pun?

53. The ostrich egg turned hard hat is for people who like to stick their heads in the sand.

54. How many garage doors does it take to open up a neighborhood?

55. How many gallons of people will a stadium tank hold?

56. Shouldn't a war over water rights be fought with squirt guns?

57. The cornucopia is hidden under the tax tables. (Shucks for bucks and the big word means *horn of plenty.* *)

58. How can you get board skating?

59.   Can you skateboard down the steps taken by the progress committee?

60.   When it comes to air pollution, many industries seem to be on an e-mission.

61.   Victoria Stiles always knows the latest wrinkle in European fashion.

62.   A Viking war whoop was used to start the annual Daytona 500. (And Helmut Gearheart as predicted was the winner.*)

63.   Let's all eat a drum roll and celebrate the music.

64.   What can we do with the noise produced at a greased pig contest? (And the winner gets a ham radio.*)

65.   Our calendar team is taking all the procedures necessary to have a *National Socks Day* built into the month of Step-tember.

66.   And then there was the day the wind blew so hard it loosened some of the fruit in the poetry tree. John Page who was sweeping up some of the rough drafts in the margins of his back yard was bopped on the head by one of the errant pieces. Page later claimed that he "wasn't even *standing under* the tree when it happened."

67.   The trap door in the belly of the Trojan horse is stuck. What will they do? (Call the Troy Crowbar Company.*)

68.   The lyrics are unintelligible. The picks are slicing into the ground and the drums thunder on. (Socrates once said that you could tell a lot about the state of a nation by listening to its music.*)

69. The new and modern Sisyphus from Greek Mythology is a heavy equipment operator who uses a dozer to push the rock up the hill.

70. Some media outlets play only lullabies.

71. The Smithereens are a branch of the military sent into war devastated countries with orders to rebuild.

72. During fall season, tribal leaders bring out the war paint and start pounding a drum covered with pigskin.

73. What a shot in the arm; we have a map that shows where *Vaca*ville is in this *nation*.

74. Life's Olympics offers the high and the low games. (Plus, you'll find a few in between.*)

75. Today's hero sandwich is on the fast food menu.

76. Some people arrive early and stay late when the ninth floor of the Derogatory Hotel is open for criticism.

77. A capital idea for some estates will feature rooms that have unrolled the new forest floor look. It is composed of a richly organic layer of soil and debris.

78. Do you make a lot of long distance crawls? A mud turtle paper weight is what you need to anchor all the statements to your desk?

79. Two pigs that can fly are on standby status in case there is a need to prove the possibility of any highly unlikely event.

80. All genies from the vintage 1970's bottles have long since left to fulfill a wish to pursue a career in modeling.

81.   If you can detail that two-toned stick shift babe magnet, can you not tape on the vocabulary stripes that might stream line your thinking process?

82.   Recently the Public Address system announced that they can attach truth filters to the microphones.

83.   Tall-erance seems to mean that an eight foot high public issue can and should be forced upon a five-foot, ten-inch society.

84.   Do you see the bird nest on the limb that overhangs the Fine Arts Building?

85.   "We're having a difficult time trying to figure out how to relax when we go on our complication next week," Victor A. Workman told a recent Rasmussen Poll.

86.   What would be the nature of the cargo and passengers on the 2008 Mayflower ship returning to England?" (Pilgrim, you have learned the ways of a material society.*)

87.   How concerned are people that an undertoe of apathy packs a subtle kick?

88.   When it comes to the courts deciding the price of ammunition, people are less likely to be taking cheap shots at each other.

89.   Tonight's conflict involves the Sturm and Drangs (storm and stress) versus a comfort zone.

90.   Christmas Eve was observed without Adam because he was called to go fight a war.

91.   The FCC recently passed a law prohibiting companies from funding an advertisement more than six hundred times.

92.   After a prolonged bombardment the advertisement raid finally ended and a stunned people opened their eyes, looked around slowly began to exit their bunkers.

93.   On the high cyber-seas does S.O.S.Com means help? (My computer is sinking in an ocean of websites.*)

94.   The last of the well-oiled and shining armor was recycled decades ago into metal cans containing potted meat.

95.   If we can find a camera how would you like to get a picture taken with your big brother?

96.   Part of a lawsuit against the judge's favorite restaurant includes a gag order.

97.   According to our popular culture, if Big Ben were drawn and quartered each horse would get fifteen minutes of fame.

98.   Are we seeing a politically correct shakedown on variety as the spice of life?

99.   The *Tribal Encyclopedia* now includes a picture of two rams butting their helmets at Anaheim Stadium in California.

100.   Does the bull rider know how to survive divorce court or *six ways to untie the knot?"*

101.   "Trey, I wish you would leave that lamp alone. Genie's ashes are in it," warned housekeeper *Ruby* Twitchel.

102.   Luke Upton tends to scratch his head when gazing at the chemical trails that waft across the sky over his house.

103.   Is there a genre of music that can be siphoned from a deprivation tank?

104. What would you expect to see on the label of a bottle of six o'clock news?

105. Would a pendulum make a good screen saver? (Probably not. No matter how you slice it, the picture gets duller with time.*)

106. Dunlap Dipstick and Lucretia were two in a series of fans stuck in an oil slick on their way to see "Derek and the Dominoes."

107. Many people have attended The Adversity of the Southern Quarry School of Hard Knocks. (The easiest part is getting in the front door? *)

108. Uncle Sam hangs his superman cape inside a closet at the oval office.

109. A landmark decision was made to construct a building for storing unused fluoridation filters.

110. Somewhere in Silicon Valley a spider web was spun between two obsolete computers.

111. Headlines: Heavy Metal Compact Disk Trips Security Systems at Shopping Mall

112. Armon Gregara stopped by the office recently to tell us that he is willing to play the game to get his name in print. Hint, hint. (Is *gregarious* in his vocabulary?*")

113. Polly and Esther organized a line behind a stack of synthetic coats and began pelting the fur industry with slogans.

114. Are computers a form of mind control unless your web site ends with *thinking.com?*

115. Indentation? Yes, all Halloween stationary is now perforated by vampire teeth.

116. Stadium construction crews raised the Popcorn Bowl in less than two minutes with the use of microwave technology.

117. The Cirrus Patrol, equipped with air rifles, was brought in to oversee an atmospheric disturbance.

118. C'mon, c'mon, c'mon snake eyes! And a pair of die slips through the fingers and bounces to a blissful stop on the game board. (To some people, the rolling of two such cubes and the prospect of winning must be nothing less than a heavenly experience.*)

119. The team's future became much more readable once they switched to the National Crystal League.

120. Several ancient gods of war have been summoned to reserve duty on a barge docked on the Potomac River.

121. Proofreaders' marks have been placed on read alert due to the ever growing threat of illiteracy.

122. Isn't a pollywog a shape shifter?

123. Crank the handle to the Jack-in-the-box and Jack will suddenly appear and be immediately informed that he is still a part of the pop culture.

124. If you cut enough corners on the processing costs for marketing breakfast foods, you'll eventually get to the serial number.

125. Those shepherds who had heard of it refused to vaccinate their sheep for Bucolia claiming the needles "were a bit rustic."

126. Before we drop the subject, can anybody tell us the nature of intelligence behind a smart bomb?

127. Walter Hyde told the committee that he had looked through all the applications and that no one seemed to understand human transparency.

128. Who can explain why a bevy of cowboys filed into the theatre to take in a ballet? (A recent article in the "Chisholm Chronicle" calls for calf ropers to have a thorough understanding of a pirouette.*)

129. Have you ever met a physician who understood the power of a belief system to prevent disease?

Science

1. Dialogue: Newton doesn't want to discover gravity. He needs your help. (Let's put it on fast forward and ask Johnny Appleseed if he has anything that can fall out of a tree.*)

2. Take your coat off and tell us what makes weather. (And it doesn't matter *whether* or not we agree.*)

3. Tuesday, you received a patent on a cloning machine. How does it work? (Somebody in one of the back offices suggested two scoops.*)

4. Are people as self focusing as a camera?

5. Spec Trummel won the award for the best description of a rainbow. (His acceptance speech was as inspiring as it was off color.*)

6. Science tells us it's a gas. Now you tell us, what is air?

7. Why are insects attracted to light? (That's where they can get their wing shield wipers washed while reading about the latest issue of the "Flier."*)

8. Explain electricity. (Wire you asking me to do this? *)

9. Would quantum bifocals give us a more detailed look at the invisible world in front of us? (I, for one, can't see wearing them. Who wants to trip over a molecule?*)

10.   The sour grapes of physics: if you can't see them, the particle clusters must not be there.

11.   A major attraction with a noticeably small charge: To see the real St. Elmos Fire as it introduces the Tesla Coil conducting watts current in alternative sound. Look for wind lights, string flashes, static riffs, cell pops and percussion glows as the orchestra pulses to the top of the Tesla Sound. Ratchet up your cultural awareness by spending a night with the master. (Excellent plug-in.*)

12.   Why do people stare back at you? Suppose the lighthouse effect of the human gaze attracts a person who is on the same wave length. (This answer beats climbing the stairs.*)

13.   The Molecular Buildings Supply Store has an ad in the Yellow Pages that is too small to see.

14.   At Ribonucleic Central, there is a crystal transformer that converts information into actual seeable, measurable light particles.

15.   Have you heard? Researchers have confirmed that some noises can be classified as toxic?

16.   Will you find fossilized sugar cane in rock candy?

17.   The tour de quantum features a spin of electrons moving through the hills of a French landscape on their way to the visibility line.

18.   According to the physics of time, when I glance away from the clock, it'll turn into a wave of nanoseconds and disappear.

19.   A gyre is a swivel idea rotating on an axis that is capable of attracting any information worth circulating. (We'll put

this one on the mantelpiece in front of the clock. It may be ahead of its' time.*)

20. "Yes, we would like a subatomic potato (with crème), some neuron spinach, a molecular steak (round) and garnished with protons. And oh! What's the charge on an electron side dish?"

21. If you can get Warden Lightman to bend the rules, the seven colors of the spectrum will be released from prism after the rainstorm.

22. "We thought the number was frozen," they ad-melted when professors were persuaded to open the doors at the H_2O Waters Center for Convinsation Studies. FYI:

    Graduates from the H_2O Waters Center exist in three states: liquid, solid and gas, and their boundaries are a matter of degrees.

23. A simple start with gases would be learning about oxygen, hydrogen and nitrogen which makeup the elementary school of chemistry.

24. Should atoms micro-manage protons and neutrons?

25. **Beta waves are to the mind what dilithium crystals are to the Starship Enterprise.** (If it's spelled right, such crystals are not in the dictionary . . . hold on, we are now been informed that it's in a different word warp.*)

26. The reader has found a handful of white pebbles in the middle of the text. (Weren't they hidden in a white room?*)

27. The atomic weight of the human element is not to be found on the periodic chart in chemistry.

28. Could it be that the amount of friction required stop a well hit golf ball is in direct proposition to the heat generated when swinging the club? (Four! *)

29. Are there panels that convert vibrations into music?

30. Are there panels that convert problems into solutions?

31. A wrap around quantum quilt is stitched from the fabric of time. (Will this keep me warm during a subatomic winter? *)

32. So, why couldn't a physics principal suspend Grady Gravity long enough to introduce a floatation system to our faculties?

33. Micro geology: the only way to determine if this rock replicates the Grand Canyon is to trickle a Colorado stream down the bottom of it.

34. If you can get a grip on the Tuesday Doorknob Tournament, you might be invited to the magnetism, electricity and light playoffs.

35. We decided to make some waves during the Celebration of National Physics Week by turning on the lights a few hours early.

36. The instruments for measuring eternity are hanging in a storage shed behind The Quantum House.

37. Ollie Molecule is tired of being treated so small.

38. Looking into the future, T. Lee Scope was convexed that the best advice he could give his son, Mike R. Scope would be to *stay focused*. When the young man asked where he should keep his money, the elder Scope recommended a

savings and lens. (Excuse me, would you read this again, I was busy cleaning my glasses.*)

39. If you insist on proof that other dimensions of light and sound exist try blowing on a dog whistle.

Technique

1. "While reading we noticed that specific words such as *really, very, maybe, simply* and *just* are used moderately in a text with so many entries. Why is that?"

    "Variety is the name of the game. Personified, these five words became self-serving with their own agendas as opposed to being team players and would have dominated the material. They were subtracting from the quality of the material. Repetition becomes redundant so we limited their use."

2. Shouldn't a character be interviewed or auditioned for the next edition of your story?

3. A story plot had scarcely enough time to become unraveled when several sentences took prolonged lunch breaks.

4. "Novel Supply Store, may I help you?"
    "Yes, we need your help in setting loose a *Robin Hood* armed with a noose in twenty-first century America."
    "You need one anachronism and if I hear you correctly, a rope?"
    "Sure."
    "What?"
    "I said 'sure' as in Sherwood Forest."
    "Can you hang on for a few minutes? Uh, we had a rope that was a major part of a plot which has since come unraveled. I would recommend a "rob from the rich"

kit. We have several in stock and the installation is easily written."

5.　Two days before the full moon Chief Motif will take a few minutes to remind his theme braves about the need to be consistently *recurring* in order to bind each tribal story into a cohesive unit.

6.　"More (t) if?"
"Yes, I'll have one more cup. Tea seems to be a recurring theme throughout this text.
"Absolutely, the material is steeped in it and once you get to the top of the mountain, it will all make sense."

7.　After the landscape has been described, let some dialogue flow through it.

8.　Verisimilitude is known as something that is very similar to or a slice of life. Describe life in a watermelon boat. (Somebody is constantly thumping at the rudder.*)

9.　If a character is thinking something with enough intensity, all quotation marks should disappear.

10.　Herbert Hyperbole and the Little Exaggerations drove 3000 miles to see a ruby-throated toad sucker take a dust bath in Mendocino, CA.

11.　Our new water compressor can splash S's into alliteration.

12.　First, measure the distance over the head of your motif; then darn some earphones in case somebody is wearing loud clothes.

13.　"Hello, Novel Supply Co...No, we are all out of dark stormy nights. The other day I found several musty smelling Dracula capes in the closet. It does sound drab...so the fangs are out

of the question. Well, there is always the Cape of Good Hope."
"Hey, the novel isn't a comedy."

14. A *skill at* writing will call for you to cook the story long enough to bring out all the juices of the plot. (You might try placing a bottle of meat tenderizer on the manuscript before going to bed tonight.*)

15. To what extent do we understand a character until he is isolated from the group? We see his true colors during a road trip, while imprisoned or stranded on an island.

16. Puns are words that are simply doing double duty.

17. Writing is difficult because you must mix the exact verbal pigment to paint the most vivid imagery.

18. Terrance Tarantula trekked through a torrential storm to avoid being trampled by an alliteration of T's. (You're teasing? *)

19. The oxy-moron stopped and refused to move until a load of puns was thrown off and some clean dirt was piled onto the wagon bed.

20. Ozzie Moran, you're a walking contradiction. How long did it take your shirt to dry after you told your neighbors that it was raining sunshine?

21. Poetry eyes can blink out a measure of metric feet as they scan right along the elbow of a river.

22. A rare case of writer's block centered on a fiction narrative that detailed the origins of Cubism.

23. A litter-ature box filled with feline stories featuring familiar feces certainly belongs in the catacomb archives.

24.   Should dialogue for alpha male characters be printed in a **bold** font?

25.   A lot of fiction has been launched from a Cape Kennedy Keyboard.

26.   Sometimes when you're looking for a so-so motif to connect several paragraphs, you can be stuck with a needle and thread.

27.   All you have to do is punctuate your word bricks with cement and when the wall is finished and you have left room for the door, step right in and see what the story is.

28.   The Faustians gave us a human soul commodities exchange board or a chance to sell our souls to the devil.

29.   Anson was hauling a pickup load of cactus extract through an Arizona desert when he got stuck. (A few things about this topic are somewhat prickly.*)

30.   The pig with the pearl necklace motif has uprooted many main characters from their hometown plots.

31.   The man lived in complete isolation for nearly two hundred pages of the novel before somebody rode up on a horse with some dialogue.

32.   The pun is the carpenter of the dictionary: This play on words can take you to new levels of thinking. An example would be a carpenter who rides over the hill on a horse. The horse halts and wants to munch on clover. The carpenter is in a hurry; he has a ladder to build. He overrides the horse and moves on. And we don't have to consult the Gallup Polls to know that the reader has moved one rung up the ladder to a new level.

33. Do you recall the professor who hung a lanyard on the pencil sharpener to remind us that the elements in our stories should be tightly woven together?

34. The best catering is contracted to provide dialogue dishes when the guest paragraphs run out of tasty topics to talk about.

35. Myron Mosley, are you miffed by the lack of moths in myths? Some say they were pelted by the rain in Spain that fell mainly on the plains.

36. What is the tone of the script you've written for the main character on your personal stage?

37. Place a novel into a honey centrifuge and notice how the flavor of the story separates then drips down to be savored leaving the syntax to wax on into octagons.

38. How do you unquote, "two sets of two fingers in the air?"

39. He walked slowly, pouring over the wall of a rough draft, carrying a can of proofreader's marks. He stopped periodically to brush in a comma or semi-gloss a sentence with a colon.

40. Use the seed from overgrown paragraphs as quotation marks should you need to germinate some dialogue.

41. We need someone who can play their part to a T while monitoring the repartee during a tea party in Thurston Park.

42. Let's get one of the hired words to take a load of analogies down to the lower eight letters and feed that heard of metaphors. They've had little more than single definition sprigs through most of the reading season and in my book they're losing weight.

43. Will water create a craving to carve out a cave? (We'll ask a spelunker if she is thirsty.*)

44. Jo Woolworth grabbed her coat upon learning that Will E. Dutton thought nuttin' of cutting bones from mutton to make buttons. (Fascinating.*)

45. After you become familiar with a sonnet it will tend to fade into imagery?

46. Most words can be broken down into syllables that when personified are quite willing to be interviewed.

47. You might trip over the fun should you try juggling three *pun*-der balls high in the air. (We were going to skip over this entry until reminded that puns can be a fun trip.*)

48. You can drive out of the Metaphorical Hills and down to the plains where sentences are long and flat and stretch out page after page of rabbits hiding under not so wise sage grass and dogs peering over the edge of an arroyo that has gulched its last waterway. Yes, we could chase a lot of wild ink in an effort to tell you how your writing will simple go downhill without the use of metaphors, but we won't. We suggest that you move your herd of words closer to the mountains for better grazing.

49. During the first meeting at the Purgatorium, we were taught how to cleanse or rid ourselves of emotional baggage through catharsis.

50. You'll find words that (a) beam and (a) dream of being used in (b) time as part of a (b) rime (a) scheme.

51. Is fluent well written literature easy to write? (No doubt it's easier to read.*)

52. Is there any connection between *denouement* or the final unraveling of a plot and the fact that tomorrow is the *day* when you get a *new mount*? With your new horse you can ride off into the sunset; end of story.

53. The secret to reading any book is to let your mind's eye become the director as you convert the story line into a film.

Television

1. Will daytime television clean an oven?

2. The television cheering squad usually manages to soak the crowd with commercial film-flamboyance.

3. A man was overheard asking his television for permission to fix sandwich.

4. "I have no idea why I'm buying this brand of aspirin," replied the lady as she placed a copy of "TV Guide" on the counter.

5. One of the membership requirements for the stoic society would be to have a mask likeness of yourself watching TV.

6. If you want to see the northern lights, switch to the Aurora Borealis star channel.

7. "Hey, Titus, why don't you drill a hole in the bottom of the TV and drain the detritus?" questioned Iris Quigley. (Shall we throw it into the clock barrel for wasted time?*)

8. This movie might cost you several nights of restful sleep. You'll see a howling banshee terror flick featuring Vincent Price.

9. The master of ceremonies won the Hyperbole Award for most superlatives in one night.

10. Was Elmer Fudd ever given a hand dummy made from rabbit fur in his youth? (Was Fudd's life little more than a dud? Even the myopic character himself would probable tell you that the only fun he ever had was with a gun.*)

11. Anachronism: A likeness of Mr. Ed might have been stamped on the saddle bags used by the pony express. (Mr. Ed was a talking horse in the 1960's TV programming.*)

12. To perform a news bypass operation, take a scalpel and cut the cord to your TV.

13. Double driveling is not necessarily restricted to basketball in the entertainment arena.

14. When a person *ad hears,* does it mean they will stick to their promise to stop believing some of the colorful stories that people tell them?

15. Should soap offers be viewed on bleach channel four?

16. The big test with TV wants to know if you can turn the tube off and light a fire under your chemistry assignment.

17. In all the western movies I've ever had a chance to see they drink that stuff straight from the bottle as if it were tea.

18. So, who gave network television permission to deaden your sensibilities day after day with the same old inanities? (Is this the Attitude Channel?*)

19. Obviously money grows on trees or we wouldn't be able to fund such programs as "Nature."

20. Only two-thirds of the Cartwright's thinking went into the name "Ponder-osa."

21. During TV's sweeps week, the situation comedy "Knows" developed an allergy and blew its last performance.

22. The new Popeye Jack-in-the-Box is a repression identity kit. When you crack open the spinach look-alike can you'll hear the sailor say, "I yam what I yam."

23. When you finish your spinach, we'll tell you all about Popeye's nephew and how he was the first to market the Olive Oil salad dressing that turned the cartoon industry into vegetarians.

24. Is there a tamper-proof television audience?

25. The only way Wiley Coyote will ever catch the Road Runner is to step out of the cartoon, then run the film in slow motion.

26. The Road Runner was hyperactive.

27. We now have access to a stove that is fueled by the temperaments of commercial TV and stored in a profane tank.

28. The Lone Ranger Bypass has a Tonto access ramp every two miles. (Does this character hark back to the days when people used horses not Ford Rangers.*)

29. How long will Brutus control the irrigation rights to Popeye's spinach farm?

30. Take the soap opera scripts to a laundry mat so that the parts could be sorted out then thrown into a machine to let the agitator play its role?

31. Does the font size expand in proportion to the emotion in the script of a soap opera?

32. Somebody opened the media cage and immediately a swarm of advertisements consumed the leaves on the money tree.

33. When you open a corporate metaphor, you discover the people who network commercial fishing.

34. Can a whirl wind of bargains be found in the Tasmanian world of advertisement?

35. Aimsley Colt was convinced most media propa-gun-das were loaded with bullets of biased information.

36. Yes, the advertisement for butterfly coaches fluttered by unnoticed.

Time

1. Describe the automobile, circa 2050. (This one may drive you crazy.*)

2. What do you plan to be doing as a middle aged adult?

3. Write about your future aspirations. (Breath deep.*)

4. Take a trip in time. Remember, you cannot change the course of events, or can you?

5. Does the bovine in the pasture ever ruminate about the future? (You have insulted a cow. *)

6. Take a trip sideways in time. (We left at three and we'll be back at nine.*)

7. Take a moment to talk with someone about time.

8. Explain the existence of the past or has it been reduced to a memory?

9. Do you need a license to kill time?

10. Have some tea and tell me: Should a bolt in the time machine loosen, will we get to watch the Model T roll off the assembly line again and again and again?

11. Some clocks unwind by sipping some Minute Maid Orange Juice as the day goes by. (Now there's a plug-in for you.*)

12. What is it you will know at seventy that you will wish you had learned in your thirties?

13. Rotating cylinders demonstrating the relationship between the past, present and future are under a marquee at Shea Stadium.

14. What kind of telescopic lens will enable you to see into the future?

15. How long will it take you to pump the time out of that glass box?

16. A gallon of tradition should take you about twenty-five miles into the past.

17. When time becomes money, we will be issued gold plated three minute pieces.

18. We need to decide when to go, so somebody flip a clock and if it lands face up, it's time.

19. In this picture, you can see how the hands of time have fashioned an hourglass out of cave clay.

20. A one-hour rock, when placed under the momentum mill, will grind down into minute pebbles and then second sand.

21. An entire year of personification has turned Father Time into an old man.

22. If we can geometrically convert the nervous tic from the face of a second into a musical note, we can listen to the passage of time.

23. On the Beaufort Scale, a clockwise wind termed a moderate gale gusted up to sixty—seconds per minute.

24. When an eighteen century ship en route to America exhausted its supply of minutes, hours and days, it sank.

25. The new Ford 24/7 has an adjustable oscillations-per-hour dial which lets you determine when you'll arrive this afternoon.

26. Why don't restaurants have time shakers on their tables? (Would it take too long to eat? *)

27. Is the past covered in time dust?

28. If frustration has a point that you reach, how are you going to feel if you arrive on time?

29. Do clocks ever take time off? (Time can be taken off the clock at football games.*)

30. Try taking a picture of the wind by adjusting the window lens, then timing the speed of a moving shutter.

31. Should you call ahead to make sure there is a future?

32. A rural clock is housed in a tree, looks over a beehive and offers no evidence of time; an urban clock overlooks public housing and often witnesses a crime.

33. If you want time to *fly* by, attach a zipper to six and have it close at twelve.

34. Notice the harvest of seconds and minutes and hours that constantly spill from the cornucopia of time. (Can you cope with a clock in a corn field? *)

35. We are taking auditions for those people who are truly skilled at playing the delicate instrument of time.

36. At midnight the right hand of a clock paused a few second to record the minutes of a meeting with its left hand.

37. Can magnetic traces of time be mixed with ordinary house dust?

38. What goes around in late October has usually found a Halloween mask on sale before it comes around in November.

39. A watch's sweeping hand keeps the sixty seconds pushed out into the complete circle of a minute.

40. Lower the thermostat inside that clock when you want to freeze an event in time.

41. Tuesday was wrapped, insulated and isolated from the rest of the week by warm weather.

42. Put your calendar in a miter box to insure that December is flush with January.

43. Does a twenty-four carat gold wrist watch tell you how valuable your time is? (Nice!*)

44. Be looking for a time piece whose right hand will work around the clock.

45. She carried an alarm clock in her purse as a reminder when she was spending too much time and money.

46. You don't have much time *left* to switch your watch to your *right* wrist.

47. What if you could reverse the end of a time pencil to erase the lines from your face?

48.   With clocks for wheels, let's see which of these chariots will reach *next* Tuesday in first place.

49.   Six minutes times ten minutes is one mathematical hour.

50.   How long does it take for time motes to cook in a dustpan?

51.   Tell us all about your weekend at the Hotel for Past Events.

52.   How long is a routine's worth of time?

53.   Do you want time to go faster on your *watch*?

54.   You can pin a brief sequence of events on a line between two Sundays and they will dry out simultaneously.

55.   Before we fully understood that a round clock could be rolled out into a line to help us better organize our thoughts, several people tripped over a two o'clock section of sidewalk.

56.   By stitching a line of seconds down the fabric that conceals the stage, we'll know when it's time for the curtain to go up.

57.   This year's high-performance model of the clock goes from zero to sixty seconds faster than your attention span can observe.

58.   At some point in the future a time machine will have been invented that will allow individuals to travel back to meet the citizens of today or are they already here?

59.   When one hour ends, we will need a brief intermission until the next one begins.

60. "Do you remember when the clock with the rock frame fell from an airplane?"
"Yes and our resident soothsayer predicted that hard times would soon rain down on all of us."

61. A one hour rock when placed under the momentum mill will grind down into minute pebbles and then second sand. (Which you can buy at a second hand store.*)

62. The sign at the edge of the highway cautioned the motorist to *watch for seconds that pass for minutes.*

63. Time has nothing to do with it. If you are the teacher you can certainly change the *course* of events.

64. "The minute hand and the second hand obviously do not get along. They seem to meet each other in passing yet never spend much time together," noted Hayward Gilliam. "On the contrary," countered Seth Thomas, "they are together around the clock."

65. When we ran out of time talking about the eternal clock we found that it was never there.

Weather

1. Take the season dial in hand and turn slowly to loosen the green and watch the fall colors as they begin to appear.

2. School has been dismissed today because of the weather so write a snow story that is six inches deep.

3. From the weather kitchen, another batch of Cold Snaps will be served on a wintry platter.

4. Does the temperature flip the switch from spring to summer?

5. Two seasons are trying to occupy the same day. ("There's only room for one of us in this here town. You got that?" replied * as Joann Wayne.)

6. When the jet stream opens a hatch, a thunderstorm falls out.

7. The ticket to a winning breeze on a hot summer day is to have one cool lottery number.

8. How do clouds affect your moods? (Are you Cirius? *)

9. Have you heard that a cumulous jam session can produce the sound of rain? (Are you ready for "Strawberry Fields?" *)

10. A cloud fell out of the sky. They called it rain. (That's a semi-detached altitude and yet, I'll bet you still got wet.*)

11. Season switching keeps the iceberg thermometers knocked off the Gulf plumbing.

12. A thermostat north of the Canadian border was stuck below freezing. (We'll put the extra charges on Terrio's bill.*)

13. The thunder clapped after the showers popped up and the lightning struck out to end a game that was forecasted to be rained out.

14. "The ty-phone was ringing," Stormy Withers recalled, "and the wind was on the other end. The gust of what was said rotated around the I. Hence, I hung up and wondered why I was ever in a hurry to live on Cain Street. I wish it had dialed a wrong number."

15. Should a carpenter consult a meteorologist before he builds a low ceiling? (The man with the hammer may want to install the new water floor carpet covering.*)

16. During a weather meal, sometimes when unpalatable particles mix (positive, negative) the results can lead to indigestion or a stomach storm.

17. On what day of the week would Thor be pounding out a weather forecast on the anvil of a thunderstorm?

18. A jogger can slice right through the wind if he/she will run between the tightly packed isobars on the weather map.

19. Graduation day at meteorological school requires the student to wear a beanie cap with a weather vane on it.

20. How would you like to be in charge of the weather remote control?

21.   Mood meters are now calibrated according to weather patterns.

22.   A prolonged cold winter might have you waving a truce flag made from thermal underwear waving in the elements.

23.   Have you heard of the stalactite of ice that was fickle enough to melt when old man winter did a personality swing?

24.   Shouldn't *rain check* mean that the weather has been called off due to a clear day? (If the check is written in the spring, it won't be *hot*. *)

25.   Once a year replace the spring in your season gun when it's time to staple a warm weather canopy outside your window.

26.   How low does the temperature go in Tupalo?

27.   Include *occlude* when alluding to the weather, dude.

28.   Ted Thunderhead was feeling highly charged one summer evening when he drifted into a fellow rain maker with every intention of starting a rumble.

29.   A disclaimer on the form for ordering the weather reads: We are a non-*profit* organization.

30.   The last time Lorrie St. Prose announced that she was writing up a storm, several people took shelter.

        130. Who determines the contents of a culture? (Most people are content to let the media decide that. Popcorn, anyone?*)

        131. How much of an electronic iceberg is below the surface of the computer screen?

132. Veggies? Hardly. Terrie and Ann would have you to clean out those animal portions that are sliced and left on the back shelf of the refrigerator. (Don't you two believe in supporting cultural studies? *)

The Word

1.   What one word best describes you?

2.   Do we ever need a different set of symbols to interpret our experiences?

3.   Please repeat the definition for ditto marks.

4.   How valid is up and down? (Be sure to write from your left to the right.*)

5.   How valid is empty and full? (Let me put on my glasses.*)

6.   Write a highly original word combination. Ex: *a yodeling refrigerator* or *the dancing boots of a canary.*

7.   Writing students are now required to use the word *azure* when they reach the sky in their poetry. (Are you blue? *)

8.   "Encroachment!" the official yelled, throwing a hoe at the weeds in his garden.

9.   If the phonetics should go flat, some words happen to carry a spare letter: Aaron, largesse, etc.

10.   Statistically, how many times has that word been mispronounced?

11.   Unless the syllable is inflatable, it is not phonetically designed to float.

12.   One word. (Two many for one.*)

13.   Lloyd has a parallel investment in llamas.

14.   Claude, does occlude include clouds?

15.   The hunt for animal descriptions took Richard Cravens to the Thesaurus Caverns where he found upside-down a list of words hibernating for the winter.

16.   Willy-Nilly was put in charge of spending. (That was a reckless appointment.*)

17.   Do people wall themselves in or use a stack of rocks to keep the world out?

18.   The *passing away* of a euphemism might create a dearth of lightweight modes of expression.

19.   *Vel-crow:* now there is one bird that will stick to its word.

20.   If you are well read, you will know that the professor's wife likes to hear the word *erudition* while eating supper. (And what about that sink full of eru-dishes?*)

21.   Try using *gentle cruelty* to describe that team of oxy-morons grazing in your back yard. (A strange species it is and lacking in intelligence.*)

22.   Can you imagine no imagination?

23.   Do the citizens in Connecticut know that we are all interconnected?

24.   Were you in class the day we discussed the definition of *absentia*?

25. Procrastination is a long word to rest behind until you feel like doing something.

26. Experts agree that bingo playing is the best way to learn how to spell the word.

27. To win the prize, you must give us an outlandish definition of *absurd*. (And you have won a two tickets to the circus.*)

28. Being hungry for information is one thing but are you thirsty enough to know what a quaff is?

29. Is it possible to do nothing? (If I answer no, is there something I can do about it? *)

30. "I'm near the end of my alphabet and I'm running out of patience," an uneasy X complained while munching from a box of Deletes. "I've been inserted here for over three hours now and all I need to do is sign up for letter unemployment benefits."

31. Let the air out of abstract and it drops to a level of understanding. (Are balloons abstract? *)

32. Would you crawl into a box stamped *aesthetics*? (The word means *beauty* and it's time to let it out of the box.*)

33. The double play or the alley-oop of grammar:

    - barber shopped around the ears

    - coffeed into a frenzy

    - football game blimped by Goodyear

    - cities cemented by sidewalks

34. Are word carpenters at their best when working at sentence construction? (And the punctuation must keep all the parts nailed in place.*)

35. If you look it up in the dictionary, you'll find the spider to be a potential Web-ster.

36. A language purist was sent out to collect all the clichés in the neighborhood. (Awesome! *)

37. Course (what) being (size) offered (shoe) on (did) how (you) to (wear) do (when) two (you) things (were) at (ten?) once. (The shoe was made by the Multi-Tasking Company.*)

38. A two-way street light now directs traffic along Palindrome Boulevard. (Shouldn't this entry read the same forward as backward? *)

39. Offer a short definition of detail. (In one minutia.*)

40. What is before a beginning? (Does something have to end before there is a beginning? *)

41. Why do people get de-sensi-tized? (Somewhere in the middle of the word we know that pennies are of little value.*)

42. What is the function of a symbol? (The brass plates usually have some information *clanging* to them.*)

43. Today's dictionary has a drain opening at the bottom of it for outdated words.

44. We try to catch what various words sound like with an accent. (Would a late model Crowe make a *cah* sound? *)

45. Should people become agitated when you mention that they are washing their clothes with an 'r'?

46.   Is inure a rhymingly safe word to use even in an agriculture class?

47.   Ballyhoo, brouhaha and boondoggle are some of the verbal penguins *orking* about on the linguistic iceberg.

48.   Isn't it ironic how many people are not sure how to define irony?

49.   Anthropomorphism is a long stretch of a word that fences in the world from a human point of view.

50.   What can you learn about a person by listening to their speech patterns?

51.   Alright, you have the two of us standing side by side. Now, which of us do you suppose knows what juxtapose means?

52.   Pour a cup of euphemisms into your daily loads of discourse to soften the words.

53.   The new semantic-scope allows you to see the word (water), then focus deeper on its symbolic meaning (wet), then deeper still, understand the power of the symbol. (Isn't it time to call 911 dictionary man? *)

54.   Penny plays the cornucopia in a band whose music reminds us how well off we are. (The horn of plenty.*)

55.   Modus Operandi is a method of operating in which Latin terms are used to impress the reader.

56.   While up in the attic, Morgan noticed the red nose repair kit was resting on top of a 20,000 piece puzzle; both of which had been placed between the inflatable clown and a Jules Verne movie poster. (And the attic fan goes around and around.*)

57. Does the power of a symbol lies in its ability to evoke emotional energy?

58. The leader of the retinue slid off the ice covered road en route to the revenue office.

59. He left the 'r' out of vertigo during a dizzy spell.

60. Carrying a bowl of story solutions, deus ex machina was lowered from the helicopter into a party whereby a family of parodies immediately approached him saying, "You don't look anything like you are pronounced." (If a topic ever needed the intervention of a supernatural force to save it, this one does.*)

61. In any minute now a phonetician will walk through that door and teach us how to pronounce dues ex machina. (We might need supernatural intervention.*)

62. We see no point in disputin'. Rasputin was a holy man of political influence during his rime in twentieth century Russia.

63. *Plethora* has had plenty of time to decide how, when and where her name should be mentioned in this book.

64. Our bailiwick wants a special domain in a topic. He claims to understand all legal enunciation within his juris-diction. "Sustained!"

65. Say, Boone, let's hike the Cumberland Gap with a warm coonskin cap all the while looking for the right appellation or name for this mountain range. (The trail here is not very well marked.*)

66. Have you ever been so tired you could not feel the 'b' in numb?

67. If you shake a bag of homonyms, you'll notice that individual groups of two or three sound alike (are even spelled alike) and yet are different from the rest.

68. The common athwart is nocturnal and will travel in one night the entire length of a dictionary with trouble on its mind.

69. Anybody who can pronounce maxixe will win three lessons on two step ballroom dancing. (Kudos. A topic with a built-in definition of the word.*)

70. Meet Rhyme, a passive sort who spends most of his time in close correspondence to sound. Meet Rhythm, the renegade cousin who would drop a rock into a flow of sound to make waves between the strong and weaker elements.

71. Innocuous doesn't sound harmless. It sounds like an unlicensed tattoo parlor.

72. If ire were a mineral on the periodic chart of human emotions, it would probably get mad for failing the scratch test.

73. Al Truism was a highly moral man of principle in charge of discipline at Harry Truman High School, south of L.A.

74. With much sorrow, we report that lachrymose isn't the residue that collects at the bottom of a molasses filter.

75. We had planned to be spontaneous.

76. Can a cantaloupe be melon-choly? (Only if it is parked next to a large, friendly, tan dog sitting on the front porch.*)

77. When a word is repeated a number of times, it is reduced to a hollow vibration.

78. Oregano should not be a mint. The phonetics are closer to a switched on instrument designed to settle complicated moral issues. (In Oregon it is used primarily during the rainy season.*)

79. The rarest of the rain forest species, the phantasmagoria, can be seen at the Exotic Word Zoo.

80. A retort would be an anti-sweet remark, pasted back at the speaker.

81. Numerous unhatched grenades were incubating at the bottom of a machine gun nest.

82. Erewhon: When you play the dialogue backwards you'll find that it went nowhere.

83. Can you tune a word? A misplaced accent mark will emit the wrong vibration and the power of the symbol is weakened.

84. The alphabet evolved from the ground up through clay tablets to your daily dose of *dirt cheap, down to earth* or *dig it*.

85. Efforts are being made to reroute the definition of *mainstream* to include everybody.

86. An editor was scrounging around the floor of an attic when he found the skeletal remains of several dead words. The coroner reported that *great, like* and *I* were deceased due to neglect and overuse. (Awesome!*)

87. A washboard design was found on the front of a soil resistant T-shirt.

88. "Well," S. M. Artesian began, "let's put it this was way; I Q-uestion the ways and means by which some people try to prove their genius."

89. From a distance you could see the Ferris wheel turning. At the same time, the story came over the radio about the Dexter County fire. Was it widespread burning? No, wait! They've reported that the amusement rides are in full swing. It's a midway, a fair. If something had been combusting, they might have said, "far." (Pronounciation.*)

90. When is the expiration date on *great*? (Cheese is the exception.*)

91. Drop onomatopoeia on your toe and it will sound as painful as the thud that describes it.

92. "What's he doing?"
    "Renunciating."
    "I've noticed he hasn't been his old self."
    (All things aside, the word means
    "to step outside yourself." *)

93. The Latin word for spider was dangling above an English description of a web.

94. The mobility to till a garden of T's teaches not only stability but turns over a sense of futility into the versatility to utilize our abilities.

95. Ladies and/or gentlemen, would you prefer lectern or latrine?

96. How much of our culture hinges upon the information received through *Rod's last doornailism*? (Film at eleven.*)

97. How the *deuce* was a wordsmith able to roll the vocabulary dice and come up with such an odd word that has very close connections to hades? (Nicely handled.*)

98. A congregation of safety monitors was taut that a red flag would go up pending the firing of the second syllable in conflagration. (The fire, excuse me, conflagration is out. The trucks have left and it's time to go home.*)

99. Backstage after the premiere of *Poltergeist,* several players witnessed the ghost of a turkey that appeared long enough to throw the NBC peacock out the dressing room window. (For the record, the peacock lost its plumage and was retired a long time ago. *)

100. Think about it. Would you decorate your room by placing an *orna* above the mirror if you wanted the place to look mental?

101. The 'g' in grain is a consonant that will add fiber to your vocabulary.

102. Would Circum locu ville include all the talk around the town that will certainly grow into Verbose city?

103. The innuendo glass window pun has more ups and downs than any other access to the house of humor.

104. To give in to the request that one ton rocks should be hurled fifty yards through walls of a medieval castle is to capitulate to catapult.

105. Talk about deforestation. Since they cut the log out of dialogue, quality conversation has been overrun with clichés and inanities and will soon be on the endangered species list. (I noticed that you left out profanities.*)

106. The first thing you need to do is to learn to spell priority.

107. When we tell people what an askance glance is, they always look at us sideways.

108. To laminate or lament is to regret that the L shaped roller broke into a vowel and "I couldn't finish the wall."

109. An *ob* shaped pond sitting on a hill might have enough of a *lique* to drain it.

110. Would a confessor be in charge of admissions to the assessor's class? (We admit that we do not know.*)

111. If you're wondering what you can do with *peripatetic*, try slipping it into the backpacks of hither and thither, that pair of pathetic and ever moving lost souls. (The word in italics is defined as *wandering about*. And, yes, a few people have been wondering about this topic.*)

112. The more incorrugated inmates are restricted to playing solitaire in cardboard boxes.

113. Methodically, step by step, Rich Ewual went about his life demonstrating that a person's name tells a lot about them. (We'll be the first to admit that we have never met anyone by that last name before.*)

114. An *astic* bag will not hold anything without a *pl* attachment.

115. How is it that the first runner up the mountain comes in second place?

116. "Albion, my way has been proven to faster and more efficient and if you don't believe me I have other places to be."

117. Frag-ment-ed? (Let's *defrag* and pretend that that's what the topic originally meant.*)

118. "We keep telling people to look us up when they get to town," noted Arlis Articulation.
"Where do you live?"
"Webster Heights in Page County, Bookampton."

119. In order to explain the meaning of their name, Phil and Ann Thropy took the Charity Drive to the intersection of Hugh and Main Street where they turned right. Three blocks later, they arrived at Givens Hall where a group of people had gathered, notebooks in hand, to better understand, in a word, the rarity of a Phil and Ann.

120. Excerpt from the Marsupial Monitor: "Ouch, Joey, will it take it easy on the pouch? I happen to be in the middle of court."

121. A female Gila monster might be called a Sheila monster.

122. Most sea gulls would raise a flap if they knew the literary definition of a gull.

123. Late breaking news: "We have confirmed that a set of two quotations marks recently had some words between them."

124. Do people ever dress their vocabulary up with an old fashioned word?

125. "They told me that it would be an *atrocious*, but I, Bill the inspector, am here to tell you that the folks in *Cali.* did a *super* job of imploding the *Fragisitic* office building. Excuse me, the *Expeali* Dynamite Co is on the phone."

Zoology

1. What are we to learn from animals?

2. What is the smartest animal you have ever seen? (Does he speak pig Latin? *)

3. Do whales ever talk at length about water spouts? (Only when someone mentions a province in the British Isles.*)

4. Wow! We asked a dog what was on his mind and he stepped back and took a bow and began to wag his tail as if it was a *rough* question.

5. What do frogs think about? (This should keep you riveted.*)

6. Describe a night as a bat. (Try to hit a home run.*)

7. Describe a day in the life of a falcon. (If you can't think of anything, wing it.*)

8. What would it be like if all the wild birds were tame? (Let's take this topic out of the text before a cat comes along.*)

9. Describe those creatures at the bottom of the ocean. (Don't leave us in the dark.*)

10. Tell a snake story. Would you get rattled if it was accepted by the *Reptile Gazette*?

11. Write the dialogue between two deer concerning all those guns pointed at them.

12. Describe being a squirrel in a snowstorm. (Make it a long tale.*)

13. On that day when the earthworm and the fish sat down for a little chat, did the trout relate that he the worm was the bait? *)

14. Do cows ever stall for time while room-inating in the barn?

15. What does your horse feel about that saddle on his back? (He says he doesn't want to stirrup trouble.*)

16. Hallie was one of the first people to understand the need to protect our whales and dolphins.

17. What is the advantage of being a marsupial? (Remember, the answer is in your left hand pocket.*)

18. "A riddle?" "No, we need something drier."
    "How about *arid* as in desert?"
    "Sure, that'll work. If you have a camel license in your pocket, you can give us an account of your latest Safara."
    "If that's what you call it. And by the way I am a member of the All-Safara Band."
    "What instrument do you play?"
    "I play the drum-edary."
    "Well, that beats being stuck in the dune without any water."

19. How many students instinctively know which courses to take if they want to study animal communications?

20. An armadillo saw the deer crossing sign and now he wants the same highway protection.

21. Chapter four of *Cat Tracks on My Car* by Mussie Feline describes coping with dogs.

22. Lester Lizard stole my sunglasses. (He told us he's planning to give them to his Sheila Monster because she needs to look cool in the dessert.*)

23. Take a picture of the bat as he flies out of the attic. (He appears to have won a game of bat-minton with a bird.*)

24. The confused identity of a dog named Checkers wants to hop through eight lives and keep the ninth one in check.

25. Headlines: Ventriloquist Dove Hosts Benefit for Passenger Pigeon (*Cool.**)

26. Is there enough room in the *Guinness Book of World Records* for a whale to be having a calf?

27. An o-*ring*-utan assured us that he will behave himself while locked in a zoo if only he can listen to the sound of his mobile phone. (I wonder how many bars this cell has.*)

28. According to the latest survey vines do make up the jungle transportation department.

29. After the dog days of summer have ended, most turtles close early for the night and head down to the Shell Hole for a quick mud bath.

30. Are you one of the rare people who slow down their busy life long enough to help a turtle cross the road?

31. Huffington is busy bidding on three used pig stories. (They should sell for more than enough to pay the taxes on my brick house.*)

32. If the convention has a concession stand, there will be peanuts aplenty to feed my pet elephant.

33. The training of a new breed of pygmy goat will entail upsetting order of anthills.

34. Dogs do think with their noses more than a minute amount. (If the dictionary man is out walking Fletcher, *scin-tilla* would be a good word to use here.*)

35. Horses are good at throwing their own shoes.

36. Would you expect to find a silhouette of a dog rolling around on his back at the flea market?

37. Caribbean investments are backed up by a green species of piranha stock.

38. Headlines: Zoology Club Toasts to Crust-aceans

39. Cyril Squirrel called in from the Walnut Tree Apartments wondering if we had any bark siding that wood cover the damage left by a woodpecker. (That report was filed by Jill Chisel, owner of Forestry Central.*)

40. Were the bald eagles of colonial New England a symbol of the Whig party?

41. Some people have much more of a touch tone connection when calling to their pets.

42. "Let's fly!" implored Gary the goose. "It's not time," honked Jeri his spruce, "and I'm worried about you. Have you been losing your DNA regulated capacity to read those electromagnetic shifts that resonate

to us any climatic fluctuations?" (Glenda thinks that Gary has been way out of line lately.*)

43. Porky Barrow felt a little guilty about his roots as a razorback but even that came to an end when he completed his rite of sausage.

44. "Pass me the goggles," honked the lead goose as he winged the gaggle through a wall of north wind.

45. Sheer poetry calls for editing the animal that has a rime scheme of Baa-Baa.

46. A stampede of sea horses is trapped at the O.K. Coral Reef. (Are they still trapped there from page 110? We'll have to find some equestrians who know how to harness a scuba tank.*)

47. You don't size down the fish industry, you scale it down.

48. The silhouette of a skillet against the backdrop of a dimly lit road created a wolverine preparing to pounce.

49. ICU's are for people. A barn is the best place to stabilize a horse.

50. The tuba is the elephant of the horn section.

51. When the writer misspelled a word that described the rabbit's coat, the animal looked at him rather quizzically as if to say, "I had a hutch this would *hop*pen."

52. A passenger pigeon had his feathers fluffed before boarding Aviary Airlines.

53. You can talk about lemmings until the cows come home and yet nobody seems to notice there is an elephant in the room.

54. The claw of a hammerhead fish could be used to extract barnacles from the side of a ship.

55. Some birds are public speakers. Others are more private in the impeccable ways in which they use their beaks.

56. A squid with headphones was listening to the "Ink-Spots."

57. Would a chart depicting the erratic trail of an ant be similar to the neuro-brain pattern activated during a chat with your mother's sister?

58. A moth and an elephant sat down over some apple cider to discuss both ends of the earth's unyielding gravity grip. (The calendar tells us that it was the year of the elephant or the moth of May. Hey, pass me some cider.*)

59. A hardback book on mobile homes was found on a turtle's library shelf.

60. Noah P. Tourist was seen in his Ark-ansas mobile home double-parked at the edge of the San Francisco Zoo.

61. A vicious dog meeting was scheduled to determine why humans had not been properly trained to take better care of their pets.

62. Two dogs were out walking a human. (Was her name A-leish-a?*)

63. One of Cole's hip suggestions: To balance the beast as you ride across the bottom of the pond, insert the words

hippopotamus and *bituminous* in the saddlebags, strap them over the big guy's rump and take off.

64. In rodeo time, you can bet your bottom boot that a spur of the moment isn't very long.

65. What African animal might sport rhinoculors to correct its blurred vision?

66. "You know the drill. We don't cheetah lion out of his noon supper steak unless of course we have a hot grill waiting at home," reminded the fishing angler, part time cat training.

67. The sound runway is currently occupied by the barking of a departing *Aire*dale.

68. While at the rodeo, the three monkeys, Speak, Hear and See No Evil each found a horse and decided to participate in the barrel racing just for a laugh.

69. The red headed woodpecker discovered while working on his family tree that he was descended from Ireland.

70. This warranty so stipulates that the entire contents herein listed have been inspired by the ancient events in Egypt that occurred well below *a ridge* along the *Nile*. (Yes, they are all original.*)

71. This is one of those topics that should be written in longhand. The idea is to thank the reader for being such a wonderful person (and feeding your little dog hushpuppies to keep it quiet at night) and in the mathematics of friendship you are indeed one half of the buddy system. Now you can frame this note and prop it on the coffee table in your living room to add a personal touch to the decor. —Sara Bellum

The Pun Playground

Welcome to the pun play ground.
  When you look around
    in the middle of Lexicon Park
    next to the trees
        you'll hear and see
        dogs that bark
        and walk their humans as they talk.

  Here in the light of day
    they're talking about word play;
        A syllable dance that will make words rhyme
        and perchance the puns will do double time.

The swing is the way so to speak;
  to bring the humor to reach its peak
  So, give me a push to get started.
      to and fro-to and fro . . .
            Whoa!
  Not for the feint hearted.

  If you prefer a lesser thrill
  with a pull of gravity that's just as real
    half of the swing is the downhill side
    to insert an 'L' to find the slide
        It's quick and slick and can't be beat
        and certain to land you on your feet.

  Hay (is for horses)
    Pardon the cliché

But we're not through yet
  and you can surely bet
    there is a merry-go-round
    and accordion to our sources
    Mary has found
        the horses
      that move with a circus sound
      around and around and around
        there's nothing like a carousel
        to ring the humor bell.
    It has a beat-an uplifting jingle
        a saddle for a seat-a horse called Pringle.

From Mary to Barry and a sea-saw-scene;
His eyes are wide open-his wits are keen.
  Lo! He spies the teeter-totter;
  to rime with otter
      is a splash of wit:
      Barry just wants a place to sit.
        Up and down, down and up.
        it takes two to fill the cup

Just what unlocks
        the sandbox?
Imagination is the key
And world can be what you want it to be.
  The micro-beach is for Little Ben
  and he's flashing one big grin.
      He's fashioned a whale;
      the beginning of a long tale.
    Of course, the beach would be fun to teach;
    just count the students that you could reach
        Of brains and tiny grains
        pouring pouring, pour on some water
        it's never boring, just ask the otter.

  In the distance we hear a gong
  the park will close before too long

Big Ben is calling Jungle Jim
It's about time for him
   to swing through the poles and bars
   and there you are.
     The clock is tick-talking:
       He's reached the end
       and so have we, my friend.
Don't be tethered to a frown
come on down
to the pun playground.